Motorcycle Turbocharging, Supercharging & Nitrous Oxide

A Complete Guide to Forced Induction and its Use on Modern Motorcycle Engines

by Joe Haile

A Tech Series Book
Whitehorse Press
North Conway, New Hampshire

Whitehorse Press books are also available at discounts in bulk quantity for sales and promotional use. For details about special sales or for a catalog of motorcycling books and videos, write to the Publisher:

Whitehorse Press
P.O. Box 60
North Conway, New Hampshire 03860-0060

ISBN 1-884313-07-8

5   4   3

Printed in the United States

Caution

High performance motorcycles are by their very nature potentially hazardous. This book deals with methods for increasing the power output of motorcycle engines and involves both machinery and chemical substances which can be dangerous if care is not exercised in their use. All participants in the modification of high performance vehicles must assume responsibility for their own actions and safety. The information contained in this book cannot replace sound judgment and good decision-making skills, which help reduce risk exposure, nor does the scope of this book allow for disclosure of all the potential hazards and risks involved in such activities.

Learn as much as possible about the activities you participate in, prepare for the unexpected, and be safe and cautious. Your reward will be a safer and more enjoyable experience.

Contents

Acknowledgments

Books about power boosting the internal combustion engine cannot be written without input from professionals who, to borrow an old phrase, have been there and done that. Books such as this one are usually a compilation of data and information supplied by people who have dedicated their entire lives to the high science of hot rodding, whether on four, three, or two wheels. To be useful as an educational tool, a technical book should present up-to-date, state-of-the-art information to the reader on a particular subject. Previous books focused on a single subject—just turbocharging, or just nitrous oxide. But this book was to be different. We wanted to present the complete range of high-performance options, and although this book deals specifically with motorcycles, we wanted it to be a valuable information source for anyone contemplating power boosting any type of internal combustion engine.

With the technical advice and professional expertise so kindly contributed by the following industry leaders—representing the entire spectrum of the power boosting industry—this, the most complete book ever written on turbocharging, supercharging, nitrous oxide injection, electronic fuel injection, and fueling motorcycles is now yours to enjoy. I take my hat off to these individuals and companies, as I couldn't have done it without them:

Bob Behn – RB Racing
Greg Bennett – First Choice Turbo Center
Bill Bushling – Magna Charger
John Camden – Camden Superchargers
Matt Capri – South Bay Triumph
Mike Chestnut – Horsepower Unlimited
Paul Civitello – Mad Max Enterprises
Gary Evans – Writer/Engineer
Mark Fageol – Fageol Superchargers
Tony Foster – PCS
Bob Franzke – Nitrous Oxide Systems, Inc.
Bill Hahn, Jr. – Hahn Racecraft
Rick Head – Turbonetics, Inc.
Bruce Hendel – VP Racing Fuels
Terry Kizer – Mr. Turbo
T.K. Langfield – Highpower Systems
"Mad Mel" Mandel – the original turbo biker
Michael McIntyre – Team Mr. Honda
Robert Miller – Turbo Motorcycle International
    Owners Assn.
Jim Newkirk – Westech Development
Carl Pelletier – Competition Motorcycles
Gerhard Schruf – Aerodyne Turbochargers
Mark Vanderwald – Writer/Engineer
Society of Automotive Engineers

Introduction

Forcing a fuel-air mixture under pressure into internal combustion engines has taken many forms over the years and the effects are quite well documented. Still, many misconceptions surround abnormal forced induction. So our main purpose for this book is to answer these three questions:

1. What benefits are derived from forced induction?
2. How does it increase horsepower?
3. How is it properly applied to motorcycles?

First, let's answer a question with a question. Why do people who want more power from their engine perform modifications such as head porting, increased camshaft duration (and/or overlap), larger carburetors, and free-flowing exhaust systems? Because each of these modifications can, and usually will, increase the amount of air and fuel available to the engine, thus increasing the horsepower proportionately. Why? Because your engine will only draw so much air and fuel each time a piston goes down on its intake stroke. This is regulated by normal atmospheric pressure, which is approximately 14.7 pounds per square inch at sea level. So we must rely on the suction of the piston going down, drawing air at 14.7 pounds per square inch through ducting, air cleaners, carburetors, ports, and valves in the head.

While it is relatively easy to increase the amount of fuel going into an engine, it is much more difficult to increase the amount of air. It's not just a matter of increasing the carburetor size. The problem is that the bigger the carburetor opening, the slower the air velocity will be at lower rpm, thereby hurting low-end and mid-range acceleration. This principal can be demonstrated by putting your thumb over part of a garden hose end: the smaller the opening, the greater the velocity but with less volume. The trick is to ram more air into a given sized orifice so you have the best of both worlds—high velocity *and* high volume.

With ram air induction, supercharging, or turbocharging, more air and fuel are forced into the engine than it would be able to draw "normally aspirated," that is, if only normal atmospheric pressure pushes it along. Logic tells us that the more air and fuel you pack into your engine, the more power it will put out. High performance motorcycle engine designs have already improved to such a point that further power increases are expensive and difficult to achieve. You can easily cause more harm than good as you try to improve on thousands of factory engineering hours. The days of easy horsepower gains on high performance bikes are over; don't expect to see any big improvements from the manufacturers. If you are after serious horsepower improvement without sacrificing drivability and reliability, the only practical solution is to forcibly aspirate your engine through the use of a ram air, supercharger, turbocharger, or nitrous oxide system. Welcome to the exciting world of *power boosting*.

Kawasaki was the first to introduce ram air induction on street-legal OEM motorcycles. With the success of the ZX-11C came the ZX-11D dual inlet ram air system, which then led to later models ZX-6, ZX-6R, ZX-7, ZX-7R, and ZX-9R. This cutaway and stripped view of the ZX-9R ram air system reveals the twin (large) openings at the front of the fairing under the headlight, and the oversize ducts channeling air to the specially designed plenum chamber that attaches to the carburetors. Part of the secret to proper ram air induction is keeping the ducting to the plenum chamber as large and as smooth as possible to minimize pressure drop.

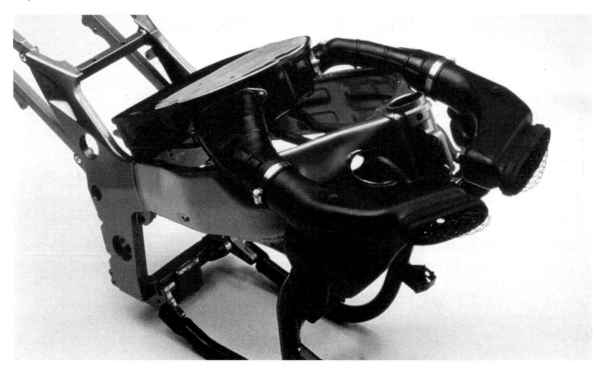

C H A P T E R   1

Ram Air Induction

To demonstrate how ram air works, here's a funny little experiment for you to try. If you have an open-faced helmet, open your mouth while traveling down the highway. Notice how your mouth becomes pressurized, forcing your cheeks outward, sort of like those old newsreels in the 1950s showing the face of a man on a rocket sled ride. If you allow this pressurized air past your larynx, you will feel the slight pressurization affect your lungs, or at least the ease with which you can breathe and fill your lungs. (Hopefully at this point, no bees or June bugs have entered the test area.) If this cooler, denser, slightly pressurized air is allowed to enter the air box of your engine, it will actually decrease the amount of effort the engine needs to "breathe." It might have about the same effect as bigger carbs, porting, longer duration cams, and bigger valves—only without the expense.

If by now you haven't been stopped by a cop wondering why you are cruising along with your mouth wide open and your cheeks flapping at 55 miles per hour, you will definitely stand a good chance of being stopped at the 100+ mph at which ram air induction makes a noticeable difference. Of course, the big drawback to ram air induction is that it doesn't do a lot of good below the century mark. On the track this is okay, but on the street? Well, let's put it this way. The cop says, "So, gotcherself one of those new ram air Kawasakis, eh?" And you say, "But officer, the ram air won't work below a hundred!" Have no fear. You'll make new friends down at the county courthouse, and your insurance company will make sure any future "E" ticket rides will be without their sponsorship. Look at all the money you'll save!

At lower speeds (under 100 mph), ram air improves throttle response and provides slightly better acceleration, but the real gains only appear at triple-digit speeds. While most riders spend little time at these velocities, the slight improvement at lower speeds makes the bike feel stronger, which can help make riding more enjoyable. Perhaps the best feature of ram air induction is that it's essentially free.

Until recently, ram air induction was fairly well ignored by the motorcycle industry, even though it has actually been around for a long time in various forms. All the major race car, race bike, race boat, and race plane builders have used it on everything from "Cowl Induction" Camaros and "Ram Air" Olds 442s to full-on sports race cars, Indy cars, dragsters, drag bikes, Bonneville bikes (and cars), unlimited hydroplanes, P-51 Mustangs and the like. Still, motorcycle manufacturers have steered clear. For the past 25 years they've made plenty of other performance improvements in ways that affect horsepower at the speeds ordinary riders usually travel. Many will say the modern sporting motorcycle is fast enough. Who needs more, especially at 180 mph? It would be better for the factories to make improvements in areas that affect acceleration through the quarter-mile and handling.

Recently, when the industry performance standards seemed to have equalized among manufacturers and temporarily peaked, along came Kawasaki to stir the horsepower pot once again—Kawasaki can never leave well enough alone. Just when everybody is happy and content, they introduce some new high-performance concept that blows everybody into the weeds. And of course Honda, Yamaha, and Suzuki are not going to take this lying down, are they? Of course not!

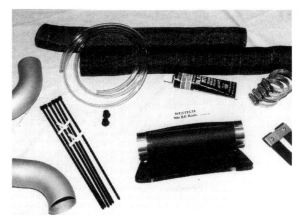

In addition to the Kawasaki Ram Air Enhancer system, Westech also makes a complete Ram Air kit *(right)* for the CBR900RR Honda. The air scoop is mounted just below the headlights on the fairing, and splits into two air feed hoses that supply cooler, denser, pressurized air to the modified air box. Bolt it on in a couple of hours, and you get an impressive 11 percent horsepower increase at full speed.

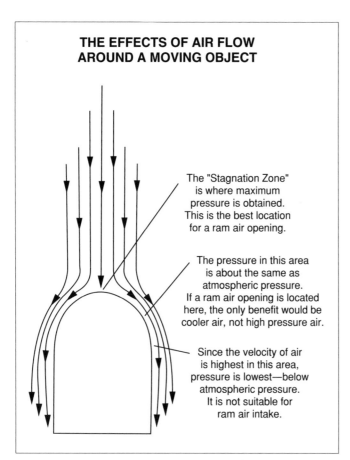

THE EFFECTS OF AIR FLOW AROUND A MOVING OBJECT

The "Stagnation Zone" is where maximum pressure is obtained. This is the best location for a ram air opening.

The pressure in this area is about the same as atmospheric pressure. If a ram air opening is located here, the only benefit would be cooler air, not high pressure air.

Since the velocity of air is highest in this area, pressure is lowest—below atmospheric pressure. It is not suitable for ram air intake.

Figure 1-1: This illustration shows the effect of a body moving through air, with points of maximum relative velocity (lowest pressure) and minimum relative velocity (maximum pressure).

Kawasaki first introduced ram air induction on the mighty ZX-11, still near the top of the heap in the quarter-mile and top end departments. Then they quickly adapted ram air systems to the ZX-6, ZX-7, ZX-7R, and ZX-900R, making all these models the performance leaders in their respective classes. Then Honda followed suit with their CBR600F3 and more recently the XX Blackbird. Suzuki jumped in with the GSXR750 and then recently applied ram air to most of their sportbike lineup. Yamaha countered with the ram air YZF600 Thundercat. With that success Yamaha also adapted ram air to the new YZF750 and 1000. We assume Ducati will be next.

How Ram Air Induction Works

The idea, which is pretty simple, is to locate an opening at or near the center of the fairing, as close as possible to the front, where it can pick up the greatest amount of air pressure, and duct it to a pressure box connected to the mouths of the carburetors. At high speed, the air entering the opening in the front of the fairing pressurizes the air box, forcing more air and fuel into the engine. As described by the Bernoulli Principle, as air accelerates, its pressure falls, and as it decelerates, pressure rises. A turbocharger compressor housing works on this very principle: air entering the scroll's small end is compressed and then decelerated through the diffuser's larger exit port at a higher pressure.

So how does this principle pertain to pushing a projectile through the air? Picture looking down on the fairing of a motorcycle (see Figure 1-1). As it moves through the air, the blunt nose of the fairing becomes a high pressure zone, or more accurately, a "stagnation zone." The air converts all of its kinetic energy into pressure in the central region—and this is where the streamline effect ends. Any air to the left or right of center gets back into the streamline. Note that the idea of kinetic energy—that is, the energy of a moving mass—is a bit different here. The air is actually sitting still while the motorcycle is moving through it. However, the principle still holds, since the velocity of the air *relative to the motorcycle* is what's important. From the viewpoint of the motorcycle, the air is moving until it comes to rest at the stagnation zone.

Bernoulli's theorem describes the pressure variations that occur with moving air. Applying it to the case of pressure rise at the area directly in front and center of your fairing at varying speeds, there's a simple formula that tells the story. Where P is the pressure rise in psi and V is the speed of the motorcycle in mph:

$$P = \frac{V^2}{57,600}$$

This formula is plotted in Figure 1-2 to show the pressure rise at the stagnation point for various speeds.

Referring to Figure 1-1, we see that the stagnation point in the air stream occurs directly in front of the fairing. At this point, air comes to rest at the fairing surface and shows its highest pressure increase. As air moves around the nose of the fairing it picks up velocity and loses pressure. At some "neutral" area, the pressure will have dropped back to atmospheric pressure, where no pressure gain exists. Then farther along the fairing, as the velocity increases, the pressure drops further and will actually be below atmospheric pressure. With all of this considered, the best location for a ram air intake opening would be as close to the stagnation area (in the middle of the fairing) as possible: about where your mouth is on your head, or just below the headlight on your motorcycle.

All right, so we agree on the location of our opening, but what shape should it be? A velocity stack shape or funnel shape might seem to be the most efficient, but this isn't necessarily true. The main goal is to decelerate the incoming air smoothly, while it converts its kinetic energy into pressure. A funnel shape does not accomplish this goal. It will accelerate air through the small end, ultimately causing a pressure drop, not an increase. The opening can be round, oval, square, rectangular, or triangular in shape, just as long as it doesn't immediately funnel down in size. The edges of the

PRESSURE RISE OF AIR
UPON COMING TO REST FROM VARIOUS SPEEDS

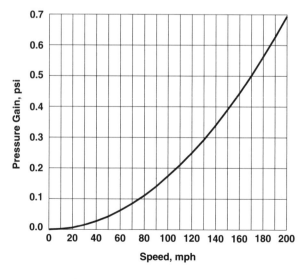

Figure 1-2: This graph shows what Ram Air is all about. The faster you go, the more pressure boost you have available.

Westech, in Wimberly, Texas, makes a Ram Air Enhancer system for the early single opening Kawasaki ZX-11. It consists of an additional air intake scoop just below the headlight that adds a second duct to the air box. This eliminates flat spots and depressions, and increases horsepower over the stock system.

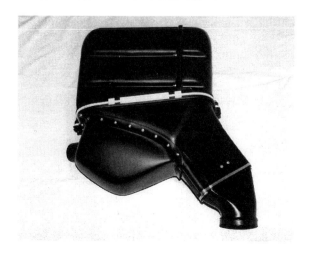

Most Formula USA bikes run some version of ram air, usually one of Air Tech's systems. This Suzuki GSXR1205 belonging to Hyper Cycle in Van Nuys, California, has extensive carbon fiber body work and ram air induction of Air Tech's making. *(Right and far right)* Note the flexible ducting. It is smooth on the inside, so as not to disturb air flow, and wire reinforced on the outside to hold its shape. This bike weighs 375 pounds, runs 9.90 ETs at 140 mph, and goes 190 mph, all with the same gearing. Without the ram air it could lose up to 10 mph on the top end.

opening should be rounded slightly to help direct the air in smoothly and the ducting should be of large diameter all the way to the air chamber connected to the mouths of the carburetors.

The air box should be large enough to supply a constant stream of pressurized air to the carburetors at full throttle. Think of it as a pressurized storage tank. Most modern sport bikes have enormous air boxes that are well sealed and are ideal for ram air pressurization, and as we will discuss shortly, some aftermarket companies are taking advantage of this fact.

Great! We've pressurized the air box at 100+ mph and gained a mild supercharging effect. How much pressure are we talking about and what will it buy you? Not much on either count, but enough theoretically to net a minimum 4 percent increase in horsepower at top speed. About the difference between 175 and 177.3 miles per hour, or a gain of 2.3 mph. Figure it this way: The *force* needed to overcome air drag goes up as the *square* of the speed you're traveling. Power is force times speed, so the *power* needed goes up as the *cube* of forward speed. The calculation does not correct for rolling resistance, friction, or volumetric efficiency (cylinder filling capability). The speed-gain factor is therefore the cube root of 1.04, or 1.013 (that is, 1.3 percent). That, multiplied by 175 miles per hour, buys 2.3 miles per hour, or 177.3. This all results from a pressure gain of six-tenths of one pound per square inch, and that's about as much as you can expect for the

factory ram air systems now available. However, the increase of inlet pressure is not the only advantage of ram air. By paying attention to the size and shape of the inlet passages, flow losses can be reduced, with the effect of increasing the mass of air delivered to the engine at any given engine speed.

Volumetric Efficiency

This seems a good place to define the term *volumetric efficiency*. It means the ratio of air volume (or mass) actually flowing through an engine, to the volume (or mass) of air that would flow if there were no flow restrictions. For example, a four-cycle 1000cc engine attempts to draw in 1000cc of air-fuel mixture every two revolutions of the crankshaft. Depending upon engine speed and many other factors, the volume (or mass) of air-fuel mixture it passes is normally less than 1000cc. High performance engines typically have a volumetric efficiency approaching 90 percent, meaning that they actually pass approximately 900cc of air-fuel mixture every two revolutions.

As we will show throughout this book, the key to making more power is to make the engine draw in (and efficiently burn) more air-fuel mixture. In later chapters you will see how supercharged and turbocharged engines can have volumetric efficiency well above 100 percent.

Fueling a Ram Air System

It always gets back to this: if you add more air, you must also add more fuel. If you know anything about blow-through turbocharging, you will have no trouble understanding this concept. Here's the problem: adding a slight amount of ram air induction without jetting changes can cause a minor lean-out condition at full speed. You will need to add a small amount of extra fuel to match the additional air being supplied. That's pretty basic. What you may not know, however, is that fuel delivery through a carburetor is based on a metering signal, or the pressure *difference* between the venturi and the float bowl. When the pressure in the air box rises, the pressure in the venturi rises equally. If the float bowl pressure doesn't rise along with the venturi pressure, the fuel metering signal decreases and so does fuel delivery.

The solution to this problem is simple. Just hook the float bowl vent lines to the air box. That way the float bowl(s) will realize exactly the same pressure the venturi(s) are seeing and everything is equalized. An air/fuel ratio meter should be used to dial in the proper mixture at top speed, as you will need to be richer at high speed to achieve that 4 percent or more horsepower increase. All the pressure in the world is useless without the appropriate amount of fuel.

The Aftermarket

Two companies, Air Tech and Westech, have made a specialty of ram air systems for motorcycles. While Air Tech's systems involve fairing modifications, and in some cases whole fairings, Westech's approach is either to enhance an existing ram air system (as they have done with ZX-11C Kawasakis) or to offer complete systems using the stock air box. Air is taken in through a special duct below the center of the fairing.

Air Tech's ram air systems are a little more roadrace oriented, while Westech's are intended more for street use and the occasional blast through the quarter-mile, although there is no reason they couldn't be used on roadracers as well.

Westech

Jim Newkirk, owner of Westech (and a ZX-11 Kawasaki), became interested in ram air induction when he noticed a few strange things happening on hard acceleration. First, he noticed better acceleration in first and second gears by short-shifting, but normal acceleration in the higher gears (at higher speeds), shifting at redline. Secondly, after sustaining a high speed cruise at 125 mph at part throttle, when he whacked it open, the bike would explode forward and then slow before picking up steam and charging ahead to terminal velocity. Third, under wind shear conditions the bike would seem to die from fuel and/or air starvation.

First he studied fluid dynamics in some engineering manuals and, as he puts it, "approached the ZX-11 project through the back door."

Newkirk installed three pressure transducers on his bike: one in the intake tract, one in the front section of the air box (before the filter), and one in the rear section of the air box. Later he added a pressure gauge on the float bowl vent line. By measuring pressure changes and differentials over the entire speed range of the motorcycle, he came up with some very interesting observations.

1. At high rpm in first and second gears, a pressure reduction occurred in the air box which didn't occur in the other gears at any speed. Simply stated, the engine needed more air than was available or entering the air box at these high rpm, low speed situations.

The first Kawasaki ZX-11s had only one air intake opening, slightly offset to the left. Westech improved on the system by adding an additional scoop and increasing the size of the stock air box to eliminate flat spots and transitional problems. The original single scoop was also affected by side winds, or wind shear. With the addition of the extra air inlet, the problems associated with wind shear disappeared. ZX-11Ds now come with twin air inlet openings in the center of the fairing and dual ducting to the larger air box.

2. At 125 mph, he had an elevated pressure reading in the air box and ducting. When he opened the butterflies abruptly, the pressure dropped instantly. It took 3 to 4 seconds before the pressure would stabilize and continue to increase.

3. At higher speeds, he could see a dip in the entire intake tract ducting pressure when a stumble occurred. At lower speeds he did not detect any pressure changes, so he added a pressure gauge to the carburetor float bowl line. Sure enough, he detected either a rise or drop in pressure when a stumble occurred. If he was cruising at 100 mph with nothing in front or to the side to obstruct the air flow, an adequate amount of air would flow through the stock ducting. But in a 15 mph side wind, less air would flow into the opening. Normally this wouldn't be noticeable to the engine operation, but since the ZX-11 picks up its float bowl venting in this same opening, any flow variance showed up as a stumble, creating too rich or too lean a mixture, depending on the wind shear speed and direction. The opening in the fairing didn't allow for restricted air flow or the additional air demands of a modified engine.

After Newkirk added his Dual Forced Air Enhancer Kit—an extra duct that starts just below the headlight

and an added air box chamber for increased volume— plus an optional air/fuel ratio monitor, he made the following observations.

1. The engine pulled right through redline in first and second without slowing, and the pressure in the ducting and air box didn't drop at high rpm as they did with the stock intake tract.

2. The pressure dropped just as quickly when the throttle was opened rapidly, but the bike felt as if it pulled longer and didn't seem to slow slightly before it took off again. The pressure in the intake stabilized in less than one second and recovered within two seconds.

3. The stumbles that occurred before adding the enhancer kit had been reduced to, at most, a slight hiccup. The added scoop picked up air from *under* the fairing, so a wind shear didn't affect the airflow into the scoop as it did with the factory opening. Since the ducting adds another sensor line to the float chambers, this also helps smooth out any pressure variations. The "D" model ZX-11 does not have these deficiencies and is a much better design than the "C" model, as are all of the other forced-air Kawasakis.

In the course of his work, Newkirk found that in a ram air system with an adequate-sized opening, a larger opening will not create more pressure. Having more inlet area may sound desirable, but it could cause turbulence and pressure eddies, making the carburetors act out of sync. Not a good thing.

Newkirk then applied all the knowledge he had gained through these experiments to create a completely new ram air system for the Honda 900RR. It has a snorkel that catches air just below the leading edge of the fairing, below the headlight. The high velocity air is then directed through two lightweight fiberglass hoses into the factory air box.

At 100 mph, the highest pressure boost that can be achieved is about 0.17 psi above atmospheric pressure (see Figure 1-2). At 170 mph that figure is 0.5 psi. Admittedly, this in itself isn't really a big deal, but you are supplying cooler, denser air on top of that. The 0.5 psi boost, plus the other benefits of a more efficient air tract may actually account for 8 to 10 percent more horsepower on a stock engine with a volumetric efficiency of 90 percent. In testing, Newkirk has seen the top speed of a stock Honda 900RR increase by 6 mph with the addition of ram air. Calculations indicate that ram air increases horsepower by a whopping 11.5 percent!

Air Tech

Air Tech has always been at the cutting edge of aerodynamics and materials technology. Walk into the plant and you are greeted with wall to wall fiberglass and carbon fiber. This company has also been making ram air systems for a number of years, mostly for high-end road race machinery.

Kent Riches, owner of Air Tech, is actually one of those "started in the home garage" success stories. Even in the beginning, his main objective was to make the finest motorcycle body work possible; over the years he has learned quite a lot about aerodynamics. An avid roadracer, Kent's products reflect his involvement in the sport. Just about any road race bike you pick will have some body component made by Air Tech. Now, the canyon racer set is taking a big interest in ram air induction, too. Air Tech's offerings will probably start showing up at local motorcycle shops as knowledge of this technology spreads.

Air Tech makes ram air systems for a small array of motorcycles: the Honda CBR900RR, the 1991 and '92 ZX-6 and ZX-7 Kawasaki, the '93 to '95 Suzuki GSXR1100s and 750s, the YZF750 Yamaha (three air boxes to choose from), and the TZ250 Yamaha road-

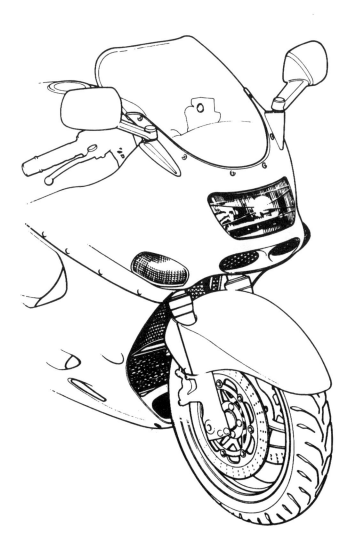

Kawasaki ZX-11D air inlet openings.

racer. Air Tech starts with a stock air box and, through redesign, makes it larger and smoother inside, eliminating any bumps and lumps that don't need to be there, to help air flow and increase volume. These air boxes come in fiberglass or carbon fiber.

Air Tech offers two ways to go: air intake snouts that you mount into your stock fairing, or complete fairings that have the ram air intake openings and ducting installed. Generally speaking, most motorcycle sport fairings are not the well-rounded shape shown in Figure 1-1. They are usually broader across the front, almost flat. This makes it possible to locate the ram air openings to the right and left side of the headlight and still pick up air from a stagnation zone. Kawasaki's stock fairings are more rounded; accordingly they locate the ram air openings in the center, under the headlight.

Above and opposite page: **Air Tech manufactures the widest variety of ram air systems today. They make many different types of air boxes and intake openings that can be mixed and matched to your needs. Notice how the intake ducts in this fairing have a large cross-sectional area at its entry, and then dump into large ducts that supply the massive air box. Keeping all air paths large and obstruction-free is the secret to ram air pressurization.**

Conclusion

An 11 percent gain in horsepower really isn't too bad, even if it is at "let's get crazy" speeds. And with no belts or pulleys or special exhaust systems to deal with, it's maintenance-free as well.

If you enjoyed this lesson, you'll really like what's coming up. We'll be talking about mild to serious boost levels and 30 to 200 percent horsepower gains from supercharged, turbocharged, and nitrous oxide-injected motorcycles.

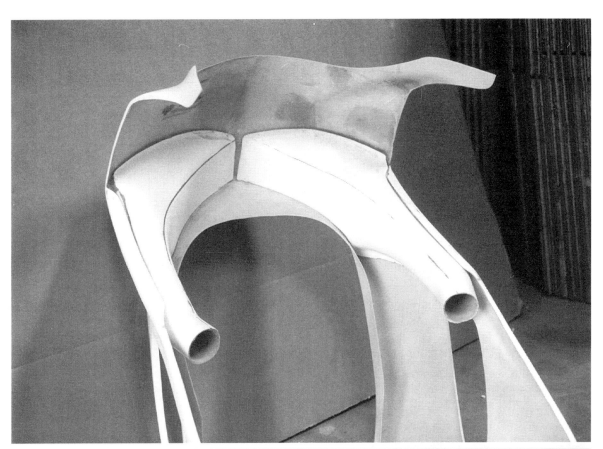

Honda's Dual-Stage Air Intake System for the 1995 CBR600F3 . . .

The most noticeable change in the CBR600F3 is its all-new air intake system, which introduces a high-volume stream of cool, fresh air into the intake system to boost overall engine performance. Unlike other systems of this type, which are generally designed to be effective only at higher speeds, the CBR's dual stage system realizes a boost in performance at all speeds, accompanied by sharper throttle response and smooth power bands. This is achieved with an innovative two-stage system that balances the air pressure within the carburetors' float and vacuum chambers with the air flowing through their bores, thus reducing air pressure differentials that can adversely affect carburetor performance.

The system consists of one outer set and two inner sets of intake ducts. They feed pressurized air directly into the carburetor chambers to ensure optimal performance at both low and high speeds. The inner sets consist of a pair of main air intake ducts that route air to the air box and air cleaner, and a pair of smaller secondary ducts that lead to the carburetor float and vacuum chambers.

Under 12 mph

The system's set of two outer ducts extend directly from the two front intake ports located near the headlight. Closed off by the system's solenoid control valve until the ignition is turned on, these ducts increase air pressure to the carburetor float chambers at speeds up to 12 mph to optimize fuel flow. The ducts are located approximately eight inches ahead of the induction chamber's air scoop. This effectively isolates the engine's main air intake from any low speed blowback of fuel-air mixture through the ducts, which can rob the induction system of needed fresh air and choke off performance.

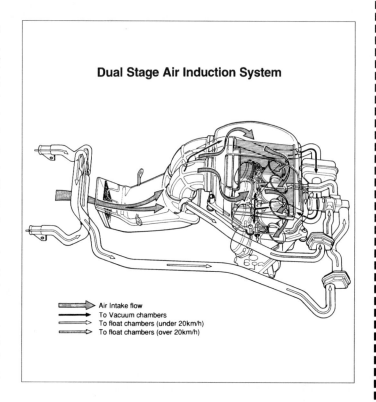

Dual Stage Air Induction System

Air Intake flow
To Vacuum chambers
To float chambers (under 20km/h)
To float chambers (over 20km/h)

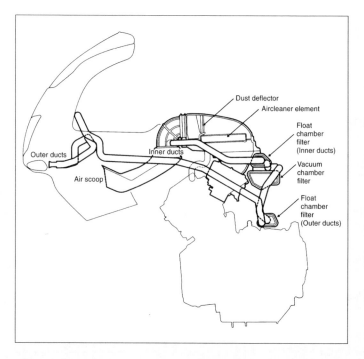

Dust deflector
Aircleaner element
Float chamber filter (Inner ducts)
Vacuum chamber filter
Float chamber filter (Outer ducts)
Outer ducts
Inner ducts
Air scoop

. . . Honda's Dual-Stage Air Intake System for the 1995 CBR600F3

At the same time, one duct of the pair of secondary inner ducts continuously balances the air pressure within the carburetors' vacuum chambers with that of air flowing through their main bores to optimize carburetor slide operation. These secondary ducts feed air directly from the system's main induction chamber, which gets its air charge from the large scoop positioned under the steering head.

Over 12 mph

At speeds over 12 mph, the system's solenoid control valve cuts off the outer ducts and opens the air flow to the second duct of the pair of secondary inner ducts. This air flows to the carburetor float chambers to equalize their internal air pressure at high speeds, thus maintaining optimal fuel flow and operation. While easily matching the power output achieved with conventional ram air systems, the CBR's new dual stage system extends this boost of performance to the lower reaches of its rev range. The result is sharper response and stronger performance at all engine speeds. ∎

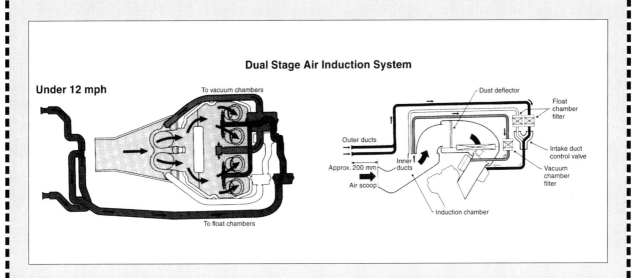

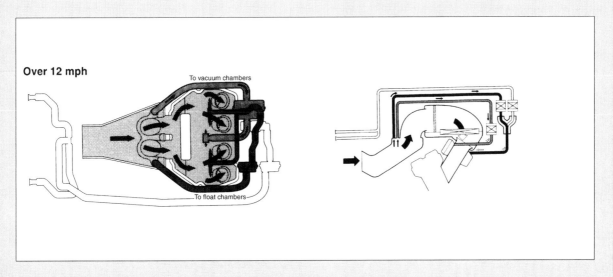

Kawasaki Ram Air Systems

Kawasaki was the first of all the motorcycle companies to incorporate ram air, starting with the ZX-11 upon its introduction, then later adapting it to the ZX-6, ZX-7, and ZX-9R motorcycles. The original ZX-11 system was somewhat different from what they are now using, with only one air intake located slightly left of center on the front of the fairing. As previously discussed, side winds had a tendency to disturb air flow into the opening, causing surging and minor flat spots, and the smaller air box caused a depression in first and second gears when the throttle was quickly opened fully. However, Kawasaki has corrected these problems by locating two openings just to the left and right of center fairing, with two separate ducts delivering the high pressure air to larger air boxes. Kawasaki's system is single stage, working only at wide open throttle and high speed, as opposed to Honda's dual stage system that affects air flow as low as 12 miles per hour.

As an example we chose the ZX-9R ram air system, which is almost identical to the other Kawasaki models. The ZX-9R employs twin ram air intakes that draw air from two ducts just below the headlight, providing the following benefits:

1. By drawing cool air from in front of the bike, the problems associated with preheated intake air are avoided, providing a more constant power supply.

2. Since air reaches the air cleaner effectively, engine efficiency does not drop and combustion efficiency is more stable, resulting in more consistent and positive throttle response.

3. The large intake swept area (air cleaner and ram ducts) minimizes intake resistance while reducing intake noise.

4. The large 12-liter air box incorporates dual resonance boxes mounted to the twin ram air intake passages to reduce intake noise, and individual collectors to catch rain entering the system. Intake air passes through a large low restriction oiled foam air filter element to the four 40 mm Keihin CVKD carburetors.

The intake ducts that extend from the mouth of the carburetors into the air box are exceptionally smooth, with the inner diameter matching the carb mouth for a smooth, relatively turbulence-free air passage. As a result the ducts exhibit the same inertia effect as the carburetor venturis, increasing mid-range torque and top-end power. The short ducts between the carburetors and the head also taper smoothly, with no dips or edges to cause turbulence. According to Kawasaki, the intake system makes a major contribution to the strong high-torque characteristics of their engines for exceptional throttle response at all riding speeds. ■

 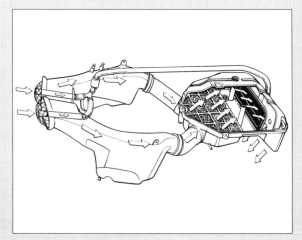

Lee's Cycle Kawasaki ZX-7/9R Formula USA bike features a unique ram air system. Air is taken in by the hole near the steering head, and with the gas tank sealing against the neoprene gasket, the carburetors are completely pressurized. When the whole carburetor is pressurized there is no need to run separate float bowl vent lines to the air box.

Suzuki GSXR750 Ram Air System

Suzuki's new GSXR750 has a lightweight perimeter frame and engine. The Suzuki fairing is broad across the face, with two large ram air openings just to the left and right of the headlight. They funnel into large ducts that route through special holes in the frame. From there, they connect to the bottom side of the air box that houses the air cleaner. Pressurized air first travels through the air cleaner, then into the large plenum chamber, thereby pressurizing the carburetors at high speed. Suzuki claims its ram air system improves air charging efficiency by 3 percent over previous models.

The carburetors are huge at 39 mm each. To compensate for their generous venturi diameter, a solenoid operated valve increases pressure above the carb slide diaphragms to prevent the slide from lifting prematurely at low rpm. This increases air velocity at the carburetor venturi, improving carburetion and throttle response at lower speeds. An igniter box, gear position sensor, and throttle position sensor ultimately control timing and carburetion functions to improve bottom end response and mid-range torque. ■

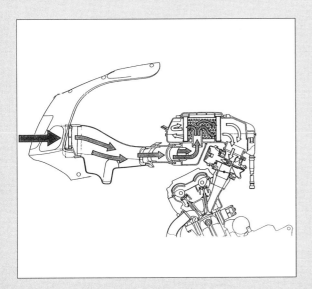

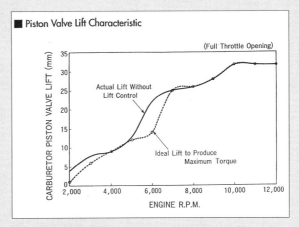

■ Piston Valve Lift Characteristic

This chart displays the difference in carburetor throttle slide lift characteristics between Suzuki's new ram air carburetors with lift control and carburetors without lift control. Positive pressure is directed to the top of the CV diaphragm and controlled by a special solenoid.

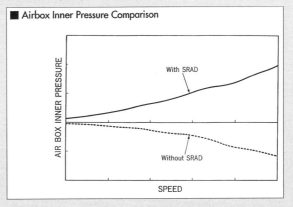

■ Airbox Inner Pressure Comparison

The dramatic effect of ram air induction can best be seen by studying this chart. As speed increases, the pressure within the air box increases proportionally with the aid of ram air induction. Without ram air, pressure actually decreases with speed as the engine demands more air.

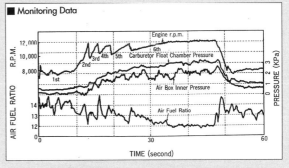

■ Monitoring Data

Monitoring data like the air/fuel ratio, engine rpm, and time in seconds reveals the effects of ram air induction. At 12,000 rpm (starting at about 35 seconds) the pressure inside the air box increases to 0.725 psi over atmospheric. Float chamber pressure is always slightly above air box pressure and the air/fuel ratio gets richer during the time of highest boost pressure. Suzuki definitely did its homework.

Superchargers and motorcycles are a rare mix on the street, but a trip to the drag strip reveals a whole other story. Top Fuel bikes are almost always supercharged—these days, usually with the Opcon Autorotor (Whipple) screw-type supercharger. In short bursts, as in drag racing, blower failure is rare, even at 35 psi! Here, Tony Lang blasts off to another routine 220 mph, low-six pass on his nitromethane-fueled Suzuki. It is presently one of the quickest bikes in the country at 6.19 seconds in the quarter-mile. *Photo by Harold Barnett*

CHAPTER 2

Supercharging

Supercharger. Just the name sounds badass. The mere mention of it in high performance circles will instantly bring reaction. "Why, I had a buddy once who had two Jimmy 6-71s stacked one atop the other," says one guy. Another will retort, "Yeah, but I had a friend with a blown double A fuel altered that'd smoke 'em the full length of the quarter-mile!" Of course, most of these people have never owned a supercharged vehicle, but what they've seen sure impressed them. Superchargers have been leaving lasting impressions on people all the way back to the industrial revolution.

Superchargers boosted the P-51 Mustang (plus various other fighter aircraft) to victory during World War II. They also set records in multitudes of race cars and boats over the years: Indy cars, Formula cars, dragsters, monster trucks, and motorcycles. Army tanks, buses, farm tractors, and stationary power plants have also been supercharged.

Superchargers became popular in the 1930s when some automobile manufacturers needed increased horsepower to haul their 5,000-pound behemoths down the road in stately fashion. At about the same time, the aircraft industry began using superchargers to increase the horsepower and altitude capabilities of fighter aircraft by packing more air and fuel into the cylinders. Once the world knew about the supercharger's contribution to increased horsepower, it became one of the racing fraternity's love affairs—and has been ever since.

The way a supercharger greatly increases the potency of an internal combustion engine is neither magical nor hard to understand. Basically, an engine produces power based on the amount of fuel and air it is able to ingest and burn. A supercharger, just like a turbocharger, is a compressor that forces more fuel and air into an engine than the engine could draw normally aspirated. Normal (or sea level) atmospheric pressure is 14.7 pounds per square inch. If you raise or increase that amount by 7.5 psi, your engine would perform (theoretically) as though it were 50 percent larger. And the more pressure you add to that, the larger your engine seems on an increasing scale.

Superchargers are driven mechanically, usually through belts and pulleys. The turbosupercharger is driven by exhaust gases passing through an exhaust housing that contains an impeller wheel. The supercharger puts out boost in relation to engine rpm, as it is directly connected to the engine crankshaft. This provides instant reaction time, with boost right off idle.

Lang's Sprintex (Whipple) supercharger cranks out 35 psi with a mixture of nitromethane and methanol. Mechanical fuel injection handles the flow to the Cooper Skull head. MTC's big block has a displacement of 1400cc and houses MTC's 6.5 to 1 pistons on special (more than big) aluminum rods. Top Fuel engines like this put out between 900 and 1,100 horsepower. *Photo by Harold Barnett*

A.S.A.P. Racing Products of Lansing, Mich. (517-484-4080) uses the Fageol supercharger on a custom intake manifold in their Yamaha V-Max system. The drive side view also reveals the Holley fuel pump and air shifter. What you can't see is the A.S.A.P. chain drive conversion and special drag-length swingarm.

However, it takes a certain amount of horsepower to drive the supercharger (this is part of the tradeoff).

Another aspect of supercharging to consider when choosing a boosting device is that it is always pumping—at 35 mph on the boulevard, while twisting through mountain roads, and on the freeway at 70 mph. The faster the engine turns, the more boost the supercharger supplies, but since it is always working, the extra loading and heat rejection requirements on the engine are increased as well. This is one reason you will almost always find street-driven supercharged vehicles (car, truck, or bike) restricted to five (possibly up to 10) pounds of boost pressure. It's not that superchargers can't put out more, it's just that they can't produce high boost pressures at high rpm for long periods of time (wide open throttle) without overheating. Superchargers also heat the intake air to high levels that can promote detonation.

Heat is the most significant enemy of any engine. Methods for controlling engine heat take many forms: coolant radiators, oil coolers, fins, fans, and fluids. However, when artificially compressing air into your engine, another type of heat problem occurs that requires even greater caution. When the compressor impeller, rotors, or screws accelerate the air or air-fuel mixture to a high velocity and force it into the diffuser, or housing, the air or air-fuel mixture decelerates and becomes hotter as it compresses. A lot hotter! This heat can promote detonation, or ping—known as the "death rattle." It's the primary cause of piston and engine failure, and superchargers are the biggest offenders. The keyword for prevention is *efficiency*. The more efficient the compressor, the less heat is generated through the compression process. Turbochargers are the most efficient, at anywhere from 65 to 75 percent. Roots superchargers, at 40 to 55 percent, are not as efficient.

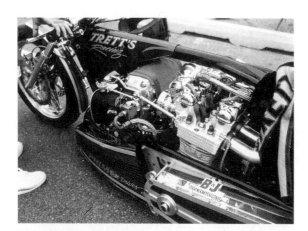

What chapter on supercharging would be complete without a shot of Elmer Trett's Top Fuel bike? Before his untimely death, Elmer had been running supercharged, nitromethane-fueled drag bikes for so long, he had become an institution. The bug catcher style scoop mounted on the mechanical fuel injection throttle body has seen the fastest top speed ever recorded in the quarter-mile by a motorcycle: 234 mph at 6.23 seconds! They say you can't steer these monsters, so you'd better be pointed real straight when you launch. *Photo by Harold Barnett*

On Ron Webb's Top Fuel drag bike, the supercharger is mounted in front of the head, as is standard practice today. The head is actually turned around so the intake ports point forward, while the exhaust exits to the rear, right behind the pilot's derriere. The supercharger blows directly into a plenum that feeds the intakes, and drives off the right side of the engine. Mr. Webb's bike has rocketed through the quarter in 6.41 seconds at over 217 mph—without the aid of a fairing! *Photo by Harold Barnett*

Let's say you start off with an ambient air temperature of 80° F and compress it to a pressure ratio of 1.9 with 65 percent efficiency (as would be the case with a properly sized turbocharger). The result would be air entering the combustion chamber at 245° F. If you think that's bad, a Roots-type supercharger at 45 percent efficiency will be putting air into the combustion chamber at a whopping 319° F. Centrifugal and screw-type superchargers operate more efficiently than the typical Roots supercharger, but still not as efficiently as a properly sized turbocharger—and the engine loading and pumping action of the supercharger also robs power in accordance with its efficiency rating. Many supercharger proponents say this loss is fairly minor when you consider the thrill factor of having boost all the way from idle to top rpm. If you are considering drag racing, you will find the supercharger more responsive than the typical Rajay turbocharger, but possibly somewhat lacking in total boost potential on gasoline. Alcohol or nitromethane often makes boost levels of 35 psi possible, and for quick bursts through the quarter-mile, superchargers seem to be right at home. And 5 to 10 lbs boost on the street will result in a sizable horsepower increase, putting a smile on any rider's face.

Superchargers can be divided into three basic types: the sliding vane compressor, the rotary compressor, and the centrifugal compressor. Within these three basic types there are various configurations. We'll look at those that best apply to motorcycle installations.

Variable Vane or Sliding Vane

The variable vane supercharger contains one rotor inside the housing, with deep slots machined into it accommodating thin vanes that are free to move radially. The rotor is seated off center in the blower housing so when it rotates, the centrifugal force acting on the vanes moves them in an outward direction. Ambient air is drawn through the intake port in the housing, then into each of several compartments in the crescent-shaped space as the volume increases. As the space between the vanes decreases, the air is compressed and then released through an exit port, and on to the cylinders.

The flow capacity of the sliding vane compressor depends on the maximum induction volume, which in turn is determined by several design parameters. These would include the housing cylinder bore, the rotor diameter (and length), the number of vanes, and the dimensions of the inlet and outlet ports. The true flow

Above and below: **Rohm Performance Products of Yuba City, Calif. (916-674-9123) fabricates this clean Fageol supercharger system for the Suzuki GSXR750. Drive is off the left side of the engine and draws fuel and air through a two-barrel PHH Mikuni carburetor. The supercharger fits neatly behind the cylinders and is fairly inconspicuous. Rear wheel horsepower tops out at 150 or so, and it'll run high 9-second quarter-miles at 150 mph. Not bad for a 750!**

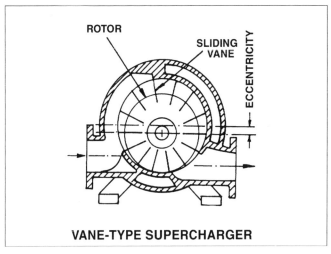

This cross-section view of a typical variable vane supercharger shows the offset single rotor in the bottom of the housing and how, by centrifugal force, the sliding vanes move outward.

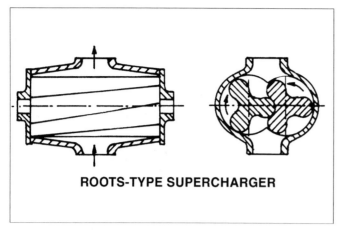

ROOTS-TYPE SUPERCHARGER

This cross-section view of a typical Roots-type supercharger shows how the twin rotors mesh together to draw air in through the top and force it out the bottom. This is a three-lobe example.

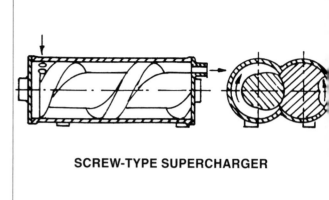

SCREW-TYPE SUPERCHARGER

This cross section view of a typical screw-type supercharger indicates how air is drawn in at one end and passed, by the screw motion of the rotor, to the opposite end. Screw compressors are very efficient.

rate and pressure rise at constant speed will be reduced due to leakage, and the volumetric efficiency may vary between 0.6 and 0.9 depending on the size of the blower, the type of design, and the type of lubrication. The compressor efficiency may be somewhat low without some form of cooling to lessen the heat buildup generated by friction between the moving vanes and between the rotor and housing surfaces. This type of supercharger is not the most efficient, but it can produce a range of pressure ratios at constant speed, making it a good choice for fast response in transient conditions.

Only a couple of these variable vane superchargers are available. One was made by Latham 30 years ago and saw duty on quite a few hot rods of that era. You might luck out and find one in a garage sale or newspaper ad—and it could make for an interesting Harley or V-Max adaptation. In the early 1980s, the Bendix Corporation started to develop a family of sliding vane superchargers, but has since discontinued their program.

Roots-Type Superchargers

This type of rotary compressor works on simple principles. Air trapped in the recesses between the rotor lobes and the housing is passed on to the exit port without a significant change in volume. As the recesses open to the delivery port, the suction side is closed and the trapped air is suddenly compressed by the back flow from the delivery port.

Roots blowers are best suited for small pressure ratios, normally 1.2:1, but larger units can be used to pump air at higher ratios if the clearance between the

rotors and housing is decreased. As with sliding vane compressors, the mass flow rate is theoretically independent of pressure ratio. However, in actual practice, the flow rate decreases as the pressure ratio is increased at constant speed. The reduction in flow rate depends on the volumetric efficiency. The performance characteristics of the Roots blower and the sliding vane blower are similar.

Several companies manufacture Roots-type superchargers sized for motorcycle use: Camden, Fageol (formally K.F. Engineering), and Magna Charger. Please refer to the sidebars on these superchargers for the technical details.

Screw-Type Superchargers

Screw-type compressors are precision machined to achieve close clearances between the rotating and stationary housing. They are designed to operate at speeds ranging from 3,000 rpm to 30,000 rpm, can attain extraordinarily high efficiency, and are known for their quiet operation when compared to Roots-type superchargers. Twin screw superchargers are similar to Roots in appearance and operate in a similar manner, but instead of rotors, the impellers are more like two large screws side by side with the threads intertwining. The screw action of the two rotors pulls air in at one end of the housing and passes it lengthwise to the other end.

Whipple Industries, Inc., is the main U.S. distributor of the Opcon Autorotor screw-type supercharger. As testament to the efficiency of these superchargers, Elmer Trett switched from rotor to screw-type and ran a 6.23 second ET at 234 mph with his Top Fuel bike.

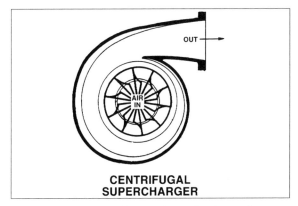

CENTRIFUGAL SUPERCHARGER

This cross section view of a typical centrifugal supercharger shows how the rotating impeller blades scoop in air through the inlet hole, compress it, and pass it on to the diffuser, or scroll outlet.

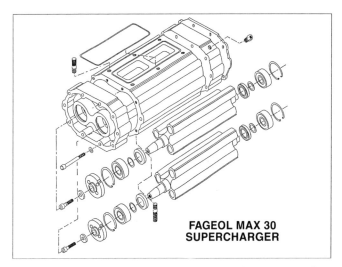

FAGEOL MAX 30 SUPERCHARGER

Superchargers are a little more complex than turbochargers. Driven by belts and pulleys off the crankshaft of the engine, they are also less efficient. Proponents of supercharging say that's okay, because having instant boost makes things much more interesting in a drag race. Shown here is an exploded view of a Fageol MAX-30 Supercharger. This three-lobe unit is popular with hobbyist performance buffs because of its small size and self-lubrication.

Centrifugal Superchargers

Centrifugal superchargers, like turbochargers, produce boost by mechanically spinning an impeller. Compared to other superchargers, centrifugal superchargers can spin up to higher rpm for longer periods of time and create moderately high boost levels.

The extremely efficient compressor also reduces outlet temperature for cooler operation, resulting in more mass airflow and greater power. Improvements in impeller design in recent years have made most modern centrifugal superchargers even more efficient. Some, like the new Powerdyne units, have design features such as ceramic bearings that require less lubrication,

and spin with less drag. This also prevents heat from transferring to oil.

Several companies manufacture this type of blower. Three of the more popular brands are Paxton, Vortech, and Powerdyne. None of these companies makes a system specifically for motorcycle usage; however, we know of one Vortech/Yamaha V-Max adaptation in process as this is written.

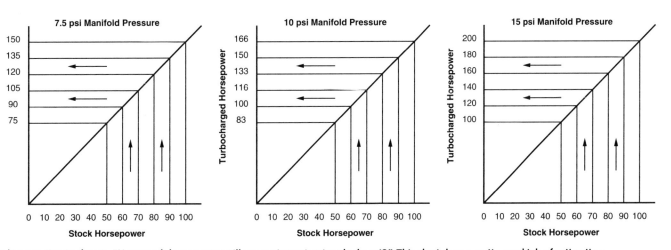

big question is always, "How much horsepower will my engine put out under boost?" This chart does a pretty good job of estimating horsepower from boost pressure. In the five years we have been using it, the chart has never been off by more than 10 horsepower in comparisons with dyno tests. Simply locate your stock horsepower at the bottom of the chart at whatever pressure level you choose (7.5, 10, or 15 psi). Follow the lines up to the horsepower rating and you've got it. This chart applies to turbochargers as well as superchargers, but does *not* reflect efficiency, due to the great variance between supercharger and turbocharger designs. This chart is more suitable for calculating the output of turbocharger horsepower than supercharger horsepower, but is fairly accurate for both.

Mad Max Enterprises of Waterbury, Conn. (203-574-7859) specializes in supercharger and turbocharger systems for the mighty V-Max. Shown here is their Camden (80 cubic inch) supercharger system, with nitrous oxide for added whallop. In street trim and at 14 psi boost, it is expected to turn quarter-mile times of 9 seconds at 150+ miles per hour. This particular bike belongs to Dennis Barch (Lodi, N.J.) and is absolutely immaculate from stem to stern. Mad Max also specializes in chain drive conversions for the V-Max, although not shown in this photo.

What Kind of a Power Gain Can You Expect From a Typical Supercharger?

A typical supercharger will operate at approximately 45 to 60 percent efficiency, so at 7.5 psi boost you really won't realize that 50 percent increase in horsepower, as the figures on paper might indicate. Some superchargers have efficiency ratings as low as 30 percent, but most screw and centrifugal superchargers have much higher ratings.

As an example, let's say your typical stock Harley Evo puts out 60 crankshaft horsepower (and that's giving it some), and you boost it to 7.5 psi. Using a supercharger with 50 percent efficiency, the engine will be putting out approximately 75 to 80 horsepower. Since 7.5 psi is considered fairly low boost by today's standards, let's kick it up a bit. At 10 lbs boost (still considered low), you'll move on up to about 90 horsepower, and at 15 lbs boost, we're talking about 115 to 120 horsepower to the rear wheel. This would be about maximum for a street blower because of inherent rotor or impeller rpm limitations.

You can only spin a supercharger so fast. A more efficient centrifugal supercharger can spin up to higher speeds than a Roots- or screw-type, but still won't come close to a turbocharger's 150,000-rpm potential.

The supercharger's real strength is its ability to create boost right off idle, which gives it the reputation for instant horsepower, the low-end punch you need for drag racing.

Most Top Fuel drag bikes running today use superchargers, as opposed to turbochargers, for two good reasons. First, supercharger boost is immediate, whereas turbocharger boost builds more slowly, but surpasses the supercharger at some point. Of course the idea in drag racing is to blast from a standing start through the quarter-mile as quickly as possible. Supercharged motorcycles usually have better 60-foot times than turbocharged ones, since they build boost at low rpm.

Second, superchargers use nitromethane fuel more effectively. Superchargers are connected to the crankshaft of the engine and turn in relation to crankshaft rpm. Turbochargers, by contrast, turn in relation to the amount of exhaust gases passing through them in conjunction with heat loading (the hotter the exhaust, the more pressure). Superchargers create more horsepower on a linear scale, which means fueling can be precisely metered—and when running nitromethane, this is very important. However, with the advent of electronic programmable fuel injection, it won't be long before fueling can be precisely metered on nitro turbo engines as well. In conjunction with today's lagless state-of-the-art turbochargers, the supercharger's days may be numbered.

Supercharger Lubrication

With the exception of the Powerdyne centrifugal, superchargers need lots of lubrication. Some, like Camden superchargers, are lubricated with high-pressure engine oil and must either incorporate a siphon system to return spent oil back to the engine crankcase or be located above the crankcase for proper drainage. Others, such as Fageol superchargers from K.F. Engineering, are self-lubricated and can be mounted anywhere. If you think you'll have a problem making lubrication hookups, choose a self-lubricating model.

Both types seem equally reliable. High-pressure engine lubricated superchargers may have a longer bearing life, less friction loss, and the ability to handle higher heat loads—but self-lubricated superchargers don't appear to increase the risk of blower failure. The choice is yours.

Above, right, and lower right: **Magna Charger of Orland, Calif. (916-865-7010)** makes this beautiful supercharger system for the Yamaha V-Max. Notice how nicely everything blends together. This hot street system can put out between 160 and 200 horsepower at the rear wheel. One of their customers bolted on the system, drove it to the drag strip, and cranked 155 mph on his first run ever. And that run included two wheel stands that forced him to back out of the throttle twice before entering the timing lights!

Blow-Through or Draw-Through

Blow-through is blowing air through an existing carburetion or fuel injection system; *draw-through* is drawing air and fuel through a carburetor.

Supercharger systems on street bikes are usually set up to draw air and fuel through single or multiple carburetors. Top Fuel drag bikes almost all use mechanical fuel injection—the supercharger just blows air, with fuel supplied directly to the intake ports. Turbocharger systems can work either way. If used in a draw-through application, the turbocharger must be properly sealed where the shaft enters the compressor housing. This keeps fuel from contaminating the oil supply through minor seepage under pressure. Most motorcycle draw-through turbo systems use one single-barrel carburetor attached to the entrance of the compressor housing.

Blow-through electronic programmable fuel injection and blow-through carburetion are becoming more popular, with better response time and horsepower than the more antiquated draw-through systems. Although you will still see a greater number of all-out draw-through turbo and supercharged drag bikes at the races, on the street it is much more important to have the flexibility throughout the entire power range which is characteristic of blow-through systems.

Supercharger Location

You can put a supercharger just about anywhere on a motorcycle that you can put a turbocharger, as long as the drive mechanism can somehow be attached to the crankshaft. On inline four-cylinder engines, the usual location is behind the cylinders where the carburetors once resided, hooked up to either the left or right side of the crankshaft. On Top Fuel drag bikes, it is common to turn the cylinder head around so the exhaust exits to the rear, while the intake ports point forward.

Horsepower Unlimited of Sophia, W.V. (304-683-5500) is assembling one of the nicest looking as well as functional supercharger systems in the business. Designed for use on Suzuki GSXRs and Kawasaki engines, the entire system is machined from billet. The belt guard (drive is off the right side of the crankshaft) acts as a rigid brace to hold the supercharger in exact position at all times. The Whipple screw-type supercharger can be geared for street or competition with a full range of boost potential from 5 to 35 psi. Street systems are fueled through a single S&S Shorty carburetor. Competition systems are mechanically fuel injected.

Harley-Davidson engines present a couple of additional problems. Most Harley riders don't want to spoil the aesthetics and natural style of the bike. It's got to fit in, or forget it. Most systems I've investigated would mount the supercharger on the side of the engine, by the cylinders, and drive the blower through a 90-degree gear drive off the crankshaft. Magna Charger (916-865-7010) mounts the blower on the right side of the engine in a more or less vertical position, which looks clean and blends in with Harley styling. Fageol superchargers have been used in many custom installations and are usually mounted on the left side in a horizontal position across the cylinders. A 90-degree drive assembly gets the belt pointed in the right direction. RB Racing (310-515-5720) is working on a Harley design that would mount the blower crosswise in front of the engine, which might be the least aesthetically offensive design.

Three companies specialize in superchargers for the Yamaha V-Max. Mad Max Enterprises (203-574-7859) is using the Camden supercharger in their kit, while A.S.A.P. Racing Products (517-484-4080) uses the Fageol supercharger. Magna Charger (916-865-7010) uses their own blower. All three of these companies mount the supercharger in the crotch of the 'V' between the cylinders, running crosswise to the engine—and as with inline designs, it's a straight shot to the crankshaft on the left side.

Choosing the Proper Supercharger

It's easier to choose the correct supercharger than the right turbocharger. If you are building a street bike, just about any of the small superchargers will do. Lower boost pressures equate to longer life, lower heat, and better efficiency. But if you plan to race, the more efficient the supercharger, the better. The trend in drag racing is toward screw-type superchargers, of which only one company offers a full range of sizes applicable to motorcycle usage: the Opcon Autorotor, distributed in the United States through Whipple Industries (209-442-1261). The rotors (or screws) are machined to close tolerances and do not require seals between the rotors and housing, leaving them free to spin without extra drag.

Centrifugal superchargers, with their odd shape, could present some installation problems on motorcycles. They are usually larger in diameter than their rotor type counterparts and much flatter. On a drag bike this may not be much of a problem, but on a street bike, one might be hard pressed to find a mounting location.

All in all, choosing the proper size of supercharger boils down to a simple formula involving cubic feet of air per minute (CFM). First, figure out how much horsepower you want your engine to put out (within reason). Then figure how many cubic feet of air per minute it will take to achieve that goal. It takes approximately 160 cubic feet of air per minute to make 100 horsepower, so if your goal is 200 streetable horsepower, you will need a supercharger capable of passing at least 320 CFM at full tilt. Now let's say your motorcycle engine puts out a factory rated horsepower of 100 at the crankshaft. It will take approximately 15 to 20 psi of boost pressure to approach 200 horsepower (this level of boost is at the high end of what's practical for a Roots supercharger, but possible in short bursts), at 320 CFM. Simply choose the model and brand that can achieve these figures, and you'll be close to correct, depending on how accurate the manufacturer's ratings and calculations are.

One of the finest examples of supercharged street bikes has got to be "Mad Malc's" Eddie Lawson Replica. It sports a Camden supercharger and runs on a combination of aviation gas and pump gas. Twin SU carburetors, transplanted from a Rover automobile, supply the mixture. It is said to be ridable and user-friendly and, according to Malcolm, has a sound all its own. *Photos courtesy of Streetfighters Magazine*

Please keep in mind that boost pressures over 10 psi on stock compression engines can create severe engine-damaging detonation problems. Without the aid of detonation controls, 15 to 20 psi boost would definitely require lower compression forged pistons and possibly race gas, which we will discuss in Chapter 8.

Conclusion

More supercharger designs and types have come out over the years than we have space to write about. The more popular types today have actually changed little over the decades, though. The biggest breakthroughs in technology have been in the areas of screw and centrifugal designs. The old rotor type of supercharger seems to be fading in the face of this competition—there is just no way they can compete in efficiency for all-out racing situations. However, for low boost street applications, Roots-type blowers work fine.

We mostly see the Roots-type supercharger on drag racing machinery, but they have been used on diesel trucks, buses, and automobiles for many years. The best-known is the GMC 6-71 blower. They too are usually driven by belts and pulleys. Twin rotors (side by side) inside a contoured housing are over-driven to spin at speeds greater than engine rpm. The longer the rotors (for any given size supercharger), the more cubic feet of air the supercharger is capable of passing to the engine. Most twin-rotor superchargers are fairly efficient (usually in the 45 percent range) and are reliable if they are not overstressed.

Centrifugal superchargers are similar to turbochargers, only mechanically driven—a turbocharger without the exhaust housing. The compressor housing and impeller work on the same principle but with a belt and pulleys used to drive them. Centrifugal superchargers generally have some type of gearing system which allows the impeller to spin up to more than 30,000 rpm.

Twin-screw superchargers, such as the Roots-types, have side-by-side rotors, but the rotors in the screw-type are like two large screws next to and intertwined with each other. Screw-type superchargers generally run quieter and are more efficient than twin-rotor superchargers.

Camden Superchargers

For more than 30 years, John Camden, president and founder of Camden Superchargers, has been involved with the design, manufacture, and application of superchargers. Camden produced the first compact supercharger for small block Chevrolet V-8s in 1957. A number of his units were campaigned in circle track and sports car racing applications, successfully competing against much larger engines.

Camden pioneered the use of aluminum rotor extrusions in 1976 and has continued to refine rotor design to achieve the present high level of operating efficiency. During the early 1970s, Camden began developing supercharger kits for smaller four-cylinder automobile engines, which turned out to be perfect for larger displacement motorcycles as well. Mad Max Enterprises uses Camden superchargers in their V-Max kit with awesome results. RB Racing is also using a Camden supercharger to design a new Harley Evo kit, to be offered through Competition Motors in Boise Idaho (208-344-7580).

Although the outside dimensions of Camden superchargers are rather large, they have many other features that make them appropriate for use on motorcycles:

1. The front rotor shafts are pressure lubricated with filtered engine oil for longer life and, according to the manufacturer, greater reliability.

2. The rotor shafts in the rear are supported by precision-bored journal bearings that are pressure lubricated with filtered engine oil. The entire lubricating system features pressure oil lubrication for low maintenance, and greater heat dissipation.

3. A special round Teflon seal runs the full length of the rotors, providing maximum efficiency.

4. The one-piece front extension provides increased strength than multi-piece assemblies.

5. A one-piece alloy steel input rotor shaft is used for increased reliability.

6. A replaceable front oil seal is incorporated in the front of the nose extension for easy servicing.

7. The multi-ribbed aluminum housing has exceptional strength and dissipates heat efficiently. It is also computer machined to maintain consistently accurate tight tolerances.

8. A one-piece steel shaft runs all the way through the rotors. They are pressed in and pinned for greater rotor strength.

If you are planning a custom supercharger installation on a motorcycle, Camden may just have the unit for you. They offer a full range of sizes that fit V-8s on down to liter-size motorcycle engines.

- Camden Superchargers, 512-339-4772 ■

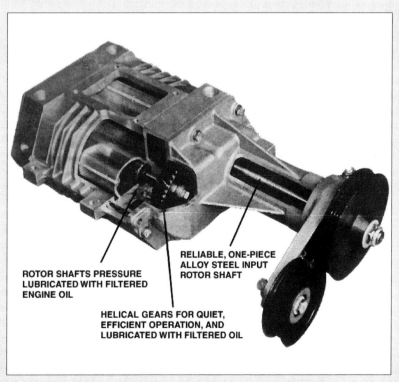

ROTOR SHAFTS PRESSURE LUBRICATED WITH FILTERED ENGINE OIL

RELIABLE, ONE-PIECE ALLOY STEEL INPUT ROTOR SHAFT

HELICAL GEARS FOR QUIET, EFFICIENT OPERATION, AND LUBRICATED WITH FILTERED OIL

Camden Roots-type supercharger

Fageol Superchargers

Fageol was formerly known as K.F. Engineering. Mark Fageol's brother retired from the business a couple of years ago, but Mark has continued manufacturing these superchargers under his own name. For many years they supplied small to medium sized Roots-type superchargers capable of boosting engines from 0.5 to 3 liters in displacement. This size range is perfect for automobile four-cylinder and V-6s on down to 500cc motorcycle engines and is currently being used in the A.S.A.P. Yamaha V-Max blower kit, and by Rohm Performance Products in their Suzuki GSXR750 kit.

These little blowers are self-lubricated, which means they can be placed in just about any location, a definite plus for motorcycle installations. No need for oil lines to, or drain lines from, the supercharger. They are available in four sizes, including 33.5, 48.3, 63.2, and 70.6 cubic inches displacement per revolution.

Fageol superchargers are made from aircraft quality materials. The gears and rotor shafts are made from 4340 steel for longer life. The extruded aluminum center section ensures sealing uniformity, and works well with the Viton rotor seals.

Various types of idler arms and pulleys are also available; units can be set up to use an 8 mm toothed belt, as well as multi-V or serpentine belts. Supercharger drives are available in lengths from 2.4 inches to 7.9 inches, and if the angle isn't right, optional 90-degree drives should do the trick.

The standard boost level is 5 psi at 5,000 rpm; however, this figure can be adjusted upward to 10 or 12 psi with the appropriate ratio change. Fageol also offers a variety of inlet and outlet adapter plates for a variety of installation applications. If you're looking for a compact, lightweight, tried-and-proven supercharger for your custom motorcycle installation, this may be the unit for you.

- Fageol Superchargers, 619-447-1092 ∎

Fageol Roots-type supercharger

Whipple Superchargers (Opcon-Autorotor)

Whipple Industries has supplied screw-type superchargers to customers in every area of the automotive, motorcycle, and industrial spectrum. Whipple Chargers are manufactured by the Opcon Autorotor Company in Sweden and distributed through Whipple Industries, Inc. in Fresno, Calif. Most of Whipple's kits are designed for cars, but even though they do not supply bolt-on kits for motorcycles, they can supply you with a range of small superchargers sized for engine displacements from 0.32 to 9.8 liters.

Twin-screw compressor technology has been used in industrial applications for more than 40 years. Screw-type supercharger technology is outstanding for durability, compactness, efficiency, and capacity. These compressors have a built-in volume ratio, which in turn gives them internal compression. This is the main reason for the high efficiency, even at high pressure ratios. The compression takes place in all rotor lobe areas simultaneously, creating constant uninterrupted pressure. The twin-screw compressor maintains its high efficiency even for pressure ratios up to 3.0.

The compressor consists of three main assemblies: the drive side assembly, the housing and rotors, and the suction side assembly. To change the capacity of the compressor, change the length of the housing and the rotors by cutting the extruded aluminum housing and rotors in various lengths. The suction side assembly and drive side assembly stay the same.

The built-in pressure ratio can easily be changed for various boost pressures. This is important to get minimum driving power consumption and keep the manifold temperature down. With the current design, a single CNC operation can vary the built-in pressure ratio between 1.0 and 2.5. This makes it possible to tailor the boost pressure over the entire speed range for each application, whether for street, strip, or cruising.

Nose drives are available from 2.5 inches to 12.5 inches. Pulley sizes vary from 2 to 3.5 inches. Many special adapters for axial and radial entry are available, as are an assortment of belts, tensioners, fuel system components, and air cleaners.

Three models should be of interest to the motorcyclist. Size range one will fit any displacement between 0.3 and 0.5 liter, QA1040 for 0.40 liter, and QA1050 for 0.50 liter. Size range two will fit any displacement between 0.6 and 0.9 liters, and QA2089 for 0.89 liter. Size range three will fit any displacement between 1.0 and 1.5 liter, QA3116 for 1.16 liter, QA3133 for 1.33 liter, and QA3150 for 1.50 liter.

Whipple Chargers are lubricated with high-pressure engine oil for long life and greater rpm potential. Size range one will spin up to 18,000 rpm. Two and three will max out at 15,000 and 13,000 respectively. The housings are made from extruded aluminum for uniformity and ease of capacity changes. A screw-type supercharger does not need rotor seals, which makes for less horsepower-robbing friction and quieter operation than Roots-type superchargers.

Full information, including technical drawings, descriptive illustrations, and brochures, is available from

- Whipple Industries, 209-442-1261 ∎

Whipple/Opcon screw-type supercharger

Magna Charger Superchargers

Magna Chargers were originally designed and developed by Jerry Magnuson in the late 1970s through the early 1980s, mainly for motorcycle drag bikes. Compared to other Roots-type superchargers of that era, they were better designed and more efficient at high boost. Most blower applications, according to Bill Bushling (president of Magna Charger Co.), "require a person with some degree of mechanical ability to install and maintain the system. This leaves out a large section of the Harley riders today." He goes on to say, "Our supercharger system for Harley-Davidsons is an extremely simple gear-driven unit that is user-friendly, maintenance-free and comes complete with a video, so anyone who owns a VCR, regardless of mechanical skill, can install the system in about two hours."

Magna Charger kits are divided into two basic groups. On stock street bikes, they use a smaller supercharger and boost is held to approximately 5 to 6 lbs, with no engine modifications needed. The hot street setup features a larger supercharger capable of boost levels up to 20 psi. Their hot Yamaha V-Max street system can put out from 160 to 200 horsepower to the rear wheel, depending on the octane level of the fuel being used. The Harley system isn't as brutal as the V-Max system though. It will really wake up a Harley, but it's still fun to ride. Magna Charger has seen 140 horsepower to the rear wheel on an 80-inch engine, and the hot street version will work fine on up to 120 cubic inch stroker engines.

Magna Charger superchargers are built for high speed. They are designed to operate most efficiently between 5 and 25 lbs of boost and can rotate up to 15,000 rpm, which is fast for a Roots-type supercharger. A patented inner web is cast into the aluminum rotor lobes, which stiffens the individual lobes to prevent growing (stretch) at high rpm. This feature allows the use of much closer tolerances in machining, making these blowers more efficient than other Roots-type superchargers. All cast parts (housing, rotors, gears, case, end plates, and drive extensions) are made from aircraft quality 356-T6 aluminum. The case itself is cast in a "waffle" pattern, making it tremendously rigid for its size and weight.

All machining of rotors, blower cases, bearing housings, and end plates is performed on a new tape controlled milling machine, ensuring total accuracy and interchangeability of components. All these super-close tolerances add up to less air slippage (compression loss), less pumping effort, and less heat generated. The one-piece $\frac{3}{4}$-inch stress-proof hexagon rotor shafts are cast in and will not come loose. The rotors also feature two-way seals on each end, and the two precision 8620 steel rotor gears are case hardened to C60 Rockwell hardness.

- Magna Charger, 916-865-7010 ∎

Magna Charger makes a slick looking Roots-type blower system for Harley-Davidson big twins. It is driven off the right side of the engine and is positioned vertically. The hot street version can pump out 140 rear wheel horsepower, and that isn't to be sneezed at! Especially when you are getting boost from as low as 2,000 rpm.

Powerdyne Superchargers

Centrifugal superchargers have been around for more than 50 years. Some units on the market today have used the same technology for the past 30 years; however, things are changing. The Powerdyne "skunk works" has come up with an innovative little centrifugal supercharger that looks promising for larger displacement motorcycles.

The extremely efficient compressor reduces outlet temperature for cooler operation, resulting in more mass air flow and greater power. A unique curved-tip impeller produces more low-end torque than conventional straight-bladed impellers and also offers improved mid-range power.

The internal Kevlar cogged-belt drive eliminates noisy, internal gear trains, and the ultra-high-speed aerospace ceramic bearings require little lubrication, thus eliminating a source of heat to the supercharger from engine lubricating oil. At this writing, the Powerdyne supercharger comes in two versions: a 6 psi model and a 9 psi model. As mentioned before, it is difficult to mount a centrifugal supercharger to a street legal motorcycle due to the supercharger's large diameter; however, a drag bike frame may accommodate one with no problem—and with just drag racing in mind, boost levels can be raised substantially.

There are several companies manufacturing state-of-the-art centrifugal superchargers that could possibly be adapted to motorcycle usage. The four top companies are:

- Powerdyne, 805-723-2800
- Paxton Products, 805-389-1154
- Vortech, 805-529-9330
- ProCharger, 913-338-2886 ∎

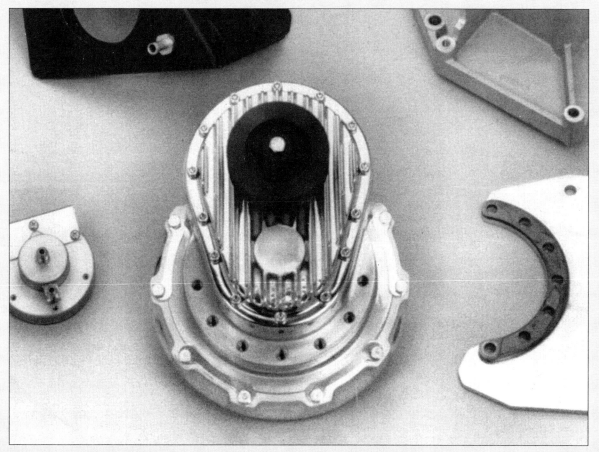

Powerdyne centrifugal supercharger

T.J. Hoftmeister, the original owner of Mr. Turbo, puts the heat to the sneaker for another 200 mph attack on the quarter-mile. The draw-through Suzuki features over-the-top headers.

Turbocharging

What if you were told there was a way to make free horsepower? Well, we all know nothing in life is free, and in one respect, that is correct—you will have to fork over what may seem like a large sum of money for your "free" horsepower. But, after the blow to your checking account, the horsepower increase is gratis.

Consider your engine's exhaust for a moment. Exhaust is hot and moves fast. Heat and motion are energy. Exhaust offers an ideal situation: a fast-moving hot gas that can be used to your advantage before escaping into the atmosphere. But how can you harness this normally wasted energy and make it work for you? Enter the turbosupercharger, or turbocharger, as it is commonly known today.

Simply put, a turbocharger is an exhaust-driven supercharger. Turbochargers use the energy of normally wasted exhaust to turn or rotate their impellers, with the only loss coming from slightly higher exhaust back pressure. However, this loss is not as great as the loss suffered by mechanical drive mechanisms.

Horsepower is "free" with turbocharging in the sense that exhaust energy, which is normally wasted, is used to drive the supercharger. Of course, the purpose of superchargers and turbochargers is to increase the amount of air and fuel to the engine, over and above what can be pushed into the engine by normal atmospheric pressure (which is 14.7 pounds per square inch, standing on the floor of Death Valley). Both methods of forcing more air and fuel into your engine produce similar results, and both methods of forced induction have advantages and disadvantages.

While mechanically-driven superchargers provide instantaneous boost from idle on up, turbochargers take a little extra time. When the throttle is opened suddenly, it takes the exhaust a few moments to overcome inertia and accelerate the impellers to a high speed. However, modern turbochargers will spin up to speed almost as fast as a supercharger, but without the sudden burst of horsepower commonly associated with superchargers—sort of a buffer zone before you go into warp speed. Some riders believe a little "turbo lag" is a good thing when it comes to motorcycles. Automobiles are another matter, but on a street bike with no wheelie bar, it's nice to have a little "ready, set, go" time.

Turbochargers have only one moving part: the turbine shaft assembly. No gears, no belts, no pulleys, no rotors. Simplicity alone makes turbochargers extremely efficient.

Compared to superchargers they are

1. Smaller and more compact
2. Lighter
3. Less complicated
4. More efficient
5. More durable

Let's Get Technical

A typical turbocharger is based on the old paddle wheel. A turbocharger consists of a rotating assembly: a turbine wheel at one end and a compressor impeller at the other, with each wheel enclosed in a contoured housing like a snail shell—small in the center, and increasingly larger toward the exit end. The two wheels are connected by a single shaft running through the turbocharger center section where it rides in a special bearing(s) lubricated with engine oil. This is known as the bearing housing. The turbocharger is connected to the engine by the exhaust pipes, which supply the drive

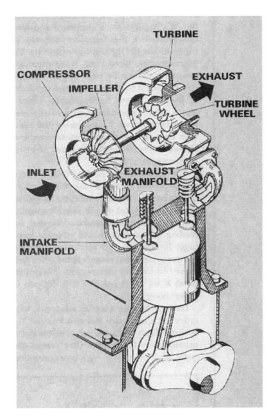

Figure 3-1.

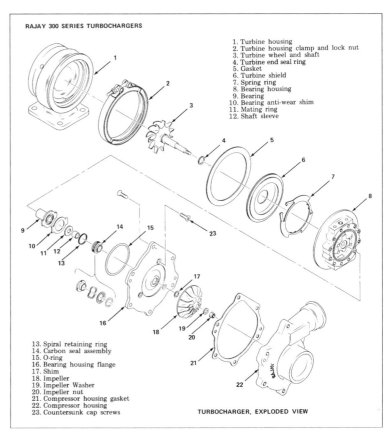

RAJAY 300 SERIES TURBOCHARGERS

1. Turbine housing
2. Turbine housing clamp and lock nut
3. Turbine wheel and shaft
4. Turbine end seal ring
5. Gasket
6. Turbine shield
7. Spring ring
8. Bearing housing
9. Bearing
10. Bearing anti-wear shim
11. Mating ring
12. Shaft sleeve

13. Spiral retaining ring
14. Carbon seal assembly
15. O-ring
16. Bearing housing flange
17. Shim
18. Impeller
19. Impeller Washer
20. Impeller nut
21. Compressor housing gasket
22. Compressor housing
23. Countersunk cap screws

TURBOCHARGER, EXPLODED VIEW

Figure 3-2.

power. The hot exhaust gases are directed against the turbine wheel blades, spinning the wheel, shaft, and compressor at high speed. With a draw-through system, the impeller in the compressor housing draws the air and fuel through the carburetor and passes it through the contoured housing, where it is compressed and sent to the cylinder(s) under high pressure. In a blow-through system, the compressor impeller draws plain air and forces it through pressurized carburetors or a fuel injection manifold. Either way, it increases the amount of air-fuel mixture available to the cylinder(s), resulting in a sizable horsepower increase. Under load, the turbocharger speed automatically increases (due to the increase in exhaust gases), providing more air and fuel mixture to meet the engine's demands (see Figure 3-1).

Turbocharger Design

It is best to understand the basic design features of the turbocharger before delving into the how-to's of motorcycle installations. The exploded view illustration of a Rajay turbocharger (see Figure 3-2) is a perfect example of just how simple a turbocharger can be. As you will notice, it is much less complicated than a super-

charger, and far more compact. However, there are minor differences in design between brands of turbochargers. Some have integral waste gates, twin bearings as opposed to single, and some may only be used in a blow-through design. Others may be self-lubricated like the Aerodyne turbocharger; however, all turbochargers are designed basically the same (see Figure 3-3).

Three major components make up a typical turbocharger: the compressor housing, the bearing housing, and the turbine housing. Exhaust from the engine enters the turbine housing, spinning the turbine wheel. The turbine wheel turns a shaft which passes through the bearing housing, where it is lubricated with engine oil. This shaft then connects to the compressor wheel, which compresses the incoming fuel and air (in a draw-through system), forcing it into the cylinder(s). In a blow-through system, only air is compressed and it is sent either through carburetors or through a plenum manifold and past direct-port fuel injectors. Each of these types of systems will be discussed in detail later.

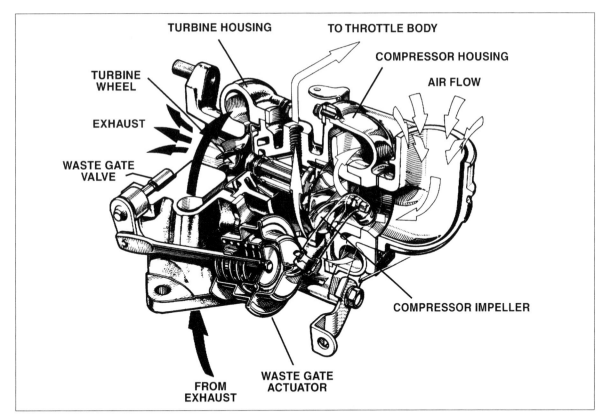

TURBINE HOUSING **TO THROTTLE BODY**

COMPRESSOR HOUSING

TURBINE WHEEL **AIR FLOW**

EXHAUST

WASTE GATE VALVE

COMPRESSOR IMPELLER

FROM EXHAUST **WASTE GATE ACTUATOR**

Figure 3-3.

Control Starts with the Turbocharger

Almost every aspect of turbocharging requires some sort of control, beginning with the compressor. The compressor impeller on the Rajay 300 series turbocharger, which is used to accelerate the air (or air-fuel mixture), comes in several major configurations. The type used in the model 300 B has curved blades on the impeller for higher efficiency. This is common among all the turbocharger manufacturers. The size and shape of the air inlet opening in the compressor housing and the size, material, and design of the impeller are key to the amount of air the scroll will ultimately be able to pass. This air flow is measured in cubic feet per minute/(CFM), as discussed in Chapter 2.

In recent years, the size, material, and blade design of the impellers has markedly reduced turbo lag time. Modern turbocharger designs (e.g., IHI, Mitsubishi, and Garrett), can realize as much as a 30 percent acceleration rate improvement over older designs. Moreover, modern blade designs make turbochargers more efficient at lower speeds. In other words, you can loosely control when you want positive boost to occur and tightly control how many cubic feet of air per minute will be supplied to your cylinders. Certain brands of turbochargers will accelerate faster than others, and within a brand, certain models of compressor housings and turbine wheels can make a major difference in efficiency.

The air (or air-fuel mixture) enters the small end of the compressor scroll passage and slows as the cross sectional area of the passage increases in size. The gas leaving the diffuser is now at a low speed and high pressure.

To determine which compressor housing will be best for your application, compare compressor maps. But first you must determine how many cubic feet of air per minute you will need to produce the horsepower you desire. Once you have decided on the proper air flow, you can then refer to compressor maps as a guide to the correct compressor and turbocharger.

In order to choose the proper air flow, you will need to assemble some information.

1. Engine size (example: 1,000cc)
2. Engine type (example: four-stroke)
3. Maximum engine rpm (example: 10,000 rpm)
4. Maximum turbo boost (example: 10 psi)

These two compressor wheels fit the same Hitachi (Kawasaki GPz750) turbocharger, but the larger is capable of pumping a much greater volume of air than the stock one on the right. Horsepower Unlimited can modify your compressor housing, install one of the larger wheels, and have you pumping to the tune of 180+ horsepower.

With this information you can calculate the correct pressure ratio and turbocharged airflow through the engine. Once you have obtained this information, you can plot it on a compressor map to help you decide which turbocharger model to use.

Pressure Ratio

Following is the formula for determining the pressure ratio. In our example we will use 10 psi as our minimum required boost.

$$Pressure\ ratio = \frac{P_b + P_a}{P_a}$$

where: P_b = Boost pressure
P_a = Atmospheric pressure

Example:

$$Pressure\ ratio = \frac{10psi + 14.7psi}{14.7psi} = 1.68$$

NOTE: Subtract 0.5 psi from the standard atmospheric pressure of 14.7 for each 1,000 feet above sea level to determine the atmospheric pressure at your specific altitude.

Volumetric Efficiency

To complete our calculation of air flow, we'll need to know the volumetric efficiency (VE) of our engine. But just what is VE anyway? It is a measure of how well the engine breathes. The better the breathing ability, the higher the VE. The VE is the ratio of the mass of air the engine actually takes in (M_{actual}), relative to

the mass of air that would be taken in if there were no losses (restrictions) in the inlet path ($M_{no\ losses}$).
Example:

$$VE = \frac{M_{actual}}{M_{no\ losses}}$$

where:
VE of stock engine in good condition = 75 percent
VE of high performance street engine = 80 percent
VE of racing engine = 94 percent

Engine Displacement

Next, you must convert the displacement of your metric engine to cubic inches.
Example:

$$Cubic\ Inches = \frac{Cubic\ Centimeters}{16.387}$$

$$= \frac{1000cc}{16.387} = 61.02\ cubic\ inches$$

Find the Density Ratio

We need to know the Density Ratio (DR) of air at the pressure ratio we've chosen. To find the Density Ratio for a given Pressure Ratio and compressor efficiency, refer to Figure 3-4. Enter the chart with the density ratio we desire. Let's assume our compressor efficiency is 70 percent. In this example, we have chosen a pressure ratio of 1.68. For that value, the Density Ratio is 1.40.

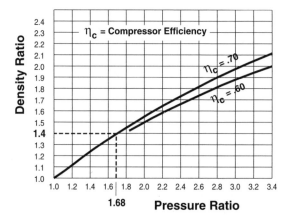

Figure 3-4.

What You Should Know About Compressing Air and Generating Heat

Heat is the most significant enemy of any engine, and methods for controlling engine heat take many forms. Coolant radiators, oil coolers, fins, fans, and fluids make up the usual assortment of heat controlling items. However, when forcing compressed air into your engine, you need to think about another kind of heat problem.

When air is pressurized, its temperature increases. A common example of heat generated by compressing air is the ordinary shop compressor. When the tank is empty, it is cool to the touch. However, when you turn on the compressor, you will notice the tank gets hotter as the pressure increases. The heat created by compressing air into your engine is one of the most important factors you will need to deal with when turbocharging or supercharging any engine. When the compressor impeller accelerates the air or air-fuel mixture to a high velocity and forces it into the diffuser (scroll), the air or air-fuel mixture decelerates, thereby causing its pressure and temperature to increase. This heat can promote detonation, or ping, and is the primary cause of piston and engine failure.

With the following series of calculations, you can figure exactly what the discharge temperature (temp) of pressurized air leaving the compressor (diffuser) will be. See Figure 3-5.

As an example, let's assume that the ambient temperature is 80° Fahrenheit, that our blower is developing a pressure ratio of 1.9 (that is, its outlet pressure is 1.9 times atmospheric pressure), and that our compressor operates at 65 percent efficiency. We have

Inlet temperature = 80° F
Pressure ratio $r = 1.9$
Compressor efficiency $\eta_c = 65\% = 0.65$

From Table 1 we must look up the factor y, which is a direct function of the pressure ratio. For $r = 1.9$, we find on Table 1 that $y = 0.199$.

To calculate the "idealized" temperature rise (that is, the temperature rise that would result if the compressor were 100 percent efficient), we take

$$
\begin{aligned}
T_{ideal} &= (460 + T) \times y \\
&= (460 + 80) \times 0.199 \\
&= 107.5° \text{ F}
\end{aligned}
$$

To calculate the actual temperature rise, we must take into account the efficiency of the compressor.

$$
T_{actual} = \frac{T_{ideal}}{\eta_c} = \frac{107.5}{0.65} = 165.4° \text{ F}
$$

We have calculated the temperature *rise*; to get the actual discharge temperature, add this rise to the ambient temperature.

$$
\begin{aligned}
T_2 &= T_1 + T_{actual} \\
&= 80 + 165.4 \\
&= 245.4° \text{ F}
\end{aligned}
$$

So, if you start with air at 80° F and compress it by a ratio of 1.9 with 65 percent efficiency, you will end up with air entering the combustion chamber at 245° F. Even worse, a Roots-type supercharger operating at 45 percent efficiency will raise the temperature to 319° F.

Further on, you will be reading more about intercoolers, water-alcohol injection, racing gas, low compression pistons, and retarded ignition timing as methods of controlling detonation. However, at this point in our discussion, it is better to understand the importance of pressure and temperature controls in designing a reliable system. ∎

Figure 3-5

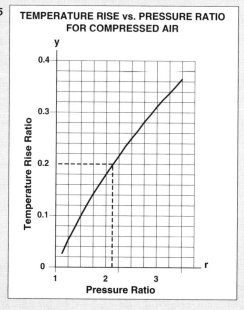

TEMPERATURE RISE vs. PRESSURE RATIO FOR COMPRESSED AIR

Required Air Flow

We're now ready to figure the volume of air flow in cubic feet per minute (CFM) your turbo engine will require. Use the following calculation to determine the air flow for four-cycle engines.

To determine the turbocharged volume of air through your engine, we multiply the Volumetric Efficiency (VE) by the Density Ratio we found in Figure 3-4. Now with our known displacement of 61 cubic inches we can compute the turbocharged air flow requirements.

Example:

$$CFM = \frac{D \times CID \times Maximum\ rpm}{1728} \times VE \times DR$$

D = Displacement factor per revolution, which is 0.5 for 4-cycle engines and 1.0 for 2-cycle engines.

CID = Cubic Inches Displacement of your engine

VE = Volumetric Efficiency (see text for your type of engine)

DR = Density Ratio (from Figure 3-4)

1728 = Number of cubic inches per cubic foot

$$\frac{0.5 \times 61 \times 10,000}{1728} \times 0.80 \times 1.40 = 197\ CFM$$

Now that we know our required air flow is 197 CFM, we can start looking at turbocharger compressor maps.

Compressor Maps

Referring to the turbocharger compressor map in Figure 3-6, locate your 1000cc engine's Pressure Ratio line of 1.68 on the left side of the scale. Then move across to 200 CFM (rounded off from 197 CFM), at the bottom of the scale. If that intersecting point is just about center, between the surge line (far left) and the 60 percent efficiency line (far right), that's about average. This should put the turbocharger at approximately 68 percent efficiency—by today's standards fairly normal. If the intersecting point is left of the surge line, you could damage the compressor. If the intersecting point is too far to the right, the compressor will be less efficient. For street or strip use, somewhere just left of center is best.

Looking at compressor maps from different manufacturers will show that some turbochargers are more efficient than others. Remember, our example indicated a Pressure Ratio of 1.68, and 200 CFM is what we'll need at 10 lbs. boost and 10,000 rpm. The compressor map shown here, taken from the Rajay model F60

turbocharger, should be an ideal turbocharger for our example engine, with plenty of boost potential for top end performance. This Rajay model F60, at 68 percent efficiency, might be a little soft on response and show significant lag. It might be more appropriately applied to drag bike usage, as it would still furnish more than enough horsepower out of the gates to light the tire while providing crucial top-end efficiency and power. This is where it becomes painfully obvious there are no set rules: if you want better low end response with boost coming on sooner, not later, you'll definitely want to compare the compressor maps for the B25 and B40 models to see if you can get the efficiency up from 68 percent. Use the same procedure when looking into other brands of turbochargers. The same rules (or lack of rules, depending on how you look at it) apply to all brands and, who knows, you may hit 75 percent efficiency with an IHI, or Garrett, or Mitsubishi.

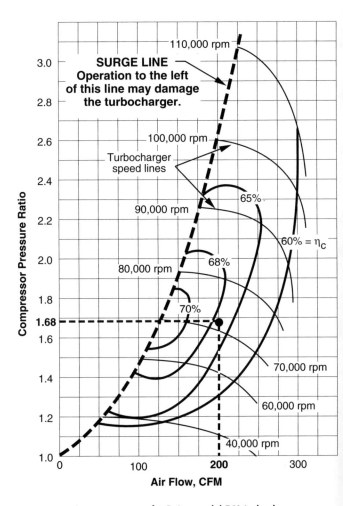

Figure 3-6: Compressor map for Rajay model F60 turbocharger.

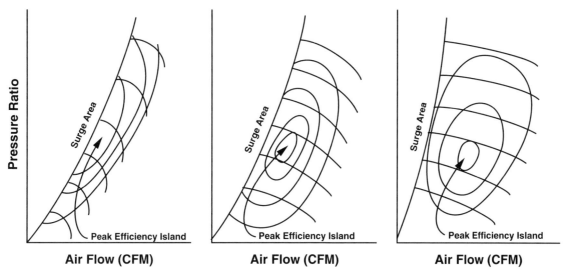

Three different compressor maps, showing the "peak efficiency island." Operation to the left of the surge line can damage the turbocharger.

Some modern turbochargers will show nearly the same efficiency on the compressor map as, say, the Rajay, but will accelerate to speed 30 percent faster. Smaller impellers, made from exotic lightweight materials, and advanced blade design have helped improve turbocharger performance over the past few years. These advances certainly help, but the rest of the story is on the opposite side of the turbocharger.

As mentioned before, today's designs can almost eliminate turbo lag if you match the turbocharger to your needs and projections.

Exhaust Turbine and Scroll Design

Just like the compressor end of the turbocharger, the exhaust turbine wheel and housing play a major role in response time, turbocharger rpm, and the total amount of boost. The turbine is vital to boost control.

Once the air flow (CFM) rating of the compressor housing has been established, the next best way to adjust a turbocharger for varying applications or usage is to change the size of the turbine housing. For instance, if you are planning to race your bike at Bonneville, you have much less need for bottom-end response. You would choose a larger exhaust inlet and outlet housing for this application to decrease the amount of exhaust back pressure, allowing the engine to breathe more efficiently at the top end, while losing some bottom-end response. For street or drag racing use, a smaller exhaust inlet housing would build boost sooner for improved bottom-end response.

The amount of exhaust gas that can be pumped through a turbocharger to produce intake pressure depends on the inlet nozzle area. A useful measure of that area is the so-called "A/R ratio," defined as the area of the incoming gas opening in the scroll, divided by the radius from the center of the shaft to the center of the opening. Larger engines typically use exhaust scrolls with larger A/R ratio. For instance, a 750cc engine might use an exhaust scroll with 0.25 A/R ratio for street or drag racing, while a 1000cc engine might use a 0.40 A/R ratio.

Exhaust turbine housings with various A/R ratios are usually interchangeable (sometimes with an impeller change) for any given turbocharger, depending on the brand and model. The smaller the exhaust inlet passage, the faster the exhaust travels, turning the turbine wheel at a higher speed. The faster the exhaust turbine wheel spins, the faster the compressor turbine wheel will turn, making for greater intake pressure. You must always try to avoid using an A/R ratio which is too small, though, as that would overspeed the turbine and shorten the life of the turbocharger.

Your challenge is to arrive at a good balance between compressor efficiency and the exhaust A/R ratio. For instance, the IHI model RHB52 turbochargers come with three different A/R ratios, all with the same 233 CFM compressor. Remember, you've already determined the required CFM and the compressor. A flow rate of 233 CFM at maximum efficiency should make a peppy little turbo for anything from a 750cc to 1000cc motorcycle. The A/R ratios available for the IHI model RHB52 are: 0.41 (good for 600 to 750cc), 0.59 (good

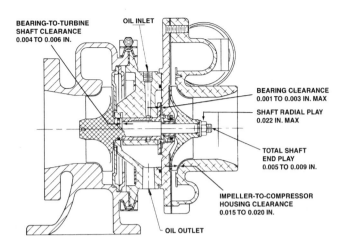

Figure 3-7

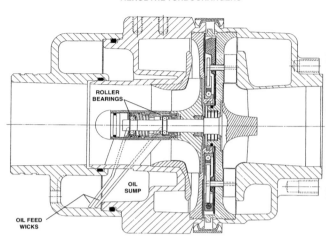

Figure 3-8: Turbochargers require reliable lubrication to prevent self-destruction at high speeds. This unit has a self-contained oil sump and feed wicks to lubricate the bearings.

for 750 to 1000cc) and 0.78 for larger engines, or for more efficient top end power.

Generally speaking, you should size a turbocharger slightly smaller than the ideal A/R ratio for any given engine. This approach will increase bottom end response and lessen lag time. Normally, choosing too small an A/R ratio would overspeed the turbine and put the turbo into a severe surge condition (remember the surge line on the compressor map?). This is where waste gates come into play. They are pressure-sensitive valves which can be preset to open at whatever peak boost level you have chosen; above that pressure they dump excess exhaust into the exhaust system or the open atmosphere, thereby maintaining your chosen boost level.

Some turbochargers come with a built-in waste gate, and some, like Rajay, do not. Turbos with a built-in waste gate are usually preset at the factory for 5 to 7 psi and are not adjustable. Built-in waste gates can be modified successfully to be used in conjunction with a dial-a-boost control and can be adjusted to allow boost levels up to the 10 to 15 psi range. Even if your turbocharger has an integral waste gate, you may want to replace it with an adjustable aftermarket unit that can be used with a dial-a-boost mechanism. Waste gates will be covered in greater detail later.

Become familiar with all the turbochargers within your performance range. Compare all the compressor maps. See which A/R ratios are available. Talk with experts and get their recommendations. Compare the results.

The Bearing Housing

It's so easy to get wrapped up in the compressor and exhaust ends of the turbocharger that we quickly forget about the part that takes all the abuse: the bearing housing.

Sandwiched between the compressor housing and the exhaust turbine housing, and connecting the two, is the bearing housing (see Figure 3-7). The shaft connecting the compressor wheel to the exhaust turbine wheel passes through the bearing housing. Here, it rotates in a floating plain bearing, or twin plain bearings (depending on the brand and model turbocharger), and is lubricated with high-pressure engine oil. Some IHI turbochargers are equipped with roller bearings for lower friction loss, but for motorcycle use the plain bearing models will be fine. Aerodyne turbochargers (see Figure 3-8) are self-lubricating and also use roller bearings. Roller bearings may be the wave of the future for turbochargers suitable for motorcycle use. Roller bearings are starting to show up in other turbocharging systems. Turbonetics in Moorpark, Calif. is now offering a ceramic ball bearing hybrid turbo based on the Garrett T2, T3, and T4 models. It shows even greater promise than the Aerodyne turbo because the ceramic bearings require very little lubrication.

Terry Kizer of Mr. Turbo fame sights in on the finish line while blasting his Funny Bike to nearly 200 mph in less than seven seconds. Note the over-the-top headers and the high mounted turbocharger. Funny Bikes must resemble a production motorcycle, but that's where the similarity ends.

When turbochargers are mounted below the crankcase, it is impossible to drain oil from the turbo housing to the crankcase without special siphon systems. Being self-lubricating, Aerodyne turbochargers can be mounted in any location, and even vertically, if necessary.

It is important to use a top brand "turbo" oil, or "turbo synthetic" oil. These oils are specially formulated to withstand the high temperatures typically found in turbochargers, and will not leave sludge deposits that eventually cook into carbon deposits. Aerodyne turbochargers require special synthetic oil available only through Aerodyne.

Since the bearing housing also contains the sump where oil collects to be drained or siphoned back to the crankcase, most turbocharger manufacturers offer specially sealed shafts to keep fuel from contaminating the oil supply when the turbocharger is used in draw-through applications.

When choosing your turbocharger you must be careful to specify the proper kind of shaft sealing. Rajay turbochargers are sealed for both blow-through and draw-through applications, but most turbos on the market today are designed for blow-through only systems. Let's say, for instance, you locate an IHI turbocharger on a Ford Turbo Escort. This turbocharger (model RHB52) is designed for blow-through use only. Do not try to use it to draw air and fuel through a carburetor, as the lack of proper sealing will allow fuel-contaminated air to bypass the shaft bearings under boost. IHI turbochargers can be ordered with the proper seals for draw-through applications, as can most other brand turbos.

Watch out for those turbos scavenged from a wrecked car. Almost all would be for blow-through only, which is fine if that's how you intend to use it.

Dennis Strickland's draw-through Funny Bike is a fine example of meticulous maintenance. When you're putting your life on the line at 200 mph, you want to be sure the equipment is up to it. The rules for Funny Bike class are fairly wide open, with most of the emphasis put on safety.

Choosing the Right Turbocharger

According to my research, six companies make turbochargers small enough to be used on motorcycle engines: Rajay, Mitsubishi, Garrett (AiResearch), Warner-Ishi (IHI), Hitachi, and Aerodyne. Most motorcycle turbo kit companies use Rajay, IHI, or Garrett turbochargers. If you are planning to purchase a complete turbo kit, one of these three turbocharger brands will probably be part of the kit.

Mitsubishi

Mitsubishi manufactured turbochargers for Yamaha 650cc motorcycles in the early 1980s. This was one of the smallest turbos ever manufactured, probably suitable only for 500cc to 650cc size motors. Mitsubishi is a major supplier of turbochargers to the automotive industry and makes small turbos for cars in the 1200cc to 1500cc range. Some turbochargers used in small car applications actually have somewhat undersized A/R ratios for their given application. This was done to build boost at a lower rpm and to help control turbo lag, while an integral waste gate controls boost at higher rpm. Some of Mitsubishi's turbos for small car applications might be desirable for large displacement motorcycle engines using a blow-through system. If you are planning a do-it-yourself installation, the Mitsubishi TC-04 turbocharger can be found on the Dodge Colt GTS Turbo, with an engine displacement of 1598cc.

These turbos are known for their ability to build boost at low rpm—as low as 2,000 rpm for the Colt. The exhaust housing will probably have to be exchanged for one with a smaller A/R ratio more suitable for a smaller motorcycle engine. Mitsubishi makes a full range of turbocharger sizes, so refer to compressor maps for the unit that will best fit your application.

Warner-Ishi (IHI)

IHI is a supplier to the automotive industry as well, and some of their turbochargers are being used on small displacement cars and trucks. They also made turbos for the Honda CX500/650 motorcycles and the Suzuki XN85 turbo bike. The Ford Escort GT, Mercury Lynx RS Turbo, Ford EXP Turbo Coupe, Ford Probe GT Turbo, and Chevrolet Turbo Sprint all come equipped with IHI turbochargers. These may be good choices for motorcycles but, again, only for blow-through applications. As with any turbos mounted on automobiles, the A/R ratio will probably be too large, forcing you to change to a smaller scroll. IHI impellers are sophisticated in design, with backward curved compressor blades for ultra-high efficiency. The models with built-in waste gates feature a compact and cost-effective design for boost pressure control. IHI turbochargers are being used by some of the motorcycle kit manufacturers because they are compact, lightweight, durable, have unique design features, and build boost at low rpm.

For a 1000cc motorcycle engine, start with an IHI model RHB52, with a part number of 5T503. It has an A/R ratio of 0.59. If you need higher air flow, a model RHB6 is the next step up.

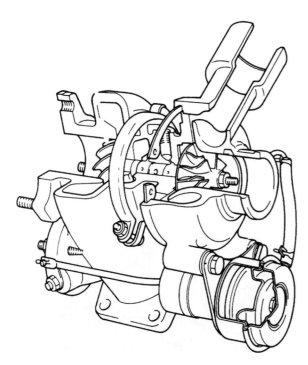

Mitsubishi

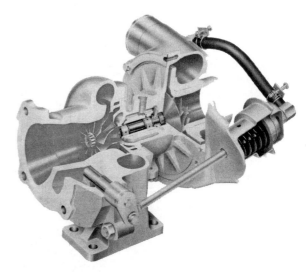

Warner-Ishi (IHI)

Garrett

Garrett turbochargers can be found in a number of applications; they too are a major supplier to the automotive industry. Garrett (sometimes referred to by their old name, AiResearch) has always been a prime mover in the development of turbochargers. Their variable vane turbo is proof of that fact. They are the only manufacturer besides Aerodyne to offer such a design. These variable nozzle turbines are currently being tested, and show promise in the future of turbocharging. The VATN (variable turbine nozzle) assemblies have multiple vanes which function as adjustable louvers. When activated by an engine's electronic boost-pressure control system, the vanes open and close, varying the exhaust flow past the turbine wheel and controlling turbocharger speed and boost level. Previously, the only way to control a turbocharger's output was to vary the turbine housing size (A/R ratio), smaller values being better at low engine speeds and larger ones offering more output at higher speeds. Of course, when a turbo is somewhat undersized in order to provide better low-end response, a waste gate is the only other alternative to the perfect A/R ratio.

Garrett is also making a small turbo known as the T15, presently slated for use on small European cars of 1.0 to 1.4 liter displacement. It features a full floating bearing and an integral waste gate. This could be an interesting turbo for 750cc to 1000cc motorcycles, as it also features full perimeter water cooling for greater reliability, and will spin up to speeds of 230,000 rpm.

There are probably more Garrett turbochargers than any other brand on factory cars. For you wrecking yard hounds, the Nissan Pulsar NX Turbo and Pontiac Sunbird Turbo use the Garrett T2 with integral waste gate.

Again, these are blow-through-only turbochargers, but new units can be ordered with the proper sealing for draw-through usage.

On a 1000cc motorcycle engine, you might want to try a T2 or T3. It should have a compressor capable of handling 300+ CFM and the A/R ratio should be in the range of 0.40 (for bottom-end and mid-range punch), up to 0.58 for greater top end power. One of the best sources for information on Garrett turbochargers is Turbonetics of Moorpark, Calif. (805-529-8995).

Hitachi

Hitachi made one of the world's smallest turbochargers for the original Kawasaki GPz750 in the early to mid-1980s. With a little luck you can still find them in wrecking yards, as the Turbo 750 was probably the most popular of the factory turbo bikes and was quite common. Parts availability is something of a problem, and I have heard of new prices for a complete turbo to be over $1,500. Horsepower Unlimited (www.horsepowerunlimited.com) specializes in rebuilding these little Hitachis and is also offering modifications that can raise the CFM level considerably. A mildly modified GPz750 Turbo Kawasaki can pump out approximately 140 horsepower to the rear wheel. However, after these special modifications (larger compressor and wheel), 180 horsepower is possible, according to Mike Chestnut. Examples of this bike, bored to 810cc displacement, have put out over 200 horsepower! You definitely do not want to use a stock GPz750 turbo on anything over 810cc, as it is almost too small for the OEM 750 engine. The part number for this turbocharger is HT-10B. It is not sealed for draw-through applications and so can only be used in a blow-through design.

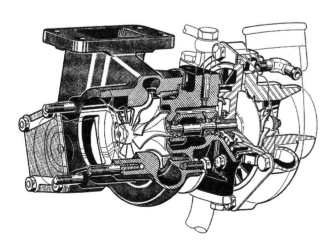

Garrett

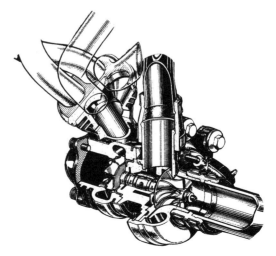

Hitachi

Rajay

Rajay is probably the most commonly used turbo for street and drag racing motorcycles. Rajay has been around since the early 1970s and their turbos have been incorporated into most of the kits being made for motorcycles. Rajay turbochargers were originally manufactured by Rajay; however, over the years the manufacturing of these popular turbos has changed hands several times. The present manufacturer is the Garrett Corporation. Mr. Turbo and Hahn Racecraft, two well-known suppliers of these turbos, can both help you choose the proper A/R ratio and compressor housing. The 300 series is the one most often used for motorcycle applications. The 0.25 to 0.40 A/R exhaust housing is about right for 750cc to 1000cc street engines.

These turbos can be rotated into 12 possible positions, providing 12 options for positioning the compressor housing to facilitate the installation, while retaining the oil outlet near the lower vertical position for proper drainage to the crankcase. Rajay turbos are fairly compact and lightweight at approximately 14 lbs. They feature a single long-lasting floating bearing. Rajay turbochargers are equipped with special carbon face seals, making it possible to use them in a blow-through or draw-through applications—the choice is yours.

A good place to start for a streetable 750 to 1000cc motorcycle engine would be the model 377B25. It has the B-flow compressor and a 0.25 A/R ratio. A model 377B40 would be the next step up. Some Funny Bike engines use different flow compressors, such as the "F" model. If your intended use is all-out drag racing, contact Mr. Turbo (713-442-7113) or Hahn Racecraft (708-851-5444) for recommendations.

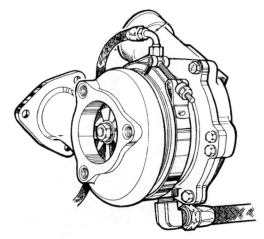

Rajay

Aerodyne

Aerodyne turbochargers use state-of-the-art aerodynamic components that produce high efficiencies and extremely broad operating ranges. The variable turbine nozzles are engineered for speed and pressure control, and improved transient response. The rotor system consists of back-to-back overhung compressor and turbine wheels supported by offset ball bearings. The bearing support is located in the compressor inlet flow path, providing a cool environment for the bearings.

Lubrication is provided in the form of a wick-fed oil mist. The oil reservoir is integral to the compressor housing, making it possible to locate the turbo in any position, including vertical (you must specify vertical or horizontal when ordering). The engine does not supply oil to the turbo bearings, and there are no drainage obstacles to overcome.

Because of the VATN (variable turbine nozzle) design, the unit acts like a small turbocharger for quick low end response and like a larger turbo for high top end efficiency. These turbochargers are available from First Choice Turbo Center, 1558 W. Henrietta Rd., East Avon, NY 14414, (716-226-2929). They are currently being used on racing (two-stroke) snowmobiles because of their self-lubricating design, apparently with reasonably good success. You would probably want to start with a model 128A777 for a 1000cc motorcycle engine, but you should ask for advice from First Choice Turbo Center before purchasing. Since the actuation of the VATN blades requires additional components, Aerodyne turbochargers cost approximately twice that of other popular brands, which can add a lot to the total cost for a system.

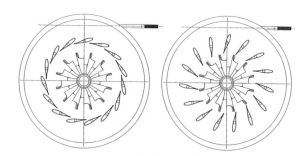

Aerodyne turbochargers incorporate a variable vane turbo nozzle (VATN) system that physically changes the dimensions of the exhaust housing internally. In a closed position the A/R ratio appears smaller and the turbocharger spools up much faster. The faster it goes, the more the vanes open, allowing more exhaust to pass without creating more pressure. In most cases, this feature eliminates the need for a waste gate.

Purchasing a Used Turbocharger

If you want to build your own system using one of the turbochargers mentioned above, you should be aware of several things first. When considering a used unit, be sure to check it carefully. A turbocharger that has been misused or poorly maintained may be in the wrecking yard for a reason!

Reach into the compressor housing with your fingers, pinch the shaft tip, and wiggle the shaft in all directions. If it wiggles a tiny bit, but the impeller blades appear not to be touching the scroll, it might just need a bearing and/or shaft assembly (the shaft that connects the turbine wheel to the compressor wheel is supported by either a single rotating bearing or twin plain bearings which, when worn, can allow the wheel blades to touch the housing) or minor rebuild. Also, make sure the shaft spins freely. A dial indicator is the proper way to check the turbine shaft for play; however, that can be awkward in a wrecking yard. If the shaft wiggles considerably and the blades show signs of touching the scroll, then forget it—unless the price is right and you just want it for spare parts, or as a core to trade against the cost of a new or rebuilt turbocharger. At the same time, inspect the compressor and turbine wheels for nicks and broken blades.

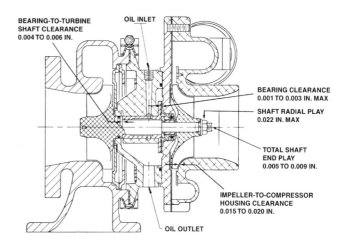

RAJAY 300 SERIES TURBOCHARGERS

BEARING-TO-TURBINE SHAFT CLEARANCE 0.004 TO 0.006 IN.

OIL INLET

BEARING CLEARANCE 0.001 TO 0.003 IN. MAX

SHAFT RADIAL PLAY 0.022 IN. MAX

TOTAL SHAFT END PLAY 0.005 TO 0.009 IN.

IMPELLER-TO-COMPRESSOR HOUSING CLEARANCE 0.015 TO 0.020 IN.

OIL OUTLET

Next, look into the oil inlet hole and drain hole to check the amount of carbon buildup. This can tell you quite a lot about how well the turbo was cared for. Turbochargers that have seen only turbo (non-coking) oil or synthetic turbo oil will show little signs of carbon buildup. However, a turbo that has seen few oil changes and only standard lubricants will be fairly crusty inside. This in turn means the bearing(s) and seals have had a tough life and should be replaced.

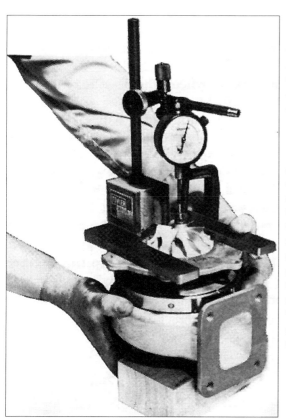

When checking out a used turbocharger, one of the first things to inspect is shaft end play *(left)* and side-to-side play *(right)*. This is usually a good indication of shaft and bearing condition and overall usability of the turbocharger. If the turbocharger is in bad condition, it can usually still be used as a core when purchasing a rebuilt or new unit. The cutaway *(above)* shows typical clearances.

Neal "Fast" Lane rode to the number one plate in 1992 and 1993 on the HRC gas-injected turbo bike. It has been ridden to a best of 7.09 seconds at 185 mph on gasoline only. No alcohol. No laughing gas. Just racing gas flows through this Kawasaki, making it one of the world's fastest bikes in its class.

Check the A/R ratio before purchasing a used "yard" turbocharger. Within the same model number, A/R ratios can vary. An IHI model RHB-52 turbocharger can come with a 0.41, 0.59, or 0.78 exhaust housing. If the turbo is to be installed on a 750cc engine, you definitely don't want the 0.78 A/R housing. The impeller size and blade design can make a major difference in turbocharger reaction time, and the design and shape of the scroll itself have a lot to do with how the turbocharger reacts at lower speeds. If the used turbocharger came from a 1400cc automobile engine, it probably has an exhaust A/R more properly suited to a 1400cc engine. However, you can swap exhaust scrolls within the same model number turbocharger—but this can be expensive. Exhaust housings are not cheap and probably the

only way you're going to get the proper size is to purchase a new one.

Don't be discouraged from buying a used turbo, but be aware you can't just pluck one off a turbocharged car and throw it on a motorcycle. You will need to know its brand, model, A/R ratio, compressor efficiency, and condition.

You can usually get this information by checking with the manufacturer or kit builder. Manufacturers will send you a complete package of information, including the all-important compressor maps, at your request. Kit builders will more than likely direct you right to the proper turbocharger for your particular application, as long as you are buying it from them. Some kit builders are reluctant to hand out free information to non-buyers, which is understandable, and actually go so far as to grind the A/R ratio off the exhaust housing so that even if you buy their kit, you still won't know the ratio.

Tell them the size of your engine, the compression ratio, and approximately how much horsepower you are looking for. Tell them what you intend to use the bike for—street, drag racing, Bonneville, or whatever. From this information the manufacturer or kit builder will be able to determine, within their brand, what you will require. Again, if the system is to be draw-through, make sure the turbocharger contains the proper seals for this type of operation. In the end, the best way to guarantee that you get the proper turbocharger for your installation is to dig deep into the ol' "play-money" safe and spring for a new unit. This way you will have first-hand knowledge of its condition and performance capabilities. It could even save you money in the long run.

If a turbocharger kit *is* available for your brand and model motorcycle and you have *no* previous turbocharging experience, I recommend you buy it. The problems involved in building your own system can be many, and until you become accustomed to maintaining and riding a turbocharged motorcycle, a complete kit may be the way to go. Unfortunately, only a handful of companies manufacture turbocharger kits for motorcycles, and the brands and models of bikes they make kits for are limited. Generally speaking, Suzuki and Kawasaki are the main choices of kit makers due to their bulletproof bottom ends and their ability to take a lot of abuse without self-destructing. However, some newer bikes, such as the Honda 900RR, show great promise also.

When Steve Rice isn't traversing the quarter-mile at 190 mph, he's tinkering on one of the prettiest drag bikes in the country. Steve works for the Kawasaki corporate offices in California as a technical adviser and does a darn good job of representing the factory at many drag events across the country. *Below:* You could literally eat off the engine, which sports a Mr. Turbo intake manifold and mechanical fuel injection.

Things You Need to Know About Turbocharger Lubrication

Oil supply to the turbocharger is vital! At turbine shaft speeds of up to 230,000 rpm, with just a small floating plain bearing or twin fixed plain bearings between the turbine shaft and the center housing, you'd better believe you need proper lubrication. The turbocharger bearings need a constant supply of cool, clean oil under reasonably high pressure at all times.

Some motorcycles with roller bearing crankshafts and counterparts have high-volume low-pressure oiling systems. Some Harleys will only put out 3 to 6 psi of oil pressure when they're hot! Early KZ Kawasakis and Suzukis also had roller bearing crankshafts; however, most modern motorcycles have plain bearing crankshafts which require a high pressure oil supply. Mr. Turbo and Hahn Racecraft offer oil pressure boosters (see Figure 3-9, overleaf) for roller bearing bikes that raise pressure to a safe level for the turbocharger. The only other solution would be to install a completely separate oil supply system just for the turbocharger. This can be complex, and sometimes unreliable.

Rajay turbochargers, with their single floating bearing, have been tested at low oil pressure and seem to survive, but operating at low pressure is not recommended. Rajay turbos need a minimum of 20 psi and twin bearing turbos may need a bit more.

In draw-through applications, the turbocharger is usually located behind the cylinders. This location is ideal for proper oil drainage from the turbocharger because everything is downhill to the crankcase. When the turbocharger is located down low and in front of the engine, as it is in most blow-through designs, it is actually lower than the oil level in the crankcase; thus, no drainage to the crankcase. Mr. Turbo, Hahn Racecraft, and RB Racing have all developed their own methods for dealing with this problem. Electric scavenge pumps can be used; however, in the past they have proven to be somewhat unreliable. But things may be changing on that front also. Westech Development of Wimberly, Texas (512-847-8918) is distributing an industrial grade siphon pump which, to date, has proven to be quite reliable. The SHURflo pump is rated for 1.4 gallons per minute at a total draw of 7 amps. It was originally developed as a water pump for street cleaners and a chemical waste pump. Perhaps its most unusual application to date would be in NASCAR race cars. Several teams have used it to circulate rear end (differential) oil through an oil cooler—definitely a severe application environment. In two years there have been no reported failures when used as a turbo siphon pump.

More complex systems use the stock oil pump (when properly modified) to scavenge the oil returning from the turbocharger. An excellent example of this type of scavenge system was developed by Bob Behn of RB Racing for V-Max motorcycles. He fabricated a special manifold to fit onto the bottom of the stock oil pump, which is cross-drilled to pick up oil from the sump as usual, but has an extra pickup spigot that siphons oil past a one-way valve mounted on the underside of the oil pan. Kawasaki ZX-11s actually have two oil pumps. One is used to supply high pressure oil to the engines vitals, while the other pumps oil through the oil cooler. Behn installs a restrictor plate above the sump for the oil cooler pump and taps in with an oil return line through the bottom of the pan, into the suction orifice leading to the pump. He uses a similar system on his Suzuki GSXR1100 installations. Where there's a will, there's a way. ∎

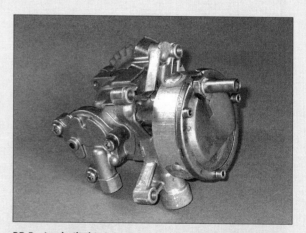

RB Racing built this interesting siphon return system for the Yamaha V-Max with low mounted turbochargers. *Right (next page):* A special aluminum manifold is cross-drilled so it still picks up oil from the sump while at the same time siphoning oil from the turbo through a one-way valve on the bottom of the pan. *Far right:* The snout sticking out of the bottom of the manifold siphons oil from the turbocharger, while sump oil is drawn through the normal opening in the shield and through the stock filter screen.

. . . Things You Need to Know about Turbocharger Lubrication . . .

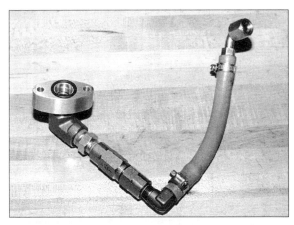

Above and top right: **Gary Evans** built his own reed style siphon system using the stock oil pump with good results. Oil returning from the turbocharger travels through the line and a one-way check valve, then through a fabricated aluminum flange block and into the siphon galley in the oil pump. The check valve keeps oil from back-flowing to the turbocharger when the engine is shut off. The special reed plate on the bottom of the pump creates enough suction on the turbo return line to draw oil from the turbocharger while still picking up oil from the sump. The faster the engine turns, the more the reed valve opens, allowing more oil to be picked up from the sump while still maintaining enough suction to draw oil from the turbocharger.

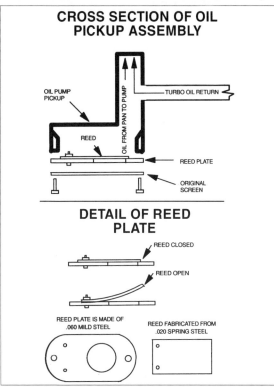

CROSS SECTION OF OIL PICKUP ASSEMBLY

OIL PUMP PICKUP

OIL FROM PAN TO PUMP

TURBO OIL RETURN

REED

REED PLATE

ORIGINAL SCREEN

DETAIL OF REED PLATE

REED CLOSED

REED OPEN

REED PLATE IS MADE OF .060 MILD STEEL

REED FABRICATED FROM .020 SPRING STEEL

Kawasaki ZX-11s have two oil pump systems. One pumps high-pressure oil to all of the critical moving parts in the engine and the other pumps oil from the crankcase through the oil cooler and back to the crankcase. RB Racing uses the oil cooler pump system to siphon oil from the low mounted turbocharger. *Right (above):* Oil is drawn up into the sump for the cooling pump through a welded-on fitting boss in the bottom of the pan. *Right:* A plate is fabricated to go over the top of the cooling sump with a small hole drilled in it to create enough suction to draw oil from the turbocharger, yet still supply enough oil to the cooler.

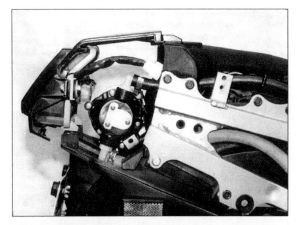

Westech hides the SHURflo siphon return pump in the tail section of the ZX-11. The pump is capable of siphoning at full capacity up to 8 feet in length and 5 feet in height, and draws a total of 7 amps.

When the turbocharger is mounted above the crankcase, gravity does the work of returning spent oil back to the crankcase, as is the case with this Suzuki Katana 750. Note the drain line coming down from the bottom of the turbocharger, plugging into a special AN fitting on the side of the clutch cover. The small line to the right is the high pressure oil supply line to the turbocharger.

Electric pumps can be used to siphon spent turbo oil and send it back to the crankcase instead of fabricating a built-in siphon system. Electric pumps were long considered unreliable, but this new SHURflo industrial grade pump is changing the image. These pumps were designed for pumping chemical waste and pumping water in street cleaners—no easy task in itself. But their most severe usage so far has been as a rear-end pump on NASCAR race cars to circulate oil through a cooler. Westech Development has been using them in their Kawasaki ZX-11 turbo kits for several years with no failures so far. WARNING: Because of the extremely high temperature of engine oil after it passes through the turbocharger, Westech makes internal modifications to enhance the durability of these pumps. If you are considering a SHURflo siphon pump, I highly recommend that you purchase it through Westech (www.westech.com).

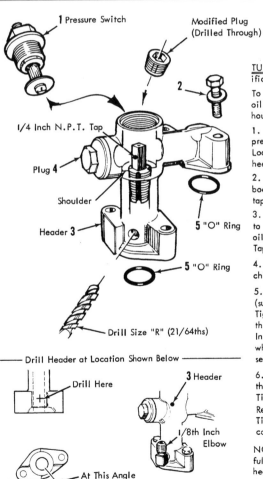

Mr. Turbo Z-1 Kawasaki Turbo
Oil Pressure Modification

<u>TURBO OIL SUPPLY</u>.... Oil Supply Header Modification.

To ensure a sufficient oil supply to Turbo, the stock oil supply header (located on top of transmission housing, at rear of cylinder block) must be modified.

1. Disconnect the electrical connector from oil pressure switch (1). Loosen and remove the switch. Loosen and remove the four bolts/washers (2). Remove header (3). Loosen and remove the plug (4).

2. Run a 1/4 Inch N.P.T. tap down into oil way in body of header as shown. Run tap in until the top of tap is even with shoulder in header. Remove tap.

3. At location shown, use drill size "R" (21/64ths) to drill hole through the wall of header to enter oil way as shown.
Tap hole using a 1/8 Inch N.P.T.

4. Now! THOROUGHLY clean all metal dust and chips from header.

5. Take the modified (drilled through) 1/4 Inch plug (supplied). Install plug in the oil way just tapped. Tighten. Apply a small amount of sealant to the pipe threaded end of the 1/8th Inch elbow (supplied). Install elbow as shown. Tighten carefully so that when tight, elbow points straight up. Remove excess sealant.

6. Reposition the original "O" rings (5). Reposition the oil header. Reinstall the four bolts/washers (2). Tighten. Replace the plug and "O" ring (4). Tighten. Replace the oil pressure switch and "O" ring (1). Tighten. Reconnect the electrical lead... that takes care of the oil supply for Turbo.

NOTE: The hole in the 1/4 Inch plug has been carefully calibrated to slightly restrict the oil flow through header to divert sufficient oil pressure/flow to Turbo. Don't try to "Second guess" us. Don't tamper with hole size.

Figure 3-9

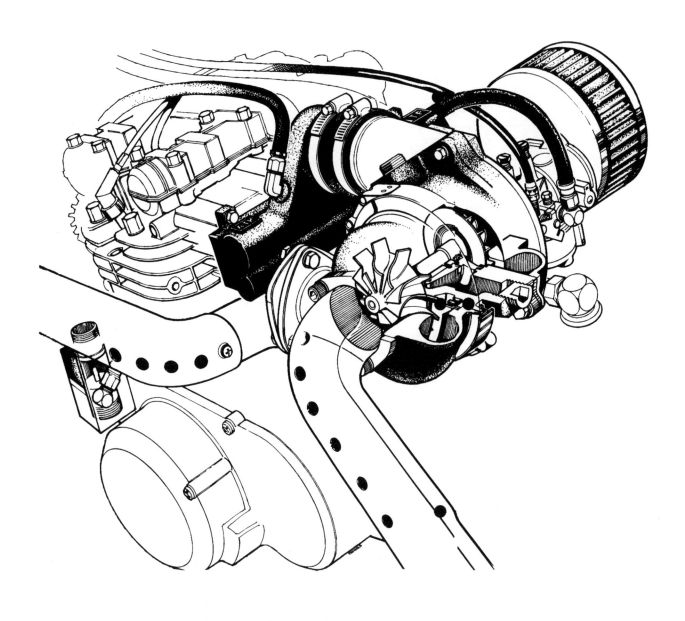

Figure 4-1: American Turbo-Pak was one of the first companies to manufacture turbo kits for motorcycles. Their draw-through designs set the style and trends for years; only now are blow-through carburetion and fuel injection beginning to get a foothold. This illustration depicts a typical draw-through system. The turbocharger is mounted behind the cylinder block in place of the carburetors. It attaches to a simple intake manifold that supplies pressurized air and fuel to all the cylinders. A single carburetor (a Bendix in this case) attaches to the compressor housing inlet and oil drains straight down to the crankcase from the turbocharger. Lower left is the waste gate on the inlet pipe running to the exhaust scroll.

CHAPTER 4

Fueling: Draw-Through and Blow-Through Carburetion

The main idea of any fuel delivery system, whether it is for a normally aspirated engine or a turbocharged engine, is to achieve the proper air/fuel ratio at all engine speeds and operating conditions. The functions of a carburetor (or fuel injection) can be summarized as follows:

1. To produce a combustible air-fuel mixture. The mixture is easiest to burn when the fuel is broken into tiny particles in the form of vapor.

2. To deliver a proper mixture of fuel and air according to the operating conditions of the engine. The ratio of fuel to air required by the engine varies with the engine's operating conditions. A proper air to fuel ratio for most internal combustion engines varies from 12.1:1 to 14.7:1 by weight, meaning 12.1 (or 14.7) parts by weight of air to one part by weight of fuel. A ratio of 12.1 is richer, with less air for a given amount of fuel, and 14.7 is leaner, with 2.6 more parts of air for the same amount of fuel in the mixture.

3. To allow an external mechanism (such as your hand on the throttle) to control the engine output by adjusting the amount of air-fuel mixture supplied to the combustion chamber(s).

Carburetion

A carburetor dispenses fuel into the intake system of an engine by using the pressure of the air passing through it. A low pressure area is created when air is forced to move rapidly through the venturi, the smallest section in the throat of a carburetor. This is where the fuel inlet holes are generally located and the suction from the low pressure area draws fuel into the air stream. The faster that air is drawn through the venturi, the more fuel it draws up from the bowl.

The problem is that the atomized fuel and air mixture often has a fairly long and irregular path to its destination, the combustion chamber. The farther or

This RB Racing draw-through system is installed on a Suzuki Katana 750 and features a Zenith carburetor with a needle-adjustable main jet circuit. With a 38 mm venturi, the system was somewhat overcarbureted and had poor transitional qualities. Later a 35 mm venturi insert was fabricated and installed and greatly improved idle and transitioning to mid-range. Top-end performance was less than desired with the smaller venturi, but it had fantastic low and mid-range punch.

Hahn Racecraft fabricates their own plenum chamber intake manifolds for draw-through systems. They are large capacity units that act as pressure chambers. This Kawasaki Funny Bike engine sports a huge S&S alcohol carburetor. S&S makes a full range of carburetors that work well on draw-through turbo systems and are the carburetors of choice for drag racing.

more irregular the path, the more that fuel is inclined to separate from the air carrying it. The fuel comes out of the carburetor in a fine mist but can condense again into tiny droplets, especially at lower speeds. This can cause a rough idle and compromised mid-range performance.

Because the carburetors remain in the stock location in a blow-through system, fuel separation is less of a problem due to the short path between the carburetors and the combustion chamber. This is one of several reasons why a blow-through configuration is so desirable when turbocharging. In a draw-through system, fuel separation is a major problem, especially at low speeds. This is because the air and fuel mixture has to first pass through a manifold at the inlet to the compressor housing, then through the compressor housing and into a log type manifold that runs straight across the ports. Talk about a torturous path! By the time the air and fuel mixture makes all these lefts and rights, you can see why it takes a richer than normal mixture even

to make it to the combustion chamber at all. Actually, the compressor impeller does a fairly good job of mixing the fuel and air, so the real problem comes after the mixture leaves the turbo and enters the intake manifold.

Draw-Through Carburetion Intake Systems

On draw-through turbo systems, the carburetor generally mounts on the opening to the compressor housing via a small connector manifold. Because space is usually limited on motorcycles, especially with perimeter frame models, small single-throat carburetors are the best choice. Mr. Turbo uses modified Keihin side draft, butterfly type carburetors on street machines, and various models of S&S carburetors on race bikes. Hahn Racecraft uses only S&S carburetors, modified for use on turbochargers.

If you have the room, some two-barrel side draft carburetors work nicely. Dellorto, Mikuni, and Weber

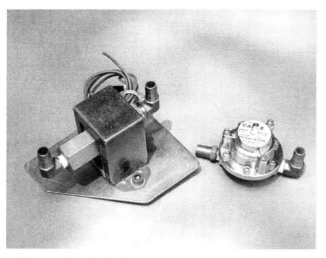

Fuel pump and Cagle deadhead regulator for draw-through turbo system

It is possible to gravity-feed a draw-through turbo system up to approximately 7 to 10 psi of boost by adding only large diameter fuel lines, a high capacity petcock valve, and a high-flow needle and seat. However, to guarantee you will never have the float bowl run dry on a hard pass, I recommend that you incorpoate a small low-pressure fuel pump into the system. Mikuni American of Northridge, Calif. (818-885-1242), can supply you with a 4 psi pump and Cagle fuel pressure regulator that works quite nicely on turbocharged street bikes. The fuel pressure regulator is vacuum-sensitive and allows only 1.5 psi fuel pressure at idle, and on up to 4 psi at full throttle. Most needle and seats become very sensitive to flow after 4 or 5 psi, which makes these little pumps and regulators ideal. High-flow petcocks are available from Pingel Enterprises of Adams, Wisc. (608-339-7999).

all make side draft twin-throat carburetors that are similar to one another and offer top-side jet removal and replacement. This makes it easy to change jetting, since you don't have to remove the carburetor from the bike to reach the jets from the bottom side. However, it can be challenging to fabricate a manifold to fit the wide space between venturis, and still keep it short to fit between the frame rails and turbo.

Some slide carburetors may stick open near idle, or when coming back down to idle. Round slides are worse that flat slides and may require stiffer return springs to prevent them from sticking open. CV (constant velocity) carburetors, like the English made SU, seem to work well and do not exhibit the same tendency toward sticking slides. Non-CV slide carburetors should be used with caution, but if no sticking is apparent, they may work adequately.

Keihin and S&S carburetors are available through Mr. Turbo and Hahn Racecraft, usually slightly modified and pre-jetted for various turbocharger applications. These carburetors will probably be your best choices. Slide carburetors and dual-throat butterfly carburetors may require slight modifications for proper operation.

Most motorcycles are equipped with multiple carburetors stock from the factory—one carburetor per cylinder. Harley-Davidsons use one carburetor for two cylinders. On a typical inline four-cylinder motorcycle, you can simply remove the stock carburetors and fit a log type manifold to the cylinder head. Four spigots slip into place where the carburetors had been connected previously and a single port on the front side of the manifold connects to the compressor housing of the turbocharger. Figure 4-1 shows the American Turbo-Pak system of the early 1970s. Most of the kit builders use basically the same design even today, a good 20 years later.

The spigot on the manifold where the turbo compressor connects is generally arranged to be a little higher than the spigots for the intake ports. This is done to keep the swirling air-fuel mixture which is entering the manifold from making an immediate left, causing the left two cylinders to run richer and the right two leaner. RB Racing actually runs a divider plate right down the center of the inlet spigot, dividing the incoming charge in half while equally distributing air and fuel to all four cylinders. Notice in the photos how the RB Racing custom draw-through manifold tapers down from the top to the ends. This is done to direct air and fuel to the end cylinders, which would otherwise run a little leaner than the center cylinders.

Hahn Racecraft makes a serious street or strip plenum manifold for Suzuki and Kawasaki motorcycles that is hand fabricated from sheet stock. They offer an extra large plenum area that, according to Bill Hahn, keeps a constant supply of pressurized air and fuel at

Carburetors for Draw-Through Application

BENDIX—These carburetors came as OEM equipment on Harleys of yore. American Turbo-Pak also used them on street turbo applications. With some minor modifications and jetting changes they can work quite well, but are considered obsolete by today's standards. Bendix carbs, parts, and jets are hard to obtain these days, but if you happen across one at a garage sale or swap meet, it may be worth picking up. These carburetors were available only in 38 mm size.

ZENITH—In basic design, size, and circuitry, this is a close cousin to the Bendix carburetor; however, it does offer a couple of distinct advantages over the Bendix. It features a tapered needle adjustable main jet, which is nice on a turbocharged engine, and it is available in two sizes: 38 and 40 mm. These carburetors are actually sold as replacements for OEM carbs on Harley-Davidsons. Both the Bendix and the Zenith are basic in design. An idle circuit, jettable mid-range circuit, and adjustable main circuit make these simplistic carburetors suitable for draw-through operation. Because of their simplicity, they are also difficult to dial in properly. Once they have been jetted and adjusted for optimal performance, however, they work well, but draw-through turbo systems really like a little more circuitry. The transition from idle to mid-range can be especially tricky, and the more circuits available, the better. Some people have added a "Thunder Jet" installation to these carburetors, which acts like an extra main jet that kicks in at wide open throttle to add sufficient fuel at full boost.

KEIHIN—These carburetors could be considered the next generation Bendix and Zenith all rolled up in one, with a little more circuitry to smooth the transitions between speed ranges. Keihins were available on Harley-Davidsons as an OEM item, but in a less adjustable EPA style. Keihins are available with all the adjustable circuitry and are available through Mr. Turbo, pre-jetted for draw-through usage. These carburetors were also used on the original Luftmeister (draw-through) systems on BMW boxers.

SU—These carburetors have been around for many years, in so many applications it boggles the mind. And yes, they have been used in draw-through turbo applications as well. The side draft SUs are of the constant velocity type, which means they will supply only the amount of air and fuel the engine demands at any given throttle opening. Quite flexible, SU side draft carburetors are really only restricted by space limitations. Jetting and other parts are easily obtainable through Rivera Engineering and can be found on many vintage English automobiles. When properly modified and jetted these carburetors work exceptionally well in draw-through applications. The SU's main drawback is height. Fairings and perimeter frames can make it all but impossible to use this carburetor.

DELLORTO—Infinite adjustability, ease of finding parts, and availability of tech information make these carburetors a decent choice. They are available in 40 and 45 mm sizes (big enough for most motorcycle draw-through applications), and are easy to jet through the top of the carburetor. Rancho VW of Rancho Cucamonga, Calif., makes special modifications to Dellorto DHLA carburetors for use on VW turbo dune buggies. Their products seem to work well. The only detraction to the use of Dellortos is their width. It is difficult to design and fabricate a manifold that is wide enough yet short enough to fit within the confines of a motorcycle. Because of their large venturi size, Dellorto carburetors are recommended for use only on engines with a displacement of at least 1100cc.

MIKUNI—The PHH 40 and 44 mm carburetors are similar to the Dellorto. These carbs are seen mostly on small displacement sports cars, sports sedans, and off-road rally type cars. They are so similar to the Dellorto they even fit on the same flange or manifold. They cost less than the Dellorto, are just as easy to get jets and parts for, and are also infinitely adjustable, with plenty of circuitry for smooth transitioning between speed ranges. Mikuni PHH carburetors, like the Dellortos, also have space limitations and should only be used on large displacement motorcycle engines. Adjustability is a pleasure when compared to a normal side draft carburetor, where jets must be removed from the bottom or bowl side.

S&S—S&S makes a full range of side draft, single-barrel carburetors that carry a great reputation among draw-through advocates. Large or small, in race or street configuration, these carburetors are the ones most often used on motorcycle turbocharger installations. Both Hahn Racecraft and Mr. Turbo supply modified, draw-through S&S carburetors that are (almost) bolt-on-and-run. ∎

Mark Vanderwald designed his own blow-through carburetion system on a 1990 Suzuki GSXR750. A front mounted Garrett T-2 turbocharger blows through an intercooler and then into the four stock CV carburetors. Jetting consisted of a Stage 3 Dyno Jet kit with much richer main jets and heavier slide return springs to slow them down a little. The bike runs on 92 octane pump gasoline, on stock compression, at 7 lbs boost and puts out 145 horsepower at 10,500 rpm to the rear wheel. It carburetes beautifully, with a smoother-than-stock idle, perfect transitioning through the mid-range, and a top end rush only fully built liter size bikes can offer. Being a 750, it is much lighter than liter class bikes and a lot of fun to ride.

the ready. Just about all the top Funny Bikes use this manifold. Also, Mr. Turbo makes cast and billet manifolds for most inline four-cylinder machines.

Getting from the Gas Tank to the Carburetor

Depending on the brand and style of carburetor you use, it is actually possible to gravity-feed a draw-through carburetor up to 7.5 psi manifold boost and, in some cases, even more. Mikuni offers an assortment of needles and seats for most of their carburetors, giving you a choice of gravity-feed or fuel pump. S&S also makes a high-flow needle and seat for their carburetors which, though expensive, can save you the cost of a fuel pump in installations requiring moderate boost levels.

In a gravity-feed system, the fuel path should be as large and free-flowing as possible, starting with the tank petcock valve. Stock petcocks and small diameter fuel lines will have to be replaced with larger items. A

Vanderwald fabricated a clamp arrangement that attaches the high pressure Walbro fuel pump to the RB Racing fuel pressure regulator, to keep from stringing fuel lines all over the bike. The heart of the fuel system is a compact package in the spot where the stock air box was located. Upper left is the fuel filter. Bypass-type regulators are the preferred method of fuel control on blow-through systems, whether carbureted or fuel injected, since they are more accurate, have less tendency toward vapor lock, and react faster then deadhead regulators.

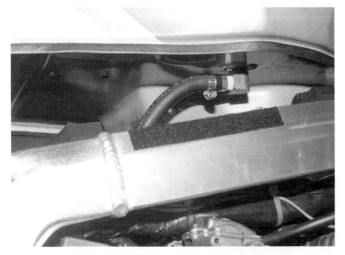

Gary Evans welded a drilled and tapped slug to the bottom of his GSXR1100 turbo bike gas tank for the fuel return from the regulator. A standpipe attached to the slug takes returning fuel to the top of the tank. See Figure 4-2.

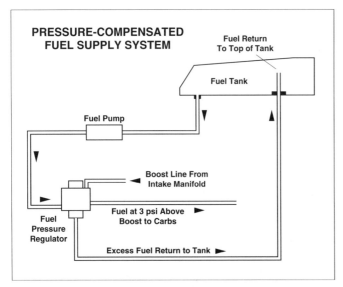

PRESSURE-COMPENSATED FUEL SUPPLY SYSTEM

Fuel Return To Top of Tank

Fuel Tank

Fuel Pump

Boost Line From Intake Manifold

Fuel at 3 psi Above Boost to Carbs

Fuel Pressure Regulator

Excess Fuel Return to Tank

Figure 4-2: Gary Evans simplifies the typical blow-through carburetion system in this drawing. Return-type systems are straightforward and easy to understand once you know why they do what they do. A deadhead-type regulator system would work also, but is slower to react and can heat the fuel before it gets to the carburetors. A return-type system constantly flows cool fuel to the carburetors, with excess being returned to the gas tank through a petcock and standpipe in the bottom of the tank. Fuel pressure is constantly maintained at 2 to 3 psi above manifold boost pressure to ensure that the float bowl is constantly filled. RB Racing makes a preset boost-sensitive regulator. Mallory makes one that can be adjusted down to 3 psi. Malpassi makes an adjustable fuel pressure regulator that saw service on blow-through carbureted Lotus Esprits and can be ordered through foreign car parts houses.

Intake plenums for carburetors and fuel injection throttle bodies can be quite simple in design. They can be made from rectangular aluminum tubing, as shown here, or round aluminum tubing like Mark Vanderwald's GSXR750. This manifold is being fabricated to fit a blow-through carbureted Suzuki Katana 750. The two threaded bosses on the left and right top side supply pressurized air to the carburetor float bowls. The boss on the back side supplies pressurized air to the fuel pressure regulator, the water alcohol injection container, the boost gauge, and the waste gate dial-a-boost controller.

Gary Evans fabricated this blow-through intake plenum for his water-cooled GSXR1100. He is using four 39 mm flat slide (non CV) Keihin carburetors. Note the two hoses running from the top of the plenum to the carburetors for float bowl pressurization. The other fittings route pressurized air to the usual places: the fuel pressure regulator, the boost controller, and the boost gauge. Pressurized air from the front mounted turbocharger is routed to the bottom center of the plenum.

Above: **By moving the oil cooler to another location, it is possible to run the compressor discharge tube up and over the top of the engine on a Katana 750, as shown here.** *Below:* **A convenient opening at the top of the frame near the steering head allows just enough room for the 1¾-inch tube to stick through. From there it's a straight shot to the intake plenum attached to the carburetors.**

high flow (³⁄₈-inch line) Pingel fuel valve should replace the stock OEM item, ensuring as much flow as possible. Pingel petcocks come equipped with a filter which allows you to eliminate other filters in the system. The ³⁄₈-inch fuel line should take a free-flowing path to the inlet spigot on the carburetor, and the inlet spigot should be able to accept a ³⁄₈-inch nose if possible. The needle and seat should be a high-capacity or competition type.

At anything over 10 to 12 lbs. boost, consider a low-pressure fuel pump. Some carburetors will require the use of a fuel pump anyway because a high-flow, gravity-feed needle and seat are not available. Mikuni makes a small, reliable electric fuel pump that is perfect for motorcycle applications. They also sell the Cagle pressure-sensitive fuel pressure regulator.

The regulator has a *fuel in* connection, a *fuel out* connection, and a connection for a vacuum line to the carburetor or the manifold between the carburetor and the inlet to the turbocharger. At idle, when only one to two psi of fuel pressure is needed, the regulator allows only that amount to pass to the carburetor. As the

The latest trend in blow-through Funny Bikes is to mount the turbocharger high and up front. This puts the turbo near the exhaust ports for better response and makes a short path over the top to connect the compressor housing to the mechanical fuel injection throttle bodies.

throttle opens and decreases vacuum, the diaphragm in the regulator allows more fuel to pass to the carburetor, constantly supplying the proper amount on up to a full 4 psi if necessary. Most motorcycle OEM (gravity-feed) carburetors, if used in a draw-through turbo application, will require a pump/regulator system similar to this if they are to be used at higher boost levels.

Draw-through systems are not complex and work adequately at the drag strip; however, in street use, they tend to idle erratically and transition poorly through the mid-range due to fuel separation problems mentioned earlier. The current trend is toward blow-through carburetion.

Blow-Through Carburetion Intake Systems

Let's start with the three advantages offered by blow-through systems. First is simplicity. The carburetor(s) remain in the stock location with no changes to throttle linkage or cables. Second is improved fuel delivery and stock throttle response. Third is that intercooling can be incorporated into the design, allowing a cooler and denser charge of air and fuel to enter the combustion chamber.

Multi-cylinder motorcycle engines will require log type manifolds connected to the carburetors at their inlet openings. Inline four-cylinder engines are the easiest to deal with. A single round tube, approximately 3 to 4 inches in diameter, runs along the row of carburetors, connecting to the mouth of each. V-four engines will require two log manifolds, each connecting two carburetors (refer to the photograph of the RB Racing Yamaha V-Max design). V-twin engines require a large round plenum chamber (approximately three times the displacement of the engine) to be attached to the mouth of the carburetor or fuel injection throttle body.

Any blow-through carburetion system will require jetting changes; you will have to experiment to achieve the proper air/fuel ratio through the entire operating range. You can expect that all jetting modifications you

This RB Racing combination air priority and pop-off valve is mounted on a Kawasaki ZX-11 turbo plenum chamber. These combination valves are fairly large, so you will need some mounting space. They allow the engine to breathe normally aspirated until boost pressure shuts the valve and traps the air. They also act as a pop-off valve to prevent pressure spikes when the throttle is snapped shut under boost.

Mark Vanderwald used an HKS pop-off valve on his homemade intake plenum. Pressure spikes of up to 50 psi can damage slides and other carburetor internals, as well as electronic fuel injection throttle bodies, turbocharger impellers, seals, and bearings. You can get along without the air priority valve, but a pop-off should always be incorporated into the design of a blow-through system. HKS pop-offs are small and compact, and work well on motorcycle turbo systems.

will have to make will be to pass more fuel, to match the greater amount of air entering the engine. RB Racing even uses a priority valve on the intake manifold that allows the engine to breathe normally aspirated at idle and closes only when it realizes boost. Whether you are dealing with draw-through turbocharging or blow-through turbocharging, the task of jetting is made much easier with an oxygen sensing air/fuel ratio meter. Hahn Racecraft, Westech, Haltech, Mr. Turbo and RB Racing all offer these meters; they are worth their weight in gold as they cut the tuning and jetting time in half. See Chapter 6 for more on fueling.

Some carburetors will require extra care in sealing, since the boost pressure can create leaks, especially at throttle shafts. In some places, you will need to use epoxy glue to assure proper sealing. Throttle shafts may require pressure sealing through the use of "O" rings or other means, depending on the brand and model. Most late model Keihin and Mikuni carburetors are well sealed in all the critical areas and should present no problems when pressurized.

When positive manifold boost pressure is applied to the venturi of the carburetor(s), fuel cannot travel its normal path to the venturi. Therefore, positive manifold boost must also be applied to the float bowl(s) via the vent line fittings, or tubes. Most Japanese carburetors have float bowl vent fittings, making this an easy task by running lines from the vent fittings directly to

the intake plenum chamber(s). However, once the float bowl has been pressurized, fuel flow from the tank through the float needle and seat will be inhibited. The solution is to install an electric fuel pump to force feed the pressurized float bowl; however, this must be done in relation to manifold boost levels. Fuel pressure must remain only one to two psi above manifold boost pressure (or float bowl boost pressure) to ensure a constantly filled float bowl.

As previously mentioned, most motorcycle carburetors come equipped with float needle and seats for gravity-feed, or for low pressure fuel pumps such as those used on the Yamaha V-Max. The needles and seats are sensitive to fuel pressure, making it impossible to use more than two to three psi above intake manifold boost pressure. If the fuel pressure is too high it will force fuel past the needle and seat, flooding the float bowl. This fine balance of fuel pressure vs. intake manifold pressure is the most difficult challenge in a blow-through carburetion system.

RB Racing designed a fuel regulator for just this purpose. For example, their turbo GSXR1100 Suzukis are seeing a maximum of 19 to 20 psi of manifold boost pressure. This means that a fuel pump capable of more than 20 psi fuel pressure is required. An electric automotive fuel injection pump supplies the pressure needed to overcome manifold boost pressure in the float bowl and a pressure sensitive bypass type regula-

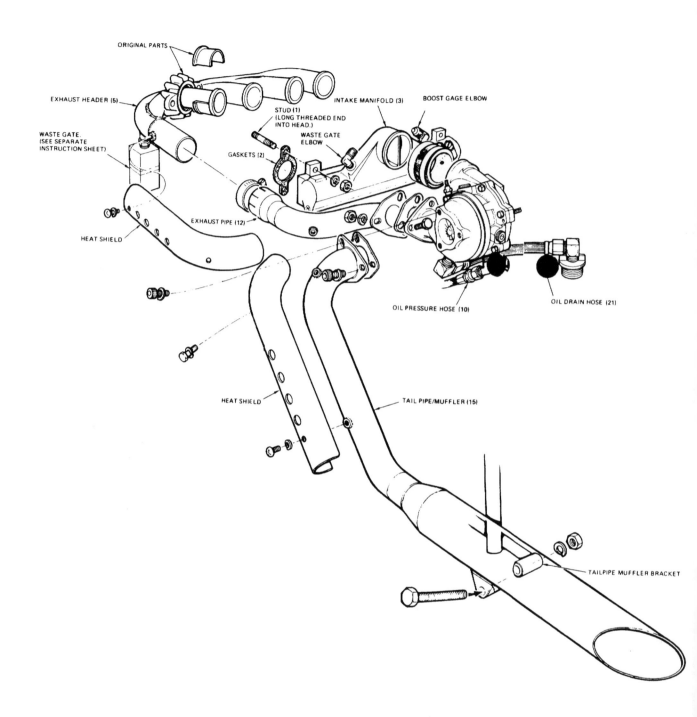

ORIGINAL PARTS

EXHAUST HEADER (5)

INTAKE MANIFOLD (3)

BOOST GAGE ELBOW

STUD (1)
(LONG THREADED END
INTO HEAD.)

WASTE GATE.
(SEE SEPARATE
INSTRUCTION SHEET)

WASTE GATE
ELBOW

GASKETS (2)

EXHAUST PIPE (12)

HEAT SHIELD

OIL PRESSURE HOSE (10)

OIL DRAIN HOSE (21)

HEAT SHIELD

TAIL PIPE/MUFFLER (15)

TAILPIPE MUFFLER BRACKET

This illustration of an early Mr. Turbo draw-through system shows just how simple turbocharging can be. Most systems can be installed in less than a day. Even today, draw-through systems are designed along these same basic lines. Spider four-into-one headers have replaced the log exhaust manifold shown here. Carburetors and waste gates have been improved, but feature the same layout with the turbocharger placed behind the cylinder block.

Gary Evans fabricated his own compact pop-off valve for his turbo GSXR1100. It features adjustability and billet construction.

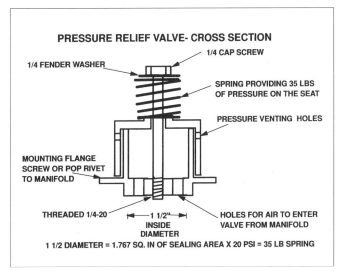

PRESSURE RELIEF VALVE- CROSS SECTION

This cross section view of Gary Evans' pop-off pressure relief valve shows how simple one can be.

tor maintains a constant 1 to 3 psi fuel pressure *above* manifold boost pressure. One end of the regulator sees manifold boost and, via an internal spring, applies pressure to a diaphragm in the middle. This diaphragm regulates the amount of fuel that is bypassed back to the fuel tank and the amount of fuel pressure the carburetor needle and seat sees. At low or no boost, the diaphragm allows more fuel to bypass to the gas tank, lowering the pressure of fuel being delivered to the carburetor. The higher the boost level, the more the diaphragm restricts fuel bypassing back to the tank, thereby increasing fuel pressure to the carburetor. RB Racing makes their own bypass regulator for their own turbocharger installations and is now offering it to the general public. These regulators are hand-made, low production items and are fairly expensive.

Malpassi in Italy makes a boost-sensitive fuel pressure regulator that is used on the Lotus 2000cc Turbo Europa. This turbo system blows through twin Dellorto DHLA carburetors, and works quite well to more than 10 psi of boost. It can be purchased through most foreign car parts houses. Mallory makes a 3-port, pressure-sensitive bypass regulator that is adjustable down to 3 psi and is available through Summit Distributing (330-630-3030) and most automotive speed shops.

Air Priority Valves and Intake Plenum Pop-Off Valves

Air Priority Valves

These valves are used on blow-through carbureted and electronically fuel injected intake plenum chambers to allow the engine to breathe normally aspirated while cruising or under vacuum conditions. In the case of blow-through carburetion, this makes it possible to use fairly normal jetting for non-boost driving, with richer main jet circuitry on standby for driving under boost or wide open throttle. As soon as the air priority valve realizes boost, it shuts, trapping the pressurized air from the compressor housing. Air-priority valves actually help smooth the transition from vacuum to boost conditions and have the pleasant side effect of improving fuel mileage due to the more-or-less conservative jetting used for cruising.

All of the factory turbo bikes of the early 1980s were equipped with air priority valves, whether they were blow-through carbureted, as was the Yamaha Seca 650 Turbo, or electronically fuel injected, as were all the others. Some people have used the Yamaha air priority

71

 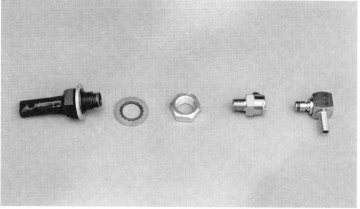

RB Racing makes this slick fuel return fitting assembly that bolts to the bottom of your fuel tank through a ⁹⁄₁₆ inch hole. This allows you to mount the fitting without welding to the tank, thereby destroying the paint. It features a crimped and welded snout with cross-drilled holes so the fuel entering the tank doesn't squirt straight up. Neoprene seal washers are used inside and outside for a leak-proof seal. Tank removal is made easy with a quick-release dry-break fitting that engages a spring-loaded seal to stop fuel flow when the two fitting halves are seperated. RB Racing's fuel return fitting is necessary only on blow-through carburetion or fuel injection systems where a full flow fuel return system is required. A larger version for blow-through carburetion may be necessary to keep pressure low at idle when the carburetor requires very little fuel.

valve on their own home-built turbo systems with great success. In some cases, on larger motors, they have used two of them on the intake plenum for even greater breathing capability.

RB Racing offers an interesting two-way valve that acts as an air priority valve while cruising and a pop-off safety valve at the same time. It is fairly large, so you will need some space to hide it, but certainly simplifies the task of supplying normally aspirated air for city driving while protecting the carburetors and fuel injection system against pressure surges.

Pop-Off Valves

Intake pressure spikes or surges are only a problem on blow-through systems. They occur when the throttle is suddenly shut while the turbocharger is spinning at a high rate of speed. When the throttle is shut while under boost, the turbocharger will keep spinning for a few moments before it can react and begin to slow down. The result is a pressure surge or spike that can instantly reach as high as 50 psi. This, of course, is hard on throttle slides, diaphragms, seals, and other internal parts of carbureted engines as well as electronically fuel injected engines, not to mention the turbocharger itself. Pop-off valves relieve this pressure buildup before it can do any damage and will save you many headaches down the line. HKS USA of Torrance, Calif. (310-328-8100), makes the most popular aftermarket pop-off valve on the market. It is compact and will easily fit onto most blow-through intake plenum chambers. Turbonetics is now offering a lightweight Bosch pop-off valve that features one-inch diameter inlet and outlet ports, and is boost-sensitive. These unique valves can be mounted remotely, away from the intake plenum.

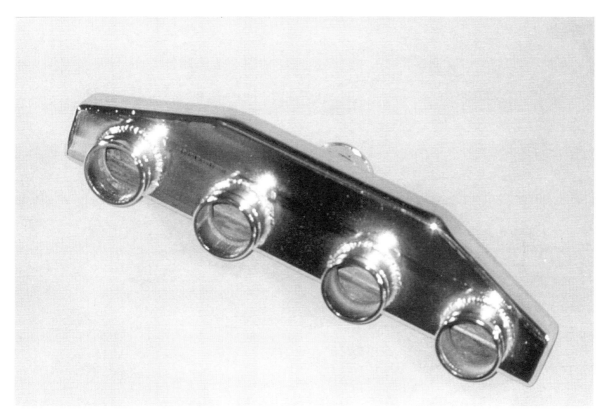

This draw-through plenum intake manifold was constructed from rectangular heavy wall steel tubing. Note the divider plate in the inlet connection, shown below. Air and fuel leave the diffuser of the compressor housing in a swirling left direction. The divider splits the incoming air and fuel before it has a chance to turn left, which would make the left two cylinders run richer than the right two.

Draw-through turbo systems are in many ways less complex than blow-through systems. Shown here is a complete draw-through system in parts *(above)* and installed on a Suzuki Katana 750 *(below)*. The S&S carburetor was eventually found to be too large for street use and was traded for a Zenith 38 mm carburetor, with needle-adjustable main jet. Even the 38 mm Zenith's venturi had to be reduced to 35 mm before it became civilized enough for street use. Draw-through carburetion systems on smaller engines can be difficult to dial in properly. Larger displacement engines can handle larger carburetors and do not seem to suffer from the same erratic idle and poor transitioning problems as smaller engines that are over-carbureted. This system features an IHI RHB-52 turbocharger that has been sealed for draw-through operation and is capable of boosting the little Suzuki engine to 130 rear wheel horsepower at only 6 psi.

Low boost draw-through systems can usually have gravity-fed fuel systems. However, higher boost operation will require a low pressure fuel pump and deadhead fuel pressure regulator. Shown here is a small 4 psi pump and Cagle regulator, both available through Mikuni American.

Blow-through carburetion systems will require a high pressure fuel injection pump and boost-sensitive return-type fuel pressure regulator. Shown here is a Pierburg pump and Mallory 3-port regulator.

Blow-through systems should also be equipped with a fuel pressure gauge. It is critical that fuel pressure go no higher than 3 psi over the boost pressure on stock motorcycle carburetors. Any higher pressure could force fuel past the needle and seats, thereby flooding the engine. A small gauge like this Mr. Gasket unit can be used inline to the carburetors.

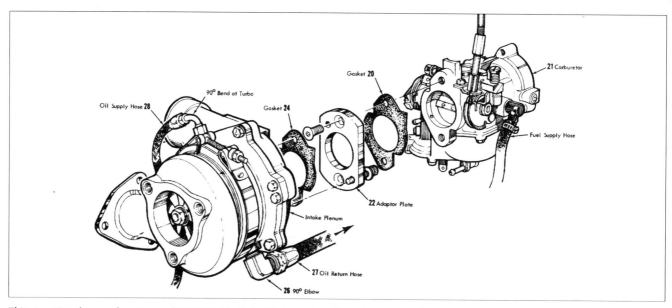

Labels on diagram:
- Oil Supply Hose 28
- 90° Bend at Turbo
- Gasket 24
- Gasket 20
- 21 Carburetor
- Fuel Supply Hose
- 22 Adaptor Plate
- Intake Plenum
- 27 Oil Return Hose
- 26 90° Elbow

This mounting diagram for a Kawasaki KZ1000 Mr. Turbo kit shows how the carburetor attaches to the compressor housing of a 300 series Rajay turbocharger. While draw-through systems appear to be simple and user-friendly, they sometimes show a rough and erratic idle, and transition poorly to mid-range. It is easy to overcarburete, making this problem even worse. For all-out drag racing, draw-through systems are still popular and work well.

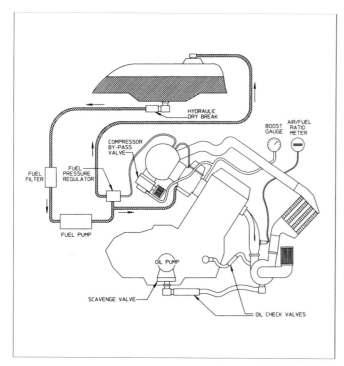

This CAD-CAM drawing of Mark Vanderwald's blow-through system tells it all. You are looking at what might take the average builder months to figure out on his own. Mark did his college internship at the Garrett Corporation's turbocharger division and did his homework. When you see the entire system laid out for you like this, you realize just how simple a blow-through system can be. Blow-through systems aren't as simple as draw-through systems, but the advantages far outweigh the disadvantages when comparing the two.

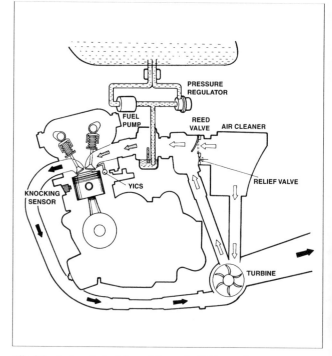

All of the factory turbo bikes of the early 1980s used air priority valves in the intake system. These valves allow the engine to breathe normally aspirated until positive boost is realized, at which time the valve shuts, trapping the pressurized air in the plenum chamber. An improved idle and transitioning to mid-range operation is the result. This diagram illustrates the Yamaha Seca 650 turbo blow-through carburetion system. Note the reed valve between the air cleaner box and the plenum chamber. The plenum was also equipped with a pop-off valve.

What's Best? Blow-Through or Draw-Through

What do you need and want from a turbocharger? This summary of advantages and disadvantages of both draw-through and blow-through systems will help you decide what will best suit your unique plans. ■

Table 4-1 Comparison of Blow-Through and Draw-Through Systems		
	Blow-Through System	**Draw-Through System**
1. Location of carburetion system and linkage	No change.	Must remove the stock carburetion system and install a single carburetor on the turbocharger. Requires new cable hookup and a plenum intake manifold in place of the stock carburetors.
2. Fuel pump	Requires a high-pressure electric fuel pump capable of producing more fuel pressure than manifold boost pressure. Also requires a boost-sensitive fuel pressure regulator and a bypass fuel system.	Requires use of stock electric fuel pump if so equipped or addition of low pressure (5 psi max.) fuel pump with a vacuum sensitive fuel pressure regulator. Gravity-feed, if properly designed, may provide enough flow for up to 6 to 7 psi manifold boost pressure.
3. Carburetor leakage	All carburetors—including throttle shafts—must be sealed properly. Alternatively, the carburetor(s) may be sealed in a pressure box. Most modern factory CV carburetors come equipped with sealed throttle shafts and are the best choice when considering blow-through carburetion. The float bowls must be pressurized if blowing directly through the carburetors.	Major jetting changes are usually needed. No other modifications or sealing are necessary. Venturi size is very important, as it is easy to overcarburete a draw-through system.
4. Distance from carburetor to combustion chamber	No change.	Much longer path, creating fuel separation problems.
5. Turbocharger oil seal	No special seal required.	Must have positive seal on compressor end of shaft.
6. Compressor surge	Can be a problem on deceleration. Requires an intake plenum pop-off valve.	Not usually a problem.
7. Compressor size	Inlet pressure is always atmospheric, so maximum capacity is always available.	Inlet pressure is below atmospheric, so a slightly larger size compressor is required in some cases.
8. A/R ratio	Same.	Same.
9. Throttle response	Near stock.	Slightly slower than stock.
10. Idle and transitioning quality	Near stock.	Poor idle and transitioning quality. Better for drag racing than street use.

Fueling: Electronic Fuel Injection

Just when you thought you had begun to comprehend the complexities of your motorcycle's carburetion system, along comes EFI. If you are a computerphobe like a lot of us, the mere mention of the words "Electronic Fuel Injection" may send your brain into full lockup. Of course, that can happen to a lot of us when we encounter something new and alien to our way of thinking. Our present subject is computerized—as opposed to mechanical—fueling, and yes, it is complicated. However, it should be comforting to know that all electronic fuel management systems operate in basically the same way; once you understand the principles, you can apply them to any system.

With EFI, eliminating the carburetor makes it possible to design the intake system to operate efficiently with high *and* low speed air flow. The beauty of fuel injection is that fuel is injected under high pressure into the air stream, not sucked into it as with a carburetor. The injector nozzles spray finely atomized fuel into the air stream, close to the intake valves. The fuel stays vaporized as it enters the cylinders, even at low rpm when air velocity is lowest. EFI systems don't rely on air pressure to deliver the goods, because fuel is supplied by a high-pressure pump. Think of it as supercharging the fuel.

EFI also makes it possible to increase the size of the ports and valves, which increases the amount of air that can be drawn into the cylinders. In effect, you have increased full throttle performance without sacrificing bottom end or cruising performance.

The most obvious advantage of EFI is drivability. There is no need for choke levers or long warmups, no slipping of the clutch to get moving, and no need to re-jet for atmospheric or altitude changes. Electronics give much more precise control over fuel delivery than any mechanical device can, whether the engine is normally aspirated, supercharged, or turbocharged. If there has been any true technological breakthrough in modern power boosting, it is programmable electronic fuel injection.

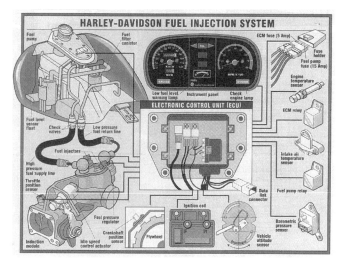

Harley-Davidson saw the EPA handwriting on the wall and teamed up with Magnetti-Marelli USA (formerly Weber-Marelli) to develop a new EFI system for their Ultra Classic Electra Glide. It uses the first split-runner intake manifold in the history of the company, uses basic components, and offers more power and improved fuel mileage than carbureted models. The 1996 Harley-Davidson product lineup includes three models which incorporate electronic fuel injection: the Electra Glide Classic, Ultra Classic, and FLHR-I Electra Glide Road King. Harley's EFI is not programmable and, at least at the time of this writing, no racing PROM chips were available.

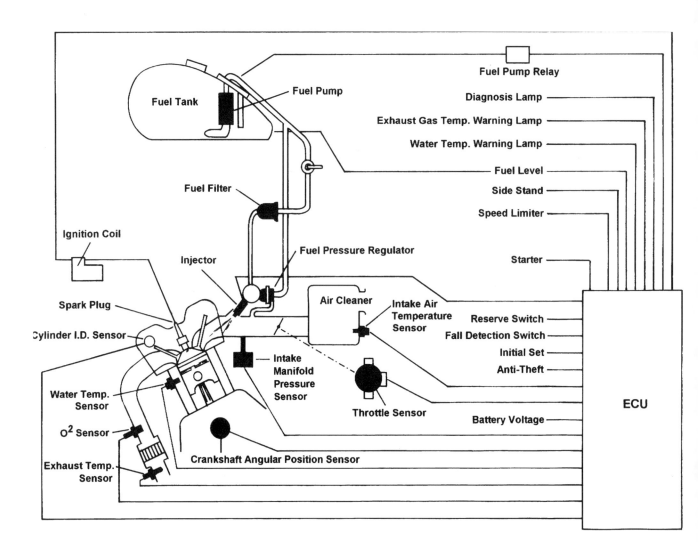

Yamaha's first ever EFI attempt is well done. What better bike than the GTS1000A on which to introduce one of the more advanced engine management systems in the industry today? Unfortunately, the bike is no longer available in the U.S. The system is a closed-loop, speed-density type, injecting fuel primarily according to engine air speed and air density. The ECU is not programmable. Any changes in calibration have to come from aftermarket performance PROM chips or programmable ECUs.

Types of EFI Systems

Electronic fuel injection systems come in three basic types:

1. Digital speed-density systems.
2. Mass flow sensing systems.
3. Closed-loop oxygen sensing in either mass flow sensing or digital speed-density formats.

Of the three, digital speed-density systems are the simplest. These designs are preprogrammed to a set of rpm and either manifold absolute pressure (MAP) or throttle angle (N-Alpha) values, which together totally control fuel delivery. Changing cams, bore, stroke, or even the exhaust system makes it necessary to change the programmed calibrations, as these systems gener-

ally do not automatically correct for such engine modifications.

Mass-flow sensing systems are extremely accurate, delivering fuel according to the actual air consumed. The Bosch LE Jetronics (flapper-valve systems installed on early BMW K100s are of this type. Although they are accurate and reliable, these designs can limit airflow. They are also less responsive, and are programmable only by exchanging the PROM chip for another that is pre-programmed for a certain set of conditions.

The closed-loop speed-density design eliminates the flapper valve, allowing individual throttle bodies for each cylinder. The pre-programmed speed-density design allows complete freedom to program all the variables, but because of its closed-loop oxygen sens-

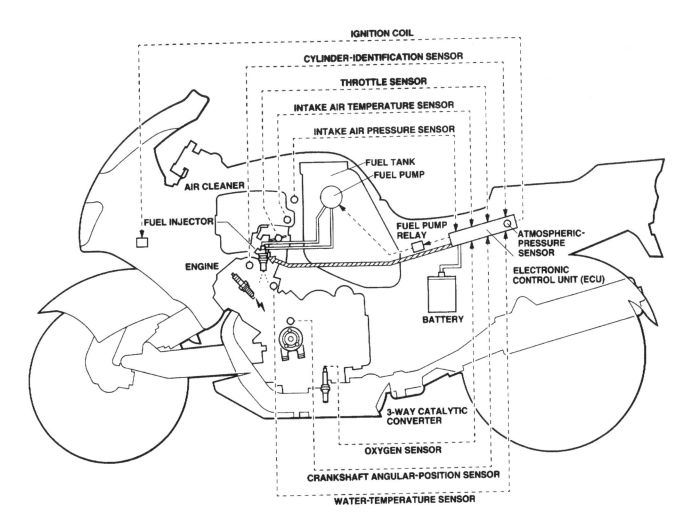

Placement of components on Yamaha's GTS1000A.

ing capability, it will automatically correct and adapt to minor changes in cams, displacement, and exhaust systems; radical changes in these areas may require a programmable system that allows you to make adjustments using your home computer. With a pre-programmed system, the oxygen sensor is set to enter the driving cycle at precise points and will automatically adjust the fuel base map memory. This means that your EFI system actually has an infinitely variable, ever-changing, multi-dimensional fuel delivery curve, instead of a single preprogrammed set of values.

How Does EFI Work?

We must first look at how the various parts of a typical EFI system work together to supply the correct amount of fuel to the engine under all conditions. The duties are divided into three basic functions: the air flow system, the fuel system, and the electrical system.

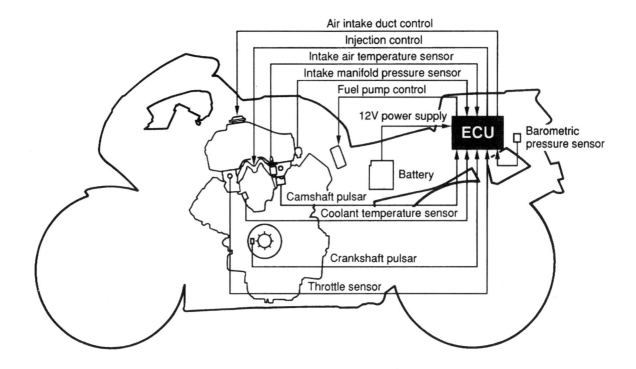

Air intake duct control
Injection control
Intake air temperature sensor
Intake manifold pressure sensor
Fuel pump control
12V power supply

ECU

Barometric pressure sensor

Battery

Camshaft pulsar

Coolant temperature sensor

Crankshaft pulsar

Throttle sensor

This RVF is not the first injected bike from Honda. They developed an EFI system for their CX500 and 650 Turbo bikes back in the early 1980s and are now back in the game with the RC45 (also known as the RVF). As we know, the RC45 is about as serious a road burner as it gets. Since one of the RC45's main development goals was to offer excellent performance on the street as well as the track, Honda opted for the precision of a digitally programmed fuel injection system. Honda offers special racing-only PROM chips available only to professional and privateer race teams. The system's four individual throttle bodies feature large 46 mm bores to ensure optimal airflow around their large butterfly valves. If turbocharging is being installed, the stock ECU will have to be replaced with a PC programmable unit.

Air Flow

There are two basic ways to control air flow into the engine: a single, large-bore throttle body connected to a tuned port intake manifold, or multiple throttle bodies (one for each cylinder). In many cases, systems with a single throttle body mount the throttle body some distance before the inlet manifold, and contain a throttle plate that is connected to the throttle via linkage or cable. In most cases, the throttle body will also contain an idle speed adjustment screw which varies the amount of air flow bypassing the throttle plate to establish a proper engine idle speed. Some systems use a bypass port in the throttle body housing that is controlled by either a fast idle valve or an idle air control motor (IAC) which puts bypass air under control of the electronic control unit (ECU). Single throttle bodies are commonly used in automobiles and trucks. Individual throttle bodies, one for each cylinder, are seen more on motorcycles because of their higher performance. They are generally more responsive and less restrictive.

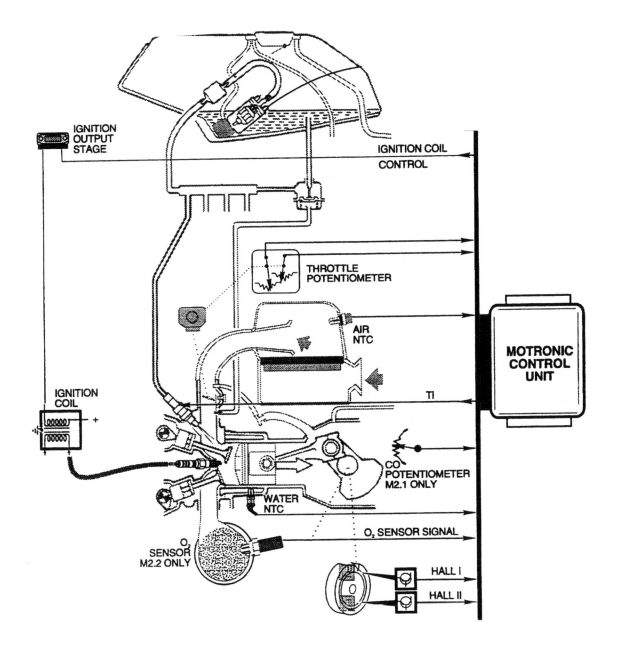

The EFI game is old hat to BMW. They've been using LE Jetronic and Motronic systems for years. If you have ever had the pleasure of riding an R1100RS or K-series Beemer, you know exactly why EFI is the wave of the future in motorcycle fueling. With the introduction of the 1990 K1, Motronic made its debut on US-market BMW motorcycles.

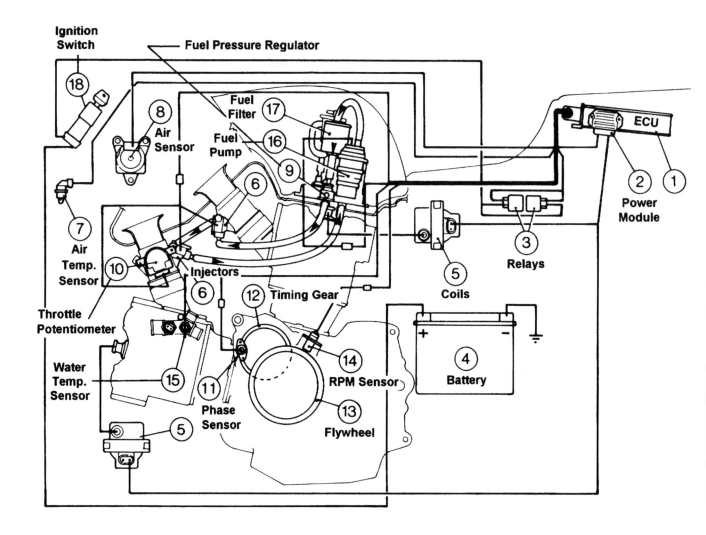

Ignition Switch — 18

Fuel Pressure Regulator

Fuel Filter — 17

Fuel Pump — 16

Air Sensor — 8

9

6

Air Temp. Sensor — 7

Throttle Potentiometer — 10

Injectors — 6

Water Temp. Sensor — 15

Phase Sensor — 11

5

Timing Gear — 12

14

RPM Sensor — 13

Flywheel

Coils — 5

Relays — 3

Battery — 4

ECU — 1

Power Module — 2

Ducati, like BMW, has been offering electronic fuel injection for a number of years on certain models, the most recent being the 851 and 916. Their EFI is an integrated system manufactured by Weber-IAW that controls both fueling and ignition. The individual throttle bodies are a gigantic 51mm, one of the main reasons for considering EFI. PROM chips for racing-only are available from Ducati; however, like the RC45, the ECU is not programmable.

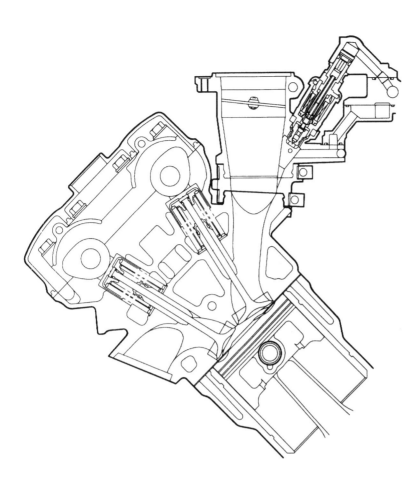

This cutaway illustration of the Honda RC45 throttle body and head shows the injector location, the straight-down path to the intake valve, and the immense size of the 45 mm throttle body. Because fuel is being injected under high pressure straight into the intake port, the intake tract can be much larger. This allows more air and fuel to enter the combustion chamber, increasing horsepower substantially.

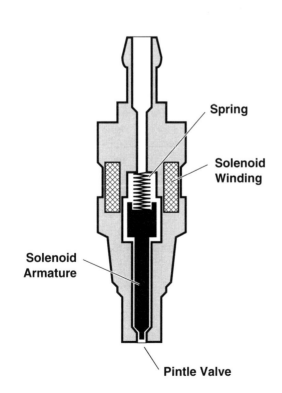

Spring

Solenoid Winding

Solenoid Armature

Pintle Valve

In a typical EFI system, each fuel injector is controlled by electric pulses from the ECU. When the solenoid winding is charged, the solenoid armature and the attached pintle valve rise, allowing pressurized fuel to spray into the inlet tract. As long as the solenoid is not charged, a spring holds the pintle valve closed, preventing fuel flow.

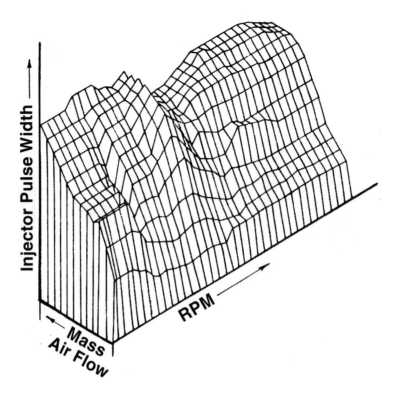

This fuel map illustrates how the injector pulse width varies for changing engine rpm and mass air flow. When an EFI system is developed, the ECU is programmed to provide precise fuel delivery for hundreds of engine operating conditions. The research involved in developing a fuel map for any given engine is what you are really paying for. The hardware is nothing compared to the thousands of hours it takes to program the ECU.

Fuel

The fuel system is composed of the fuel pump, fuel pressure regulator, injectors, and sundry lines and filters. A high-pressure fuel pump supplies fuel to a fuel pressure regulator which ensures that pressure in the rail feeding the injectors is held at a fixed level relative to intake manifold pressure. Accurately regulated fuel pressure is required at the injectors to provide precise metering. Usually, a diaphragm-operated pressure regulator maintains fuel pressure at 44 to 50 psi (depending on the system) above the vacuum or pressure in the intake manifold. A spring is installed in the manifold side of the regulator for pressure preload, and excess fuel is routed back to the fuel tank.

Electrical

The electrical system consists of the ECU and sensors, which may include an air flow meter, throttle position sensor, coolant temperature sensor, air temperature sensor, exhaust oxygen sensor, manifold pressure sensor, barometric pressure sensor, and engine output sensor. Some of the sensors vary, depending on the system.

The Brain

The brain of the typical EFI system is sometimes referred to as the "Electronic Control Module," or ECM. It is referred to here as an ECU, which means "Electronic Control Unit." Some people even refer to it as the "black box." Whatever you call it, its job is to receive and process all of the information from the various sensors and transmit an electrical signal to the injectors, turning them on at precise moments for precise durations. More sophisticated systems also process information communicated to and from the ignition system (for example, Yamaha GTS1000A, BMW K and R bikes, and the Ducati 916).

We are just beginning to see a few aftermarket motorcycle EFI systems offered to the general public. Shown here is the RB Racing RSR Electronic Control Unit mounted on the license plate bracket of Matt Capri's turbo injected Triumph Daytona 1200. This is a user-friendly, PC-programmable system. Even computerphobes should have no problem adapting to RB's EFI. Others makers are Hahn Racecraft, ET Performance, and Mr. Turbo.

Here's the business end of RB Racing's EFI system. Note the fuel log which feeds the injectors.

Mr. Turbo offers EFI in some of their recent turbo kits. They use a single throttle body on a tuned port intake manifold; tuning is performed through potentiometer adjustments. Shown is a Honda 900RR system.

The ECU often functions on analog signals, but some ECUs process digital signals. To receive a signal, the ECU must first send a constant voltage electric current of about 5 volts to a sensor. Each sensor then returns a current of reduced voltage, which tells the ECU what is happening at the sensor. Let's say the ECU sends out a constant 5 volt signal to the coolant temperature sensor, which is calibrated to sense from zero to 80° C, and a 2.5 volt signal returns. The ECU then knows the engine is still heating up, because the coolant temperature is at 40° C, and would know to send a longer pulse to the injectors, enriching the mixture. At the same time, the ECU may be receiving a signal from the TPS (throttle position sensor) indicating the throttle has been opened beyond a 40-degree position angle. This lets the ECU know the engine is under heavy load, like hard acceleration or pulling a

hill. The ECU increases the pulse width to add the needed fuel.

So how does the ECU module figure out these increases and decreases in injector pulse width? It's actually pretty simple. For any set of sensor conditions, a corresponding injector pulse width has been tabulated or "mapped" into the ECU. This "map" is worked out by the EFI manufacturer using a dyno, a computer, and a lot of equipment you don't have to worry about, until every possible combination of engine operating conditions has been assigned a specific fuel injector pulse width. The performance goals used while creating the fuel map can involve fuel economy, power, boost pressure (if supercharged or turbocharged), and emission control.

The map, stored in the ECU's memory bank, covers hundreds of engine operating conditions. As an

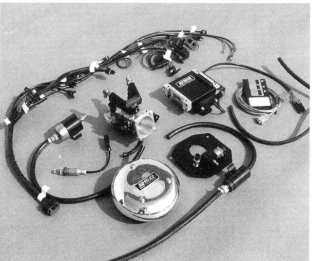
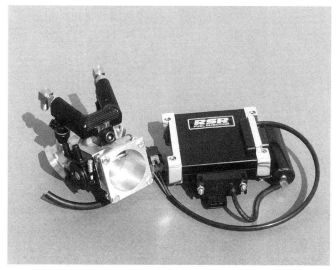

RB Racing makes multiple-throttle-body EFI systems for V-4, inline 4, and Harley-Davidson engines. They can also custom design a complete system for any motorcycle made today. For about $2,500, you can be the first on your block to shelve those carburetors.

example, let's say the engineers found that at 6,000 rpm, at normal operating temperature, with the throttle opened beyond the 40-degree point, the engine produced optimum power with an injector pulse width of 9.7 milliseconds. This information, along with hundreds of other map reference points, is stored in the black box's memory. Later on, when the engine is operated at 6,000 rpm and the throttle is opened beyond the 40 degree point, the ECU looks up this information in storage and finds what pulse width is needed for that particular situation. The ECU then sends a 9.7 millisecond pulse width signal to the injectors in response to that input.

Under normal conditions, the air flow sensor is one of the most critical sensors. Since air density changes with ambient temperature, air flow alone is not enough for accurate fuel metering. The air temperature sensor is also located in the air flow meter; the ECU calculates air *mass* flow from the air flow and the temperature of the incoming air.

The ECU also receives other input signals to vary the injector pulse width (the amount of time the injector stays open). These sensors differ according to the particular type of system you are dealing with. Water-cooled motorcycles may include a coolant temperature sensor. Most will have an engine speed sensor, which is usually connected to the ignition system. Some EFI systems will have a manifold absolute pressure sensor (MAP), a barometric pressure sensor (BARO), a camshaft position sensor (for sequentially timed injection

RB Racing is putting the finishing touches on a new EFI system for the mighty Kawasaki ZX-11. Single or dual injectors per cylinder will be available for everything from normally aspirated to 550 horsepower turbo systems.

systems), and a vacuum-atmospheric pressure (VAC) sensor. The latter reads the difference between manifold vacuum and atmospheric pressure.

Most EFI systems have a throttle position sensor (TPS). The Bosch TPS has two sets of contacts. One monitors when the throttle is closed, and the other when the throttle plate is opened past 40-degrees. Both sets of contacts are attached to the throttle body and are activated when the throttle shaft turns. Generally, when idling or decelerating, the throttle is closed and both contacts close. If, while the engine is idling, the control module receives a signal from these points (indicating that the throttle has just been opened), the pulse width is widened to enrich the mixture. However, if the ECU senses the engine is running at 4,000 rpm, and the TPS points are closed (because the throttle has been closed), it figures the engine is coasting and shuts off fuel to the injectors to reduce fuel consumption. When the engine speed falls below 1,700 rpm, the TPS points open, allowing fuel to continue past the injectors. During

high load, when the throttle plate exceeds 40-degrees, the points stay open for a longer pulse width period, increasing fuel flow by approximately 8 percent for maximum power.

The exhaust oxygen sensor, or "Lambda Probe," is technically known as the EGO (exhaust gas oxygen) sensor. It is common to most EFI systems today and is fitted in the exhaust system, close to the exhaust manifold. It is a metal-coated ceramic probe that works like a small battery. It produces approximately 100 millivolts when the oxygen content in the exhaust is high, which means the mixture is lean. When this condition occurs the voltage increases, signaling the ECU to increase the injector pulse width.

A PROM (programmable read-only memory) chip is a replaceable memory chip containing detailed information which makes up the fuel map for a given set of engine specifications. A PROM from a factory system maps the correct amount of fuel for any set of operating conditions, as long as the stock exhaust, pistons, cams,

Hahn Racecraft has developed a new EFI system for Suzuki GSXRs, shown here on Scott Crippen's Pro Mod drag bike, blasting off to another 200+ mph run in just a shade over 7 seconds. *Below:* Special single injectors cover a wide range of operation, thus eliminating the need for two injectors per cylinder in most applications. Street and race systems are available. This is the quickest electronically fuel injected bike in the country.

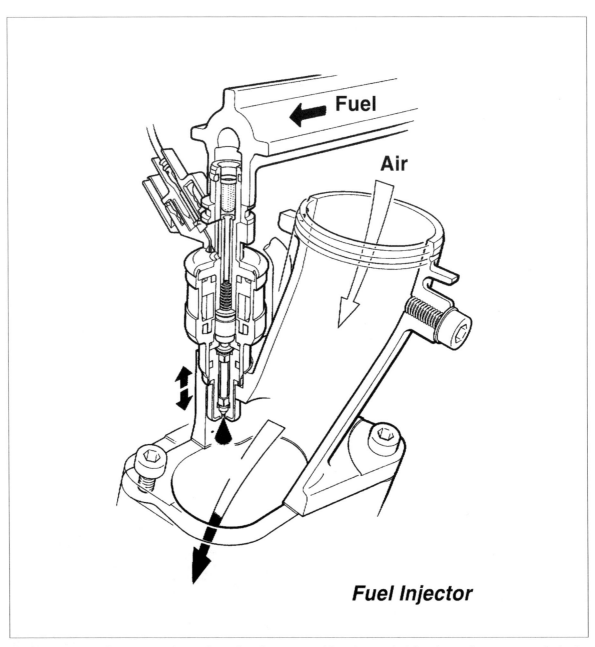

Fuel

Air

Fuel Injector

The fuel injector usually mounts as close to the intake valve(s) as possible and injects fuel directly into the air stream. A fuel rail (top of illustration) runs across the row of injectors, supplying high pressure fuel at all times. Fuel is constantly recirculated back to the gas tank, which keeps it cooler and at a consistently even pressure under all operating conditions. Shown is the throttle body and injector assembly for the Yamaha GTS 1000A.

and other equipment have not been altered. If you change the specifications of a fuel injected engine, you will need to exchange the PROM chip for one that has the proper injector pulse width values for the new specifications. These (usually aftermarket) chips are commonplace today, and are simply PROMs with a fuel map designed to maximize power, while the stock chip is designed to balance power needs against emissions control. Both Honda (for the RC45) and Ducati (for the 916) offer replacement PROM chips for racing purposes only. If you can prove you're a racer, they're available. Other fuel injected motorcycles such as the Yamaha GTS1000A and the Harley-Davidson Ultra Classic Electra Glide are stuck with the factory chips unless an aftermarket programmable ECU is adapted to the machine.

Aftermarket IBM PC programmable systems use sophisticated microprocessors with electrically erasable programmable memory functions. This allows you to program the fuel injection ECU using a personal computer, even while the vehicle is running. This eliminates the need to replace PROM chips. If you are considering turbocharging or supercharging, this is the type of system you will need.

RB Racing, for example, offers a programmable EFI system that features Autocal,™ a computer program that allows anyone to write a complete ECU calibration without having to be a Detroit-level fuel systems engineer. By simply entering data on engine displacement, number and size of fuel injectors, fuel pressure, etc. the Autocal™ program automatically generates:

- Complex 3D fuel curves
- Exact horsepower outputs
- Accelerator pump calibrations
- Warm up curves
- Deceleration fueling
- Idle control calibrations
- Manifold pressure bar calibrations
- Closed-loop parameters
- Air temperature correction
- Maximum power and idle fuel curves

RB Racing's Autocal™ program makes anyone an expert. You can change fuel injector size, fuel pressure, or even engine displacement without starting from scratch and automatically generating a complete ECU calibration. Letting the computer do the work is sure a heck of a lot easier than starting from scratch with little or no guidance and having to enter hundreds upon hundreds of digital entries which are all interrelated in a complex manner!

The WhiTek EFI system for Harleys replaces the standard carb and manifold with a neat little package. The throttle body and electronics are all together, not strung out all over the bike. The adjustable LED control monitor mounts on the handlebars or dash. This system uses the Motorola 68HC11 microcomputer, state-of-the-art microelectronics developed specifically for controlling small engines.

This is RB Racing's ECU. It is typical of the electronic control units made today. Microelectronics make it possible to condense these packages down to motorcycle size, making installation much easier. This ECU is fully programmable, operates in either open-loop or closed-loop modes, and features the Autocal™ program.

Programmable systems can replace the stock ECU on motorcycles with factory EFI systems. Some wiring and sensor changes may be necessary when converting to a programmable system, and one must always be aware of environmental standards in certain states like California, where it is forbidden to alter emission characteristics. But for racing and forced induction motorcycles, programmable electronic fuel injection is the wave of the future.

Open- and Closed-Loop Systems

We've mentioned open- and closed-loop systems. In a closed-loop design, the ECU constantly monitors the voltage generated by the exhaust gas oxygen (EGO) sensor. The ECU uses the voltage of the EGO sensor to determine whether the fuel mixture is richer or leaner than the theoretical ideal mixture (stoichiometric ratio) of 14.7:1 air/fuel ratio. The ECU's microprocessor calculates the degree of error and modifies the output signal to the fuel injectors (the calculation being the combination of many factors) to bring the air/fuel ratio, at the next injector firing, back into line at 14.7:1. Although the details of these computations vary with the designer's intent, the computer code which controls the closed-loop fuel injector operation can typically shift preprogrammed outputs as much as 50 percent. In other words, while a fixed, preprogrammed fuel map determines the nominal fuel injector operation for a set of conditions (temperature, throttle setting, engine speed, etc.), the information fed back to the ECU from the EGO sensor can alter fuel input to the engine by as much as 50 percent more or 50 percent less than the preprogrammed values, to compensate for actual engine operation. Figures 5-1 and 5-2 show the flow of information in both open-loop and closed-loop fuel control systems. You can see how the term "closed-loop" got its name, by the way the information fed back from the EGO sensor to the ECU "closes the loop" back to the ECU.

Is It Worth It?

A properly designed fuel injection system should be capable of a 15 percent horsepower increase over carburetion— with no other modification. With non-emission-controlled vehicles, this figure could jump to a 25 percent increase! Teamed with supercharging or turbocharging, the increase in performance of EFI systems over draw-through carburetion systems is unbelievable.

Obviously, this performance gain is not free. EFI systems are more complex and more expensive than carburetor equivalents. Is EFI worth the money? In the future that decision will not be yours to make. The EPA has motorcycle manufacturers in a stranglehold, just as it does the auto companies. The fact is *you will have fuel injection,* whether you like it or not! Why? Because Uncle Sam says so. Looking at the brighter side of this situation, however, a gain of up to 25 percent more horsepower (normally aspirated) and an increase to your fuel mileage are positive benefits stemming from EPA-mandated emissions requirements. The EPA's demand for tighter emission controls has stimulated interest in motorcycle EFI. You might say that motorcycle manufacturers are practicing for what is inevitable.

This, of course, is good news to power boosting enthusiasts because turbocharging or supercharging a motorcycle already equipped with EFI is not only easier, but will produce better results. Motorcycles with factory-equipped EFI include the Honda RC45, the Yamaha GTS1000A, Harley-Davidson's Ultra Classic, the 916 Ducati, and all of the BMWs. Others will follow in time.

Aftermarket EFI systems for motorcycles are beginning to emerge as well. WhiTek (805-481-7710), RB Racing (310-515-5720), Mr. Turbo (713-442-7113), ET Performance (805-563-2386) and Hahn Racecraft (708-851-5444) all offer bolt-on EFI systems for most popular motorcycles. EFI Technologies, MoTeC, and Electromotive offer electronic packages that can be adapted to motorcycles, and programmable ECUs that can replace factory preprogrammed units.

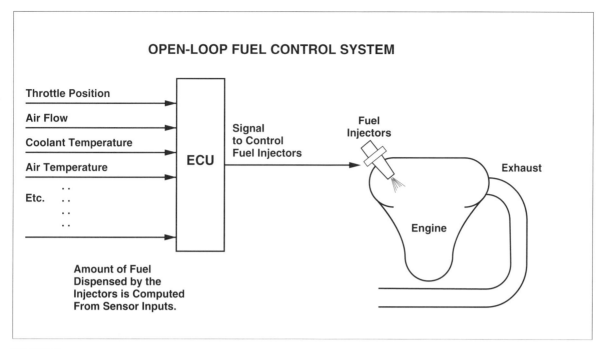

Figure 5-1

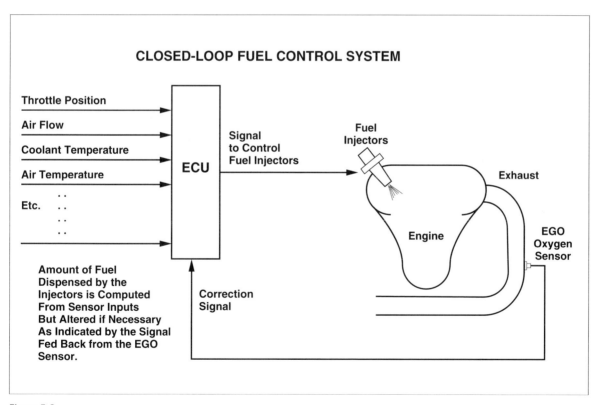

Figure 5-2

ET Performance makes this EFI system for big twin Harleys that features fully programmable fuel and ignition functions (four injectors can be staged and there is programmable output for nitrous oxide), two programmable accelerator pumps (low and high speed), programmable rpm limiter, and open-or closed-loop operation with a programmable oxygen sensor.

 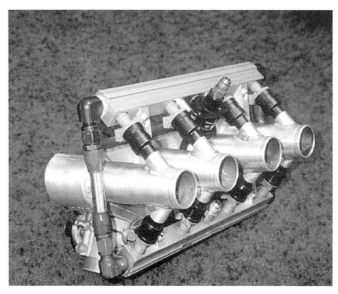

Hahn Racecraft makes cast alloy throttle bodies for inline four-cylinder engines having either one or two injectors per cylinder. The single injector system uses special broad range injectors that work well up to 300 horsepower.

TURBO/D.F.I. SYSTEM

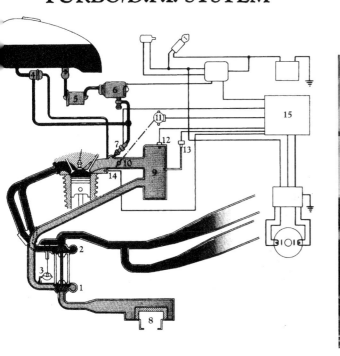 

Kawasaki first used electronic fuel injection in the early 1980s on the GPz750 Turbo bike. This system can be modified to fuel up to 215 horsepower, like this Horsepower Unlimited example belonging to John Voter.

The air/fuel ratio meter is small enough to mount just about anywhere on a motorcycle. Here it is mounted next to the boost gauge on this turbocharged Katana 750.

CHAPTER 6

Fueling: In search of the Perfect Air/Fuel Ratio

The quest for the perfect air-fuel mixture began ages ago (before dynos and exhaust gas analyzers) as a ritual involving the inspection of spark plugs and exhaust pipes and punctuated with numerous carburetor jet changes and gallons of gasoline spilled on the garage floor. The most determined high-tech tuners would compare mileage and performance gains (usually measured by top speed) until they were satisfied they could do no better. Things have progressed quite a lot since those days. Thanks to the EPA, automobile and motorcycle manufacturers are forced to adhere to strict standards regarding the ratio of fuel to air entering the combustion chamber. One might think this is a bad thing for the go-fast set, but it has actually proven a blessing to the motorcycle and performance industry, since we might otherwise have continued to use carburetors until all of humanity had vanished from the face of the earth. This is not to say that carburetors don't adequately perform the job of supplying atomized fuel mixed with air. It's just that electronic programmable fuel injection (a direct result of EPA mandated standards) can do it better, while improving performance *and* fuel economy.

Carburetors haven't been relegated to the scrap heap quite yet. So far, motorcycle manufacturers have been able to adjust to EPA guidelines with carburetors, but are just now bringing out EFI on a limited basis. The carburetor's replacement is under way, though, and, like automobiles, all motorcycles will eventually be equipped with EFI.

Specialty carburetor jetting companies were the first to take advantage of the EPA's mandates. Anyone who has installed a low restriction exhaust pipe or low restriction air cleaners on an EPA standardized motorcycle has undoubtedly discovered the incredible loss of horsepower with stock jets. Of course this loss occurs because more air is able to enter the combustion chamber but, without the required extra fuel to go along with it, a lean condition is the result. The need for "green" translates to excessively restrictive exhaust systems (to create higher back pressure) in conjunction with extra lean air-fuel mixtures to cut emissions. Companies such as Dyno Jet of Belgrade, Mont. (406-388-4993), have been developing and marketing motorcycle carburetor jet kits for a number of years and are well known to both racers and street riders.

Generally speaking, manufacturers of jet kits will develop two or three jet packages for any given motorcycle. This would include a set for stock exhaust and air cleaners or with low restriction air cleaners; a set for low restriction exhaust and low restriction air cleaners (street applications); and a set for full race, unmuffled, open intake applications. One of these jet kits will get you close to optimum; however, without tedious spark plug readings, trial and error needle height adjustments, and main jet changes, you probably won't hit all the proper air/fuel ratio combinations. You'll have a little lean spot here and a little rich spot there. When you are supercharging or turbocharging, things get even more complicated and the process of dialing in the proper air/fuel ratio can sometimes mean a burned piston—or worse.

But have no fear—meet the digital air/fuel ratio meter. Originally developed to aid in the mapping and programming of electronic fuel injection systems, these relatively inexpensive ($100-$250) devices can also calibrate carburetion systems. When you install your jet kit, high performance exhaust pipe, and low restriction air cleaners—or supercharger or turbocharger kit—you can accurately (and at any engine speed or load situation) see exactly what the air/fuel ratio is. It's a great tool to have and a lot more accurate than peering up your exhaust pipe to check its color.

Air/fuel ratio meters are relatively easy to hook up. An oxygen sensor port fitting must be welded into the exhaust header as close to the exhaust ports as possible. This is because the oxygen sensor has to be heated to at least 600° F to operate properly. On turbocharged motorcycles, mounting the oxygen sensor is usually not a problem, since the head pipes dump into a collector close to the exhaust ports. The collector makes an ideal spot to locate the oxygen sensor. On normally aspirated bikes with a four-into-one exhaust system, the collector is usually quite a distance from the exhaust ports and may not get hot enough in that location. In this case you can simply install an electrically heated oxygen sensor. This will heat immediately and greatly shorten the wait before the digital meter begins to operate.

The oxygen sensor is wired to the meter and grounded to the battery. The meters are small in size and can be located just about anywhere. Opening this chapter is a photo of a turbocharged Katana 750 on which the air/fuel ratio meter is mounted next to the boost gauge. Computer or no computer, developing a fuel curve for a motor is a time-consuming process; there are many points to calibrate in a "digitized" system in order to develop a base fuel map. The use of the digital air/fuel ratio meter has equal validity in carburetor jetting. Whether you are tapping computer keys or changing needles and jets, you are after the same thing: the correct air/fuel ratio.

Air/Fuel Ratio

The mixture of the air and fuel can be expressed in three ways, all based on a common point called the "stoichiometric ratio." Stoichiometry is the determination of the correct proportions in which chemical materials combine. The stoichiometric ratio for gasoline and air—the proportions at which the most complete combustion takes place—is 14.7 parts of air to one part of

fuel by weight. Table 6-1 correlates three ways in which the air and fuel ratio can be expressed.

	Table 6-1	
Ratio of Air to Fuel	Ratio of Fuel to Air	"Fuel Ratio" = Ratio of Actual Fuel to Stoichiometrically Correct Fuel
9.80:1	0.1020	1.5
10.50:1	0.0952	1.4
11.30:1	0.0885	1.3
12.25:1	0.0816	1.2
13.36:1	0.0748	1.1
14.70:1	**0.0680**	**1.0**
16.34:1	0.0612	0.9
18.38:1	0.0544	0.8
21.00:1	0.0476	0.7
24.50:1	0.0408	0.6

Mixture Requirements

The proper air/fuel ratio for each particular set of operating conditions is most conveniently broken down into two categories: steady state running, and transient operation. Steady state running is continuous operation at a given speed and power output with normal engine temperatures. Transient operation includes starting, warming, and the process of changing from one speed or load to another.

Steady-State Fuel Requirements

Idle. Due to low port velocity and frictional losses, idle mixtures are typically set at a fuel ratio of 1.2, or expressed differently, 12.25:1 air/fuel ratio. Your motor will idle at the stoichiometric air/fuel ratio (14.7:1), or possibly even leaner, but this would result in misfiring and, if operating temperatures have not stabilized at a high level, the motor will die. For example, operational fluid temperatures can vary from 150° F to 250° F and inlet air temperatures can easily vary by 100 degrees. These variations in temperature all necessitate different mixture requirements, so it is far better to keep the fuel ratio in the 1.2 region to preserve idle quality and off-idle responsiveness.

Steady State Throttle. At a given rpm, under steady state load conditions, your mixture strength should be a 1.1 fuel ratio, or 13.36:1 air/fuel ratio. At this ratio your engine will develop its highest peak cylinder pressure or Brake Mean Effective Pressure (BMEP), which is the point at which internal combustion engines oper-

The black wire from the air/fuel ratio meter must be grounded at the battery to prevent the meter from picking up trace electrical signals from other electrical grounds. These other signals will cause false readings and can cause the display to malfunction.

ate most efficiently. When developing a fuel map for programmable electronic fuel injection (EFI) systems, the base fuel ratio is generally centered around this value. Being 10 percent richer than the stoichiometric ratio, it lies within the correction range of a closed-loop oxygen sensing system. This allows the base map to be programmed for maximum power without excessive fuel consumption and still allows the closed-loop operation to self-adjust, when necessary, to 14.7:1. Of course, to obtain a 13.36:1 air/fuel ratio with a carburetion system, you will have to make changes to needles and mid-range jets. The air/fuel ratio meter will indicate necessary jetting changes at varying steady state rpm levels.

Transient Fuel Requirements

The principal transient conditions are starting, warming, acceleration (increase in load), and deceleration (decrease of load).

Starting and Warming. A cold engine needs an abnormally rich air-fuel mixture. The air/fuel ratios must be reduced during the warmup period until the engine will run satisfactorily with the normal steady-running air/fuel ratios. Starting or cranking fuel is also tempera-

ture dependent, with more cranking fuel required in lower temperatures. Air/fuel ratios on initial startup in cold weather should easily be 50 percent richer than the stoichiometric ratio—somewhere in the range of 11.0:1 to 10.3:1 air/fuel ratio.

Acceleration. When the throttle is opened for acceleration, it increases the manifold pressure and additional fuel must be supplied to prevent misfiring, backfiring, or even complete stoppage of the engine. Injection of this acceleration fueling must take place simultaneously with opening of the throttle. In an EFI system this is done by increasing the pulse width of the injectors via the electronic control unit (ECU). The ECU, of course, receives its input from the various sensors on the engine. On a carburetor, the accelerator pump supplies the added fuel. The optimum amount of acceleration fueling is that which will result in the best *power* air/fuel ratio in the cylinders. In general, this varies with the engine speed and throttle position at the start of acceleration, as well as fuel volatility, mixture temperature, and rate of throttle opening. Since partial or slow opening of the throttle requires less fuel than that required at full acceleration, the amount of extra fuel is usually made roughly proportional to the throttle

Work, Power, and BMEP

If you're getting involved with power boosting, you should learn some of its terminology. One common and useful term is BMEP, Brake Mean Effective Pressure, or simply Mean Effective Pressure. The term "brake" refers to the power output measured on a dynamometer (not the rear brake, as is commonly thought). Mean Effective Pressure is an alternate way to express the power being produced by an engine.

Before talking about MEP, let's define *work* and *power*. "Power" is defined as force acting through a distance over some period of time. Breaking it down further, "work" is force acting through some distance; for example, if you exert a force of one pound over a distance of one foot, you have done one "pound-foot" of work. Now, let's introduce time into the picture. If you push with one pound of force over a distance of one foot, but it takes all day, that represents a small amount of "power." You could actually do that "work" with a tiny electric toy motor if you gear it down sufficiently and give it enough time to get the work done. But now suppose you push with the same one pound of force over the same one-foot distance, and do that in one second. That's a horse of a different color; it takes much more "power" to do that same amount of work over a short interval of time. The definition of one horsepower is doing 550 pound-feet of work in one second. The following situations are all equivalent to one horsepower: pushing with a force of 550 pounds over a distance of one foot in one second; pushing with a force of 55 pounds over a distance of 10 feet in one second; or pushing with a force of 550 pounds over a distance of two feet (that's twice the work) in two seconds (give ourselves twice the amount of time).

Now, let's go back to Mean Effective Pressure. Suppose we have a two-cylinder engine with a three-inch bore and a four-inch stroke. The piston area represented by a three-inch bore is $\pi \times r^2 = 3.14 \times 1.5^2 = 3.14 \times 2.25 = 7.07$ square inches. Now suppose we have a constant pressure, let's say 100 pounds per square inch (psi), acting on that piston as it travels the length of the stroke of the engine—four inches. As the piston travels the distance of the stroke, work is being done. The pressure (100 psi) acting on the piston area (7.07 square inches) will exert a force of 707 pounds (pressure times the area). That force (707 pounds) acts through a distance (four inches) to do work, the amount of which is 2,828 pound-*inches* of work (force times distance), or (dividing by 12) 235.7 pound-*feet* of work. Now let's consider the effect of time. On each revolution of our two-cylinder engine, one piston goes through its power stroke, the other piston on alternate strokes. Suppose our engine is running at 3,000 revolutions per minute, or 50 revolutions per second. This means that 50 times each second, 235.7 pound-feet of work is being done. In one second, that adds up to 11,785 pound-feet of work. To calculate horsepower, divide that number by 550 (550 pound-feet of work per second equals one horsepower) and we get 21.42 horsepower.

To put this into perspective, we all know that engines don't really see constant pressure in the cylinders during the combustion process. We've used as an example an *average* pressure of 100 psi all the way through the power stroke. In reality, the cylinder pressure varies widely through the combustion process. It starts out low; then as the air-fuel mixture ignites, the pressure builds rapidly; as the piston moves away from the cylinder head—increasing the volume occupied by the charge—the pressure falls again. Engineers find it useful to relate the power output of an engine to the *average cylinder pressure that would be required to produce the same amount of power.* That figure is Mean Effective Pressure and it is strictly a theoretical value that equates to power. You'll be interested to know that street engines typically have a MEP rating of 130 to 140 psi. High performance street engines have 165 to 185 psi rating. Racing engines will have MEP ratings more like 185 to 210 psi.

A simple way to relate MEP to horsepower is the following formula:

$$MEP = \frac{hp \times 792{,}000}{displacement \times rpm}$$

$$\text{or,} \quad hp = \frac{MEP \times displacement \times rpm}{792{,}000}$$

where: *hp* is horsepower;
MEP is in pounds per square inch;
displacement is in cubic inches;
rpm is revolutions per minute.

∎

opening and the angle through which the throttle moves. Mixture strength under these conditions may be as rich as 12.7:1 on warm engines and perhaps as rich as 12.1:1 on cold engines. When an engine reaches normal operating temperature we should not see acceleration fueling richer than 12.7:1.

Deceleration. Under closed throttle deceleration, fuel must be controlled to prevent rich conditions or leanness-induced backfires. This controlled fuel shut-off can be monitored with the digital air/fuel ratio meter. Deceleration fueling should be no leaner than 17.1:1.

Digital Air/Fuel Ratio Meters

Air/fuel ratio meters display your exact air/fuel ratio digitally through a series of LEDs. The number of LEDs depends on the brand; in addition, there may be operational differences from one brand to another. However, most operate on the same general principle. As an example, the RSR gauge has ten lights divided into four colors: three green, three yellow, two orange and two red. The air/fuel ratio display is shown in Figure 6-1.

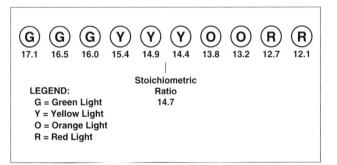

Figure 6-1

To the upper right of the display is a small window which houses an ambient light sensor. This automatically dims the display at night. Using this display, you will be able to adjust your base fuel map (EFI systems), or carburetor jetting under conditions of:

- steady state running
- starting and warmup cycles
- acceleration fueling
- deceleration fueling
- full throttle operation

Note that high quality air/fuel ratio meters have very fast (almost instantaneous) response to changing fuel conditions, making them useful for analyzing transient as well as steady state operation. Some poor quality

instruments respond slowly to changing conditions and are of questionable accuracy. If you're serious about fine-tuning fuel mixture, buy a solid, high quality instrument.

Using a Digital Air/Fuel Ratio Meter

There is no magical, absolute, digitized way to develop your application's fuel requirements. You must drive your machine and apply a considerable amount of judgment in such areas as cold start, warmup, acceleration fueling, idle quality, and drivability. Each motor is different, and the calibration will be only as good as the effort you put into it. Much subjective decision making will take place and the air/fuel ratio meter will not give you all the answers. Stopwatches, elapsed times, lap times, horsepower, and your own opinions as a tester are equally valid. There are some limitations to keep in mind:

1. Your O-sensor must reach 600° F for the display to become active. It will not "read" any exhaust gases until it reaches this temperature, which takes one to two minutes.

2. If you run leaded racing gas, your O-sensor will become contaminated and the display will no longer give true readings. Use unleaded pump gas to keep the O-sensor reliable for 50,000 miles or more.

3. Nitrous oxide will confuse the sensor because it reads free oxygen content; the nitrous will add oxygen molecules to the system, giving false readings on the meter.

Reading Your Air/Fuel Ratio Meter

The ten-LED readout can be used either on a dynamometer or when you actually drive the machine. The lights can go out if the mixture is way too lean, but the last red light will stay lit no matter how rich the mixture is beyond 12.1:1.

If the lights go green under any condition but hard deceleration or during rapidly changing engine conditions, you are too lean. If the last red light goes on, you are so rich the vehicle will stumble. You should concentrate your development so that the operating range centers around the two orange lights. This is approximately 13.8:1 to 13.2:1 air/fuel ratio, or about 10 percent richer than the stoichiometric ratio. Acceleration fueling will need to be richer than this, to the first red light while under load. Full load steady state maximum power is indicated by the second orange light, at about 13.2:1 air/fuel ratio.

Steady state operations under light load can occur in the yellow lights, but not leaner than the stoichiometric ratio. On carbureted vehicles, or EFI systems that do not feature closed-loop operations, maximum economy will occur at the stoichiometric ratio, or 14.7:1. This is the middle of the display.

Idle can vary from the last yellow (14.4:1) to the first red light (12.7:1), depending on how cold the engine is on starting. Again, judgment is a major factor in determining idle fueling after start enrichment and temperature corrections. Setting idle quality is a subjective process.

Once the engine reaches normal operating temperatures, try to keep the steady state running in the two orange lights, and full power (to include acceleration fueling) not past the first red light.

A visual shorthand version of how to read the digital air/fuel ratio meter is summarized in Figure 6-2.

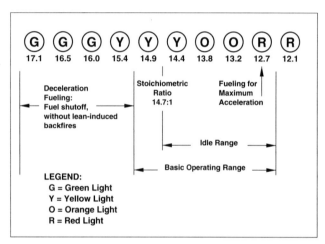

Figure 6-2

NOTE: Under closed-loop operation (EFI only), the display will "cycle" back and forth with the display trying to center around the air/fuel ratio of 14.7 to 1.

IMPORTANT: You should be aware that, on fuel injected vehicles, your electrical system's health can affect the accuracy of injector fueling. A poor charging system which cannot adequately support the injection system's demands will cause the injectors to lean out. As battery voltage drops below the system's built-in voltage correction factors, the injectors won't stay open to their pre-programmed values and the system will slowly lean out as voltage drops.

When mounting or wiring the digital air/fuel ratio meter, be sure the black wire of the meter is grounded at the negative terminal of the vehicle's battery. The other two wires—the red and the green — are attached to switched positive battery voltage and the O-sensor output respectively. If you ground the black wire of the sensor to any other location, you are in danger of picking up trace electrical signals from other electrical grounds. These other signals will cause false O-sensor readings and can cause the display, as well as the fuel injection, to malfunction.

Test Procedures

Steady/full load. To obtain different steady state load readings at the same rpm, use different gears and vary your test route by using level ground and by going up and down constant grades. Full-load readings can be observed in the lower rpm ranges by placing the vehicle in a higher gear. Stabilize at the test rpm and then go to full throttle (load).

To avoid warp velocities, you can get high rpm full load readings by using your lower gears. Just stabilize at the test rpm and then instantly go to full throttle (load). During any transitional load shifts, look at your acceleration fueling. If the meter goes momentarily lean, increase your accelerator fueling. If you see a rich stumble, decrease your accelerator fueling. On RSR fuel injection systems, you can adjust both your timed (synchronous) and your untimed (asynchronous) acceleration fueling to meet these requirements. Timed (synchronous) "accelerator pump" functions refer to additional amounts of fuel added to regular injector firing events. Untimed (asynchronous) functions refer to additional amounts of fuel added *between* the normal, timed injector firing events. By adding fuel between the regular injector firing events, lean-induced backfires and hesitations are eliminated.

Deceleration *fueling*. Adjusting the closed-throttle fueling at various deceleration rpm is important for three reasons:

1. It prevents an over-rich condition.

2. It prevents lean backfires.

3. It allows you to meter the correct amount of fuel to eliminate hesitations when you re-open the throttle.

When using the air/fuel ratio meter, you want to keep out of the red or orange lights under deceleration. You also want to avoid having the light go *off* or out of the green (lean) range, where backfiring can occur. Evaluate your deceleration fueling requirements in each rpm range to provide instantaneous throttle response when suddenly getting back on the gas. Increase the fueling in these ranges if the vehicle hesitates.

Exhaust Gas Percentages

Carbon monoxide (CO) exhaust gas content and your engine's air/fuel ratio are directly related. Your air/fuel ratio meter is not designed to set CO levels and should not be used for these purposes. Table 6-2 shows the relationship between the percentage of CO and your air/fuel ratio.

Alternative Fuels

Air/fuel ratio meters can be used with ethanol, methanol, or propane. A visual shorthand version of your ten LEDs' corresponding air/fuel ratio for alcohol and propane is shown in Figure 6-3. Tuning with these fuels is exactly the same as with unleaded gasoline. The tuning instructions previously mentioned apply equally to alcohol or propane.

Table 6-2
Relationship of Carbon Monoxide Content in Exhaust Gases to the Combustible Air/Fuel Ratio

%CO	Air/Fuel Ratio	%CO	Air/Fuel Ratio	%CO	Air/Fuel Ratio	%CO	Air/Fuel Ratio
0.1	14.71	2.6	13.53	5.1	12.58	7.6	11.68
0.2	14.53	2.7	13.48	5.2	12.53	7.7	11.64
0.3	14.41	2.8	13.44	5.3	12.50	7.8	11.60
0.4	14.33	2.9	13.40	5.4	12.45	7.9	11.57
0.5	14.27	3.0	13.37	5.5	12.42	8.0	11.53
0.6	14.22	3.1	13.33	5.6	12.39	8.1	11.49
0.7	14.20	3.2	13.30	5.7	12.36	8.2	11.45
0.8	14.16	3.3	13.26	5.8	12.32	8.3	11.42
0.9	14.14	3.4	13.23	5.9	12.29	8.4	11.39
1.0	14.10	3.5	13.19	6.0	12.24	8.5	11.36
1.1	14.08	3.6	13.14	6.1	12.21	8.6	11.31
1.2	14.03	3.7	13.11	6.2	12.17	8.7	11.27
1.3	14.00	3.8	13.07	6.3	12.12	8.8	11.24
1.4	13.97	3.9	13.02	6.4	12.09	8.9	11.20
1.5	13.93	4.0	12.99	6.5	12.06	9.0	11.15
1.6	13.89	4.1	12.95	6.6	12.02	9.1	11.11
1.7	13.85	4.2	12.92	6.7	11.99	9.2	11.07
1.8	13.81	4.3	12.89	6.8	11.95	9.3	11.04
1.9	13.79	4.4	12.85	6.9	11.92	9.4	11.01
2.0	13.76	4.5	12.82	7.0	11.88	9.5	10.96
2.1	13.72	4.6	12.79	7.1	11.85	9.6	10.93
2.2	13.68	4.7	12.74	7.2	11.81	9.7	10.89
2.3	13.62	4.8	12.69	7.3	11.78	9.8	10.85
2.4	13.58	4.9	12.66	7.4	11.75	9.9	10.81
2.5	13.55	5.0	12.63	7.5	11.71	10.0	10.78

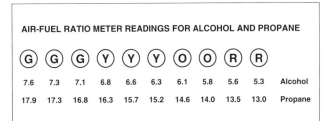

AIR-FUEL RATIO METER READINGS FOR ALCOHOL AND PROPANE

(G)	(G)	(G)	(Y)	(Y)	(Y)	(O)	(O)	(R)	(R)	
7.6	7.3	7.1	6.8	6.6	6.3	6.1	5.8	5.6	5.3	Alcohol
17.9	17.3	16.8	16.3	15.7	15.2	14.6	14.0	13.5	13.0	Propane

Figure 6-3

Summary

You couldn't ask for a more valuable tool at such a reasonable price than an air/fuel ratio meter, especially when you consider how much time it can save. Many racers have discovered the value of air/fuel ratio meters and are now adding them to the collection of information indicators already on their machines. There is no better way to monitor your air/fuel ratio on the fly, and that is especially important when turbocharging or supercharging.

High-quality air/fuel ratio meters can be obtained from several sources, including RB Racing (310-515-5720), K & N Engineering (714-684-9762), Mr. Turbo (713-442-7113), TWM Induction (805-967-9478), Turbo City (714-639-4933), and Westech Development (512-847-8918).

CHAPTER 7

Nitrous Oxide Injection

Nitrous oxide, or squeeze, as it is commonly called in the racing fraternity, is technically known as N_2O. Yes, it's the very same laughing gas that makes trips to the dentist slightly more tolerable and parties more fun. Before you invite your friends over, though, note that sulfur dioxide is added to commercial grade nitrous oxide as a deterrent to substance abuse. If you do decide to inhale the stuff, you will get very, very sick. Just say no.

While nitrous oxide can make people silly and stupid, it can also stimulate the internal combustion engine to produce unbelievable amounts of horsepower.

N_2O is commonly, and wrongly, considered an extremely volatile chemical, on a par with rocket fuel or nitromethane. In fact, it can actually put fires out. Nitrous oxide is not an inert gas (that is, one which does not react with other chemicals), but is an oxidizer, meaning that it liberates oxygen when it does react. It

The average-size nitrous oxide bottle for motorcycle usage is a two pounder, and is usually mounted on the side of the bike by the rear wheel. Notice the pressure gauge used to keep tabs on what's happening inside. On a hot day, and in direct sun, bottle pressure can increase by 500 psi. For consistent results, consistent pressure is a must.

On this Harley installation the bottle mounts near the engine and the rider's leg, which it does clear. Most installation locations involving a 2 lb or larger bottle will show. However, small 10 oz cheater bottles can be hidden just about anywhere.

is this added oxygen, introduced to a combustion process, that increases the horsepower of your engine. By comparison, nitromethane is also an oxygen-bearing chemical but is volatile because it produces oxygen as it burns. Nitrous oxide by itself is non-flammable. However, the oxygen present in nitrous oxide causes fuel to burn more rapidly. Unlike some other oxidizers, nitrous oxide is only a mild oxidizer and needs compression and combustion to fully break the bond between the oxygen and nitrogen, releasing the oxygen to combine with fuel.

Nitrous oxide is commonly stored as a liquid in high-pressure bottles. When it is released into the connecting supply lines and injected into the inlet ducts, it remains a liquid until it absorbs enough heat from the inlet charge to become a gas. This change of state from liquid to gas cools the induction charge; depending on where the nitrous is being injected, more or less heat can be removed from the charge. The farther the nitrous is injected from the combustion chamber, the greater the cooling effect. By cooling the charge, N_2O increases charge density and consequently improves the volumetric efficiency of your engine.

As soon as the air-fuel mixture fires in the engine, at 575° C, nitrous oxide breaks apart into oxygen and nitrogen. This added oxygen produces more heat, which increases the charge temperature, internal pressure, and ultimately horsepower. Nitrous oxide is a simple three-part molecule of nitrogen-nitrogen-oxygen (N_2O) and is actually similar to the air you breathe. Air is composed of approximately 80 percent nitrogen and 20 percent oxygen. Nitrous oxide has a higher oxygen content and is approximately 66 percent nitrogen and 33 percent oxygen. If more oxygen is supplied to the combustion process, the engine can burn more fuel. Just as in a turbocharged or supercharged motor, more oxygen (air) means more fuel must be added to compensate. This extra fuel must be added to maintain the proper air/fuel ratio. If you don't add enough, you might be able to inspect your rods and crankshaft through that shiny new hole in the top of your pistons— not a good thing. If nitrous oxide is allowed to run in a lean condition, it will promote detonation. On the other hand, if it is used in conjunction with an enriched fuel mixture, its cooling, shock-absorbing effect can actually lessen the chance of detonation.

Nitrous oxide injection systems operate independently of engine speed, load, and gear ratios. In a single-stage system, the flow rate of added nitrous oxide will be the same any time you push the button to turn it on. If your engine is producing 40hp before the nitrous starts flowing, it will develop about 80hp once the nitrous begins to flow. This in itself can cause some problems. At low rpm the pistons cannot accelerate away from the flame front fast enough, the end result being an engine-damaging explosion. This is why most N_2O systems operate at full throttle only. The alternative is variable nitrous controllers, which can usually be found on more serious all-out drag bikes.

Ignition timing is also important in setting up a nitrous oxide system. About halfway through the combustion cycle is the peak pressure point, which occurs between 5 and 25 degrees after top dead center (TDC). This is when the piston starts its downward stroke at the beginning of the combustion cycle—your ignition tim-

Easily installed in an afternoon, the Fogger system from NOS for Harley-Davidson motorcycles comes with everything you need. This includes detailed, easy to follow instructions, a factory filled 10 oz. (shown) or 2 lb nitrous bottle, nitrous and fuel solenoids, Fogger 2 nozzles, filters, fittings, tubing, fuel pump, T fittings, jets, switches, hose, and all the hardware necessary to turn that 68 horsepower weakling into a asphalt-pounding beast.

ing has a great deal to do with when this occurs. If you ignite the air-fuel charge too soon, the engine will experience excessive pressure before TDC; too late and you risk power loss. The faster you can burn the fuel in the cylinder during this critical period of 5 to 25 degrees after TDC, the greater the horsepower increase with that amount of fuel.

With appropriate controls, you can adjust the percentage of nitrous oxide being introduced during the combustion cycle. By varying the amount of nitrous admitted to the inlet charge, you can actually control how quickly the fuel burns, with the result of more energy released in a shorter period of time.

Weather can also play a major role. On a hot day the nitrous bottle can run up to 500 psi higher than on a cold day. For consistent results, a pressure gauge should be used to monitor what is happening inside the bottle. To reduce pressure variations, some racers use a booster bottle that pressurizes the nitrous to a constant level. The booster bottles are filled with nitrogen, an inert gas. For optimal running conditions, keep the bottle pressure at approximately 800 to 1,000 psi. If

you operate a nitrous system in colder climates, it is a good idea to purchase a bottle heater kit. Generally speaking, 70° to 90° F will give the best results.

The Hardware

Let's start at the source: the bottle. They are available in many sizes, from tiny cheater bottles (you usually run two of these tucked away in some inconspicuous location), to larger champagne sizes (usually mounted at the rear of the bike where it *can* be seen). Whatever the size, the bottle should be angled upward at approximately 15 to 30 degrees, facing forward. With the exception of 10-ounce cheater bottles, nitrous oxide bottles come with siphon tubes which take liquid nitrous from the bottom of the bottle; in order to maintain proper pickup of the liquid nitrous, it is important to mount the bottle correctly.

Some people prefer braided steel connecting lines and some use semi-rigid nylon that can withstand up to 3,500 psi. Either way, high pressure hose takes the nitrous from the bottle to the rest of the system. These

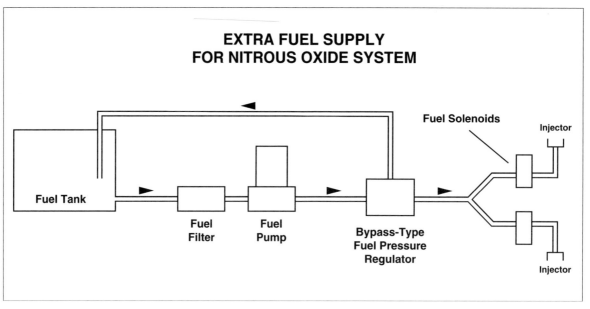

EXTRA FUEL SUPPLY
FOR NITROUS OXIDE SYSTEM

Fuel Tank

Fuel Filter

Fuel Pump

Bypass-Type Fuel Pressure Regulator

Fuel Solenoids

Injector

Injector

This is the typical arrangement to deliver extra fuel to an engine using nitrous oxide. A bypass-type fuel pressure regulator is inherently more accurate than a diaphragm type (deadhead) regulator, and responds more quickly to fuel flow requirements.

special hoses have a Teflon inner liner and a braided steel outer cover. Do not replace these hoses with standard neoprene lined braided steel hose with screw-together connections. Standard hoses cannot take the high pressures of nitrous and will become brittle at the extremely low temperatures. From the lines, nitrous flows first through the all-important filter, then to solenoid valves where the flow is interrupted. Solenoid valves are simply on-off valves which are controlled electrically.

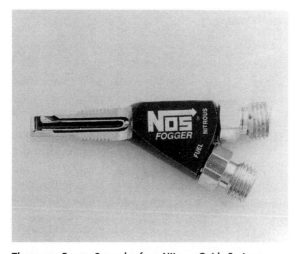

These new Fogger 2 nozzles from Nitrous Oxide Systems mixes the nitrous and fuel outside the nozzle tip to provide superior atomization of supplemental fuel as well as more even fuel distribution within the nitrous flow.

There are two control systems for the solenoids: an overall arming switch which turns the system on, and a microswitch in the throttle linkage (or a manually activated button switch) that cuts the nitrous loose at full throttle. The amount of nitrous flowing through the solenoid valve determines the amount of extra horsepower you get. The typical carbureted system will require two solenoid valves: one for nitrous oxide and one for the extra fuel needed to balance the additional oxidizing effect of the N_2O. The manufacturer of the system will let you know what your particular application will require.

Metering of the nitrous oxide is accomplished through small brass jets on the exit side of the solenoid valve. The larger the jet, the more nitrous flows, and the more horsepower you will get. There is only one jet per solenoid valve.

The nitrous injectors are used to direct the nitrous flow and spray it into the engine's intake stream. Where the injectors are located will determine whether you get a soft or hard hit when you activate the system. It is best if the injectors do not protrude into the intake tract, since the engine is running without nitrous injection more than 90 percent of the time and any obstruction causes horsepower-robbing turbulence. The important thing here is to follow the instructions in your nitrous oxide kit.

Extra fuel gets into the engine through its own solenoid valve and injector. Normally, a T fitting is installed in the existing fuel system to provide a fuel supply to the fuel solenoid valve. For carbureted engines, the T fitting should be in the carburetor fuel supply, and should deliver fuel to an adjustable pressure regulator which, in turn, supplies extra fuel through its own solenoid valve only when the nitrous injectors are turned on.

Solenoids and connecting nitrous lines should be mounted in a cool place to help keep the compressed liquid from turning to gas. If the solenoids are mounted in a location where its temperature could reach 500° F, the nitrous could start to go gaseous before it reaches the intake ports. As a precaution, any drag racer who knows nitrous will also purge the system of gaseous nitrous oxide before every run.

Engines using multi-point nitrous injection incorporate a distribution block that is used to divide the nitrous to each cylinder. In this case each nozzle is usually tapped into the intake manifold(s). On V-configuration engines, a spacer plate under the carburetor(s) commonly contains one or two nozzles.

Single- and Multi-Stage Nitrous

The typical single-stage nitrous oxide system is set to come on at wide open throttle (usually activated by a button or switch) and jetted for a predetermined amount of horsepower increase. That's it. A system with two or more stages has double or triple the hardware. For instance, stage one might be set up "soft"— that is, it introduces a small amount of nitrous to the engine, for a small power boost—and each successive stage increases the amount of N_2O released into the intake ports. Single-stage systems are usually seen on street bikes and multi-stage systems are common on all-out drag bikes.

A variant of multi-stage nitrous injection is to use only one set of nitrous injectors, but pulse the injection solenoids with a variable electronic controller, so that different amounts of nitrous will be injected for each stage of operation. This approach simplifies the hardware considerably, since only one set of nitrous plumbing and injectors is required. The electronic switching controllers are programmed to pulse the nitrous control solenoids on and off, thus regulating the nitrous flow to any particular set of injectors. The end result is a progressive and controllable delivery of power boost.

The heart of any nitrous system is the solenoid valves, which control the amount of nitrous introduced into the engine. These NOS units come standard with stainless or brass bodies and incorporate top-quality seals for long life.

This is the entire system for an over-700cc four-cylinder motorcycle engine. A stock Suzuki GSXR1100 with normal street nitrous settings will experience high nine-second and 135 mph quarter-mile performance.

Standard on all NOS systems are these high flow bottle valves. Their large, non-restrictive orifices eliminate pressure drop and freezing that causes surging and reduced horsepower. For extra safety the valves incorporate an exclusive blow-off venting system to relieve pressure in the event your bottle is overfilled or pressure in the bottle increases beyond the maximum safety level.

Nitrous bottles come in all sizes and shapes. The small 10 oz. cheater bottles are great on motorcycles because they can be hidden so easily.

NOS's Most Commonly Asked Questions

Nitrous Oxide Systems of Cypress, Calif. (714-821-0580), supplied this question and answer list that should address most issues concerning the use of nitrous oxide.

Question: How much does nitrous oxide cost?

Answer: The average cost is $2.50 to $3.00 per pound; however, it depends on your supplier. Some suppliers offer a discount to those who purchased the nitrous system from them. Also, the quantity can make a difference: the more you buy, the cheaper it is.

Question: How long will the bottle last before I have to refill it?

Answer: This largely depends on the type of nitrous kit and jetting used. For example, a 35 horsepower kit with a standard 2 lb bottle will usually offer 5 to 7 full quarter-mile passes. If nitrous is only used in third or fourth gears, the bottle will last considerably longer.

Question: How long can I hold the nitrous button down?

Answer: Theoretically, you can hold the button down until the bottle is empty. However, you would rarely need nitrous injection for more than 15 seconds. Your competition should be a tiny dot in your rear view mirror at that time anyway.

Question: When is the best time to use nitrous?

Answer: Only at wide open throttle, unless a progressive controller is used. Most street riders will wait until second or third gear before hitting the go button, as first-gear nitrous wheelies really aren't the way to start your day.

Question: How easy is it to hide the system?

Answer: There are various nitrous bottle sizes, ranging from a 10 oz bottle all the way up to a 5 lb capacity. The standard motorcycle size would be a 2 lb capacity bottle; of course, the larger the bottle, the more runs you will get before hitting the ugly word "Empty." Small cheater bottles are easy to hide. If the stock air box has been replaced with individual air cleaners, this usually leaves a void that can be used for the nitrous bottle. Some people have hidden the bottles up inside the rear fender area, but if you are using a larger bottle you will probably be forced to hang it on the side of the bike next to the rear wheel.

Question: How do I know how much nitrous oxide is left in the bottle?

Answer: The best way to tell is to weigh the bottle. When a bottle is nearly empty (about 20 percent or less nitrous remaining), you will normally feel a surging effect. It is best to refill the bottle at this point. A nitrous pressure gauge will not tell you how full the bottle is. Pressure is a function of temperature, not weight.

Question: Will I have to re-jet my carburetor(s) when adding nitrous?

Answer: No. The nitrous oxide system is independent of your bike's carburetor(s) or fuel injection system and injects its own mixture of supplementary fuel with nitrous through a "Y" shaped nozzle.

Question: What is the purpose of the blow-off safety valve on the bottle?

Answer: It is important not to overfill a bottle. A 2 lb capacity bottle should not be filled with more than 2 lbs of nitrous oxide by weight. Over-filling and/or exposure to too much heat can cause excessive bottle pressures, forcing the safety seal to blow and release the contents of the bottle.

Question: Where can I buy nitrous oxide?

Answer: Aside from the company from whom you bought the system, many performance stores offer a refill service. If you're really strapped for a supplier, try a medical supply house. Use the yellow pages and look under "gas." Every kit sold by NOS Systems contains a geographical list of suppliers within the United States.

Question: Who can install my N₂O system?

Answer: The company from which you purchased your system is a good bet. However, motorcycle shops specializing in high-performance services should be able to handle it. In fact, it's so simple that with instructions in hand, you should be able to do it yourself. A few basic hand tools and an average of 4 to 6 hours are all it takes to install a complete kit. You don't have to take the whole engine apart to install a kit. They are so complete, there shouldn't be any extra trips to the hardware store.

This NOS adjustable fuel pressure regulator is excellent for optimizing and tuning a nitrous system. Fuel pressure can be regulated from 0 to 12 psi with a simple turn of the built-in screw adjuster. It also features a boost compensating port to allow fuel pressure to be corrected for boost pressure on turbocharged or supercharged engines.

Question: Will nitrous oxide destroy my engine?

Answer: Most nitrous system suppliers will agree that modern motorcycle engines can handle up to a 100 percent increase in horsepower and certain engines will handle up to a 300 percent increase. However, specific rules should be followed to guarantee your engine's safety. Like turbocharging, nitrous adds more boost and requires greater precaution to avoid damaging things. The more "squeeze" you put in the system, the heavier-duty the components need to be to withstand the abuse. The key is choosing the correct horsepower for a given application. A kit that uses the calibration recommended by its manufacturer does not usually cause increased wear. As the energy released in the cylinder increases, so do the loads on the various components that must handle them. This is true whether an engine's power is increased by nitrous, turbochargers, or other modifications such as big bore pistons, cams, etc. If the power increase exceeds the ability of the components to handle them, added wear takes place.

The amount of wear and tear to the engine depends largely on the actual condition of the engine components. Any performance modification to an engine that is worn out or poorly tuned will have detrimental effects. However, an engine in good condition, with good ring and head gasket sealing, should be able to use nitrous at mild levels of boost without any abnormal wear.

Question: Is the use of nitrous oxide street legal?

Answer: There are no laws that prohibit the use of nitrous oxide on the street; however, there are rumors the EPA is looking into it. Note that certain modifications are recommended before using nitrous. One is a richer mixture and another is retarded timing. Both modifications can be considered tampering with the emissions system, and if your motorcycle falls under EPA guidelines, you *may* be in trouble—but only if they check.

Question: How is the power rating of a nitrous oxide kit determined?

Answer: The power rating is calculated from the flow rate through the nitrous oxide jet and is therefore theoretical. The actual power increase achieved by a particular engine depends on the following: (1) The richness of the fuel-to-nitrous ratio. Too rich means less power output. (2) The engine's particular characteristics. Different engines will produce different power increases from a specific amount of nitrous oxide. It is also important to remember that different motorcycles will lose different amounts of power through the transmission and final drive. Bikes with drive shafts will lose more power to the rear wheel than chain drive.

Question: How much power can I use?

Answer: As much as you can handle. Typically, you would start off the normal street system at a 50 percent power increase and work your way up to 100 percent or more. Some drag bikes are looking at a nearly 500 percent increase in power. That, however, would not be advisable on the street. For many motorcycle applications, you can expect an improvement of one full second and 10 to 15 mph in the quarter-mile. For example:

1994 Suzuki GSXR 1100 (stock)
Before – 10.93 at 123 mph
After – 9.97 at 138 mph

1994 Harley-Davidson Fat Boy (stock)
Before – 14.96 at 92 mph
After – 14.00 at 98 mph

1994 Harley-Davidson Fat Boy (modified)
Before – 11.55 at 114 mph
After – 10.26 at 127 mph

Question: Are any improved engine components needed?

Answer: The typical motorcycle street system should not require any internal modifications—to a point. With high rates of nitrous oxide, slightly lower compression might be a good idea, along with a solid copper head gasket. Of course, extreme power boosting will require all the engine modifications one would perform on an all-out race motor. Anything you can do to strengthen your engine can't hurt—it's just a matter of how deep your wallet is. Generally, high-quality forged aluminum pistons are one of the best modifications you can make. A set of high quality rods or shot peening, balancing, and blueprinting rods are also a good idea. The same may be advisable for the crankshaft. A high-quality race-type clutch with stiffer springs is usually advisable. A set of quality valve springs is a good idea to help deal with all the extra horsepower. All-out racing engines that are jetted for a lot of nitrous may require a modest amount of ignition retard, whereas applications to stock machines with a

The best performance gains are realized when bottle pressure is between 750 and 900 psi. A nitrous pressure gauge can alert you when pressures are low before you make a run or embarrass yourself in a street race. Fuel pressure is equally important on a nitrous system because running lean can damage your engine.

relatively mild nitrous kit may not require any ignition retard. Higher octane racing gasoline may be required, as well as spark plugs one to two heat ranges colder than normal, with gaps closed to 0.025 to 0.030 inches.

Question: Will nitrous oxide improve a highly tuned engine?

Answer: There is no reason why it shouldn't. The more highly tuned an engine is, the more efficient it is; consequently, it will use nitrous oxide more efficiently.

Question: Does nitrous oxide work on two-stroke engines?

Answer: Yes and the results indicate that for a specific amount of nitrous oxide flow, a two-stroke engine will produce better results than an equal size four-stroke engine. They do, however, suffer from certain problems sooner than four-strokes. The oil mixed with gas lowers the octane rating approximately two numbers and this makes detonation a greater possibility. The fuel-to-nitrous ratio is more critical.

Question: What are some of the advantages of nitrous compared to other performance modifications?

Answer: Nitrous is used only when you want it (5 to 10 seconds at a time in most cases), not all of the time, as with other traditional performance modifications which have a full-time effect on reliability and fuel economy. Normal operation, when you are not using nitrous, is therefore completely unaffected. Normal carburetion will also be unaffected since nitrous and supplementary fuel are injected with a separate nozzle only when additional power is required. The horsepower performance improvement per dollar is tops when compared to the high cost of parts and labor for turbocharging, supercharging, installing big bore kits, cams, headers, etc. Nitrous also has a tremendous intercooling effect by reducing intake charge temperatures by 60° to 75° F.

Question: Are there benefits to using nitrous with turbo or supercharger applications?

Answer: Yes! In turbo applications, a nitrous system eliminates turbo lag. Another benefit of nitrous on both turbo and supercharged engines is its tremendous cooling effect, which reduces intake charge temperatures by 75° F or more. Boost is usually increased as well, which adds up to even more power.

The NOS time delay switch allows you to activate a second or third stage of nitrous as a function of time. Delay is easily set from one-tenth of a second to almost two minutes, in one-tenth-second increments, by setting the small switches on the top of the timer.

Question: What is the difference between a standard bottle valve and a nitrous Hi-Flo bottle valve?

Answer: The orifice of a Hi-Flo valve is much larger than the standard valve, allowing for a larger flow of nitrous. With a small orifice, common on medical-type valves, a pressure drop could occur when nitrous flow is high, causing surging or inadequate nitrous flow. Hi-Flo valves designed for power boost applications eliminate this problem.

Question: Can high compression engines use nitrous oxide?

Answer: Absolutely. High or low compression ratios can work quite nicely with nitrous, provided the proper balance of nitrous and fuel enrichment is maintained. Nitrous kits are used in applications from relatively low-compression stock motors to applications that can exceed 15:1 compression. Generally, the higher the compression ratio, the more ignition retard—as well as higher octane fuel—is required.

Question: What type of cam is best suited for use with nitrous oxide on four-stroke engines?

Answer: Generally, cams that have more exhaust overlap and duration. Unless your engine is used strictly for racing, it may be best to choose a cam tailored more toward normal use (when nitrous is not activated), since 99 percent of your operation is *not* at full throttle with nitrous activated.

Question: Should I modify my fuel system to use nitrous oxide?

Answer: It is important to make sure that your fuel tank petcock assembly and fuel lines can flow enough fuel to satisfy both your existing fuel system and the additional fuel required by the nitrous kit under full throttle conditions. Pingel Enterprises manufactures dual fuel petcocks that allow separate fuel lines to the carbs and to the fuel pump dedicated to the nitrous system.

Langfield's Do's and Don'ts

T.K. Langfield of the TMC Group (nitrous oxide specialists in the U.K.) supplied this Do's and Don'ts list. The TMC Group, which manufactures unique nitrous oxide systems for both automobiles and motorcycles, can be reached in England at (44) 130-283-4343.

Do install a larger petcock on the fuel tank, as well as larger fuel lines. If your motorcycle is equipped with a fuel pump, you should be okay; however, you will be required to add a fuel pump in conjunction with a nitrous fuel pressure regulator.

Do check your engine compression to make sure the cylinders are uniform. Then perform a leak down test. Leakage should not exceed 10 percent.

Do fit a high-performance ignition system including high-output coils if heavy rates of nitrous are to be used.

Do replace the spark plugs with plugs one range colder. Sometimes two ranges colder is a good idea for higher doses of nitrous.

Do retard your timing approximately 2 to 6 degrees. Adjustable ignition advance/retard mechanisms are available for most modern motorcycles. Older bikes may require an aftermarket distributor ignition system.

Do have your motorcycle serviced for optimum performance. This includes synchronizing the carburetors.

Do check your head bolt torque settings.

Do replace your oil with a good grade turbo or turbo synthetic oil, at least a 20/50-weight. Two-strokes should run a high-quality synthetic.

Do use high-octane (over 100) gas or a tetraethyl lead octane booster for anything over a 50 percent increase in horsepower.

Do purge the nitrous system before leaving your bike overnight, or when it is unattended. By purging, we refer here to releasing the pressure in the nitrous line between the bottle and the solenoid valve, after the bottle valve has been shut off. This can be achieved by running the engine at about 1/3 throttle and briefly activating the nitrous solenoid after the bottle valve has been shut off.

Do use a filter in the nitrous line. Some people remove the filter, thinking it will increase horsepower. WRONG! What it will do is allow junk to pass through your system and possibly clog the seat of your solenoid valve. This means the nitrous may not shut off, even when you back off the throttle; it may also fill the intake manifold or ports with nitrous oxide and induce an explosive backfire when you start cranking the engine over. Note that with conventionally fueled engines, backfires are often the result of an excessively lean fuel charge. The presence of excess nitrous oxide in the fuel mixture has the same result: too little fuel for the available oxidizer. If nitrous oxide has accumulated in the intake tract while the engine is not running, it is important to clear the intake tract before starting the engine. This can be done by cranking the engine without ignition for 15 or 20 seconds. That is usually enough to purge unwanted nitrous oxide from the inlet tract. The engine can then be started and run as usual.

Do make sure your supplier of nitrous oxide uses a filter between his mother bottle and yours. This means less trash will end up in your bottle and means your own filter will be less likely to plug. Two sizes of filters are common to nitrous systems. The large diameter version is recommended as it has more filtering area and is less likely to plug.

Do use an engine cut-off switch as a low pressure safety on the fuel supply line to reduce the chance of engine damage and fire should you lose fuel pressure during a crash. It can also prevent internal damage due to a lean fuel condition. Put a 10 psi switch in the fuel supply line before the fuel pressure regulator. If you use an rpm switch to activate your system, use the cut-off switch as a path for ground. Discuss this with your system supplier.

Do keep the bottle full. It has been shown that a 10 pound bottle filled with just six pounds of nitrous drops head pressure 35 percent faster than a full bottle. Consistent performance will mean keeping the bottle full, or putting on a new bottle before every race. You may consider using two bottles for more consistency. A T-fitting is used to route the nitrous of both bottles into one line. The added capacity, pressure, and nitrous will help increase consistency and performance. This may put you a tad on the lean side, so you may need to enrich your mixture by 10 percent or so to dial this in properly.

Do use a bypass-type fuel regulator on your nitrous system if your engine makes more than 100 horsepower. When the nitrous system is first engaged, there is a large fuel pressure drop. The inherent restrictions of a deadhead-type pressure regulator can't keep up with the system's demand for more fuel. This can result in a lean air/fuel ratio and your pistons don't like that.

Do make sure your electrical system can handle a nitrous system. Solenoid valves can draw up to 16 amps each.

Do monitor the condition of the spark plug ground electrode and porcelain of your plugs. If the electrode is turning blue or there are specks of shiny metal on the porcelain, you may have a nitrous tuning problem. Shiny metal deposits on the porcelain means your pistons are starting to melt. Bluing of the electrode can mean a lean mixture.

Do Not operate the nitrous system when the engine isn't running.

Do Not start the engine if you suspect the nitrous system has been operated while the engine was off. Purge the nitrous from the engine by removing the plug wires and turning the engine over. (See earlier description of lean-induced backfires.)

Do Not use the nitrous system when the engine is not under load.

Do Not leave the nitrous bottle valve turned on for long periods while the engine is not running.

Do Not under any circumstances use a torch to heat a nitrous bottle. Using a direct point of heat can damage or weaken the bottle and could lead to bottle failure. On a motorcycle, this could be a bad scene. The best way to heat a bottle is to use an electric bottle heater blanket, or just to put the bottles in direct sunlight. And then make sure you check the pressure before you use it.

Do Not use medical grade nitrous oxide, thinking it will increase horsepower even more. It won't. Tests have proven that using medical grade N_2O has no advantage over the commercial grade. It's also more expensive.

Do Not put more oil in the gas (two-strokes only) than advised on the container. Oil lowers the octane rating of gasoline.

Do Not use nitrous on an engine with badly worn rings. If you build your own engine and are going to use nitrous on an engine that makes 200 horsepower or more, be sure to increase the ring gap by 0.003 to 0.005.

Do Not use components other than those supplied in the system. Incorrectly matched components may not produce the best results.

Do Not install a nitrous oxide system without reading the instructions. If you don't have instructions, get them from the supplier or manufacturer of the system.

Conclusion

If you are comparing horsepower gained to dollars spent, nitrous oxide is the king of the hill. Nothing else compares. Its one drawback is that when you run out of nitrous, the power drops to normal and some turbocharged bike (with its constantly renewable source of horsepower) will probably beat you. On the flip side, how many times do you get into five or more street races in a day of riding? For most it's more like once a week, tops. And, of course, nitrous oxide used in conjunction with turbocharging can take you to performance levels well beyond normal human capacity. Can you black out from severe motorcycle acceleration?

Special thanks to Nitrous Oxide Systems and T.K. Langfield for their assistance in writing this chapter. If you are interested in nitrous oxide equipment, they may be contacted as follows:

Nitrous Oxide Systems, Inc.
5930 Lakeshore Drive
Cypress, CA 90630
714-821-0580
Fax 714-821-8319

T.M.C. Group
Manufacturers of High Power Nitrous Systems
Rands Lane, Armthorpe
Doncaster, South Yorkshire
ENGLAND
(44) 130-283-4343
Fax (44) 130-283-3969

The Nitrous Works
Route 1, Box 1900
Dahlonega, GA 30533
706-864-7009

Severe detonation is generally caused by too high a compression ratio (especially when boosted by turbocharging, supercharging, or nitrous injection), a lean fuel mixture, excessive ignition advance, or high intake charge temperature. It usually causes burned or collapsed pistons, as seen here.

CHAPTER 8

Detonation Control

As I mentioned in Chapter 2, detonation is the number one enemy of any engine, not just turbocharged engines. Detonation is caused by one of three things, or possibly a combination of all three: high compression in conjunction with low octane fuel, a lean fuel mixture, and ignition that is too far advanced. Look at detonation as premature ignition of the fuel. The results, especially if prolonged, can cause extensive damage, including burned or collapsed pistons, resulting in valve, head, and cylinder wall destruction. And this list doesn't include what might happen if some of the debris gets into the bottom of the engine.

To paraphrase MIT Professor John B. Heywood, from his textbook *Internal Combustion Engine Fundamentals,* engine knock is the sharp metallic "noise" caused by pressure fluctuation during the spontaneous release of chemical energy in the combustion chamber. Simply put, knock (detonation) results when the pressures and temperatures in the cylinder increase excessively during charge burning. These high pressures and temperatures induce ignition of the "endgas" (unburned air-fuel mixture) before the flame front arrives. The interaction of the two flames creates the high-frequency pressure wave known as knock, ping, or detonation. This knock phenomenon transmits more heat to the pistons, valves, and cylinder walls, while transmitting less heat to the exhaust gas.

If detonation occurs with enough frequency, it can heat a particular spot within the cylinder to a temperature high enough to ignite the charge. This can lead to more massive pre-ignition, which occurs when the hot spot ignites the charge before the spark from the plug occurs. After this, a snowball effect takes place. The engine then seemingly runs on its own. Pre-ignition leads to higher cylinder pressures, which are conducive to more knock or detonation. As the temperature continues to escalate at the pre-ignition site (hot spot), it causes even earlier ignition and much higher pressures. Soon, you reach the *destruction* point, or, to be blunt, MELTDOWN.

Low compression pistons, racing gas, methanol, water-alcohol injection, intercooling, retarded ignition timing, and waste gates are all appropriate methods of dealing with the problem. The following text will describe how you can apply each of these methods.

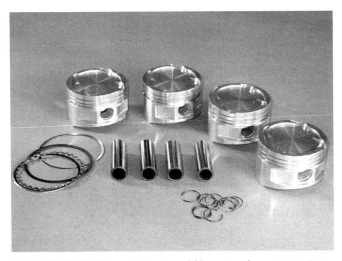

Arias (310-532-9137) made these jewel-like custom low compression pistons for a turbocharged Yamaha V-Max. The 8 to 1 compression ratio allows boost pressures of up to 18 psi (intercooled) without fear of detonation. Note the dished tops.

Wiseco (805-445-7334) makes low compression pistons for supercharged or turbocharged motorcycle engines, like these flat-tops installed in a turbo KZ Kawasaki. Lower compression is the most effective method of controlling unwanted detonation under boost.

Low Compression Pistons

Detonation can be a pronounced problem in a turbocharged engine. Boost levels above 15 psi can drive the effective compression ratio up to 14 or 15 to 1, even with 7 to 1 compression pistons. So you know right off that garden variety 92 octane super-duper unleaded isn't going to keep your engine happy. Remember, aluminum scrap is worth less than beer cans at the local recycling depot.

If boost pressures are to exceed 10 to 12 psi, the first thing to consider in your fight against detonation would be the installation of forged low-compression pistons. For most people, this is probably the most difficult obstacle to cross. But if boost levels are to exceed 10 to 12 psi, you may have to take this step—whether you like it or not. Changing over the pistons is not an easy job, and it will body slam your wallet. However, it's a lot easier and cheaper to lower the compression in the beginning than to repair a broken engine later. Just consider it preventive maintenance.

Refer to the compression ratio chart (Figure 8-1) to calculate the effective compression ratio resulting from your intended boost level. Most motorcycle turbo systems will be capable of at least 15 psi manifold pressure. For street applications this would be the maximum recommended limit for superior all-around performance. A waste gate will be required to control the boost at a level the pistons can deal with.

If your desire is to achieve 15 psi manifold pressure, the pre-turbocharged compression ratio should be adjusted down to 8 or 9 to 1. At that figure, most forms of anti-detonation controls will still have to be incorporated to avoid destroying your engine. Racing gas, water-alcohol injection, retarded ignition timing, richer fuel mixture, intercooling (if possible), waste gate pressure control, and a four-valve-per-cylinder head will all help.

Four-valve heads are less prone to detonation because four small valves dissipate heat faster than two large valves. Valves can act as hot spots in the combustion chamber and promote pre-ignition under high boost and wide open throttle situations.

Boost levels up to 12 psi can be successfully used with stock compression ratios on certain late model motorcycles, as long as intercooling, water-alcohol in-

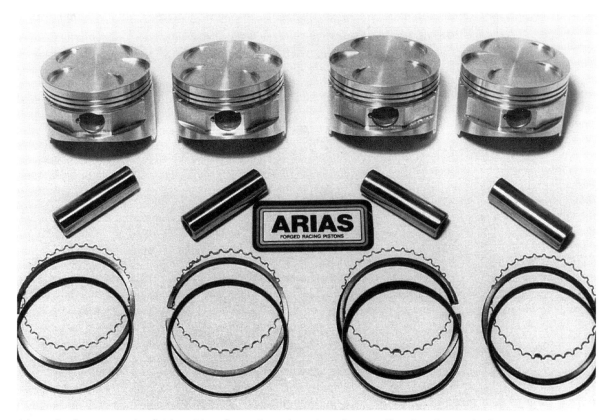

Arias makes low compression flat-top pistons for most popular motorcycles, as well as pins, rings, and valves.

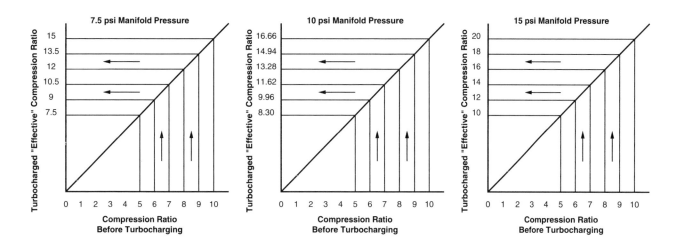

Figure 8-1: This diagram makes it easy to calculate effective compression ratio based on boost pressure. As you can see, it doesn't take a lot of boost to take the effective compression ratio to high, detonation-inducing levels.

jection, or other methods of detonation control are also implemented. It would be a good idea to make sure the engine came equipped with OEM *forged* pistons. If your pistons are cast, you may want to change over to lower compression forged units, which can take more heat and abuse. Several companies manufacture low compression forged pistons. They include Arias of Gardena, Calif. (213-770-0055), J.E. Pistons of Huntington Beach, Calif. (714-898-9763), A.P.E. of Burbank, Calif. (818-842-4952), Wiseco of Keller, Texas (800-392-0940), and MTC of Cocoa, Fla. (407-636-9480).

Table 8-1
Octane Test Results for the Top Five Racing Gasolines

	Turbo Blue	VP, C-12	Unocal	Sunoco CAM 2	Phillips Trick
Research Octane Number (RON)	116.6	106.1	111.4	114.2	114.2
Motor Octane Number (MON)	104.3	104.6	105.0	108.9	104.0
$\frac{R+M}{2}$ Number	110.5	105.4	108.2	111.6	107.6
Energy Content: BTU/lb BTU/gal	20,090 124,552	20,326.8 120,072	20,166.8 122,010	20,248.2 120,152	19,857.4 120,137
Density, lb/gal	6.20	5.91	6.05	5.93	6.05
Specific Gravity, API	58.5	67.9	63.2	67.0	63.2
Specific Gravity, g/cm^3	0.74	0.71	0.73	0.71	0.73

Almost all fuels tested exceeded their advertising claims. See Table 8-2.

Table 8-2
Advertised Octane Rating and Values

Color	Blue	Green	Red	Purple	Aqua
RON	115	110	112	114	112
MON	104.5	108	104	106	105
R+M/2	110	109	108	110	108
Specific Gravity, g/cm^3	0.74	0.71	0.73	0.72	0.73
Reid Vapor Pressure, psi	6.6	7.75	6.5	10.0	7.0
Lead (Pb) g/gallon	4.2	4.2	4.1	4.23	4.0
Alcohol/Ethanol	none	none	none	none	none
Price/gal. (average)	$3.75	$4.50	$4.00	$3.75	$4.25

The price is shown so you may better judge which is the best race gas for your money.

Racing Fuels

Aside from lowering the compression, the next best way to combat detonation is high octane leaded racing gasoline. Simply put, octane is a measurement which rates resistance to detonation. Detonation resistance is measured in units—85 being a low rating and 116 a high rating. The higher the octane, the greater its resistance to detonation. A high octane gasoline, however, does not make more power. It just means you can run a higher compression ratio or, in the case of turbocharged/supercharged engines, a higher boost level. Higher compression ratios and turbocharging/supercharging will increase horsepower, but a high octane level itself will not.

Everybody knows that gasoline is a fuel made from crude oil, but most of us have no idea how it's made, how it's rated, and why it does what it does. Gasoline is not just one chemical. It is made up of many different chemicals, each having its own purpose for being in the blend. Here's a brief summary.

Racing gasolines are a combination of molecules from chemical groups called aromatics, olefins, and paraffins or saturates. Aromatics include the chemicals benzene, toluene and xylene—basic octane enhancers. Olefins and paraffins include butane, isopentane and isooctane. Because these chemicals are made up of ring molecules, they are "packed" more densely, increasing the density of the gasoline and the amount of energy it contains per gallon (relative to the density of aromatics and paraffins).

After crude oil has been separated into all its chemical groups, each chemical is ranked into categories by the temperature at which it vaporizes. The lighter the molecular weight, the faster it evaporates. The faster vaporizing chemicals are known as the "light fractions," "front ends," or "light ends." Less volatile are the "medium fractions" and finally the "heavy fractions," or "heavy ends." Light fractions evaporate at approximately 130° F, or lower. Medium fractions evaporate between 130° and 250° F and heavy fractions between 250° and 400° F. To determine whether a gasoline is a heavy-, medium-, or light-fraction fuel, testers will establish a distillation curve by heating the gasoline and reading the temperature at which it evaporates in 10 percent increments. Serious racers consider this information to be a true indication of how a racing

Table 8-3
Comparison of Properties — Methanol vs. Gasoline

	Methanol	Gasoline
Oxygen content by weight, %	50.0	0
Boiling point, degrees F	149	95-410
Lower heating value-MJ, kg (approx.)	19.9	42.7
Heat of vaporization, MJ/kg	1.17	0.18
Stoichiometric air/fuel ratio	6.45:1	14.7:1
Specific energy (approximate)	3.08	2.92
Blending Research Octane Number	115-130	90-100
Blending Motor Octane Number	95-103	80-90

Methanol has six times higher latent heat of vaporization than gasoline, creating a cold starting problem. Gasoline can be added to methanol to help cure this problem. *Chart from the Society of Automotive Engineers*

Table 8-4
Pure Hydrocarbon Octane Ratings

Compound	Research Octane	Motor Octane	$\frac{R+M}{2}$
Cyclopentane	101	85	93
Isooctane	100	100	100
Isodecane	113	92	102.5
Triptane	112	101	106.5
Xylene	118	115	116.5
Toluene	120	109	114.5
Benzene	120+ (exceeds capability of octane rating machine)		

Toluene and benzene have always been used in the blending of racing gasolines with great success. *Chart from the Society of Automotive Engineers*

gasoline will ultimately perform under given conditions.

Racing gasoline that has more light end chemicals will tend to start easier, especially when it's cold. However, it will also have less heavy fractions, which means it will be less dense and will not contain as much energy per gallon. Most racing gasolines are formulated toward the heavy end, but when purchasing racing gasoline, it would be wise to compare formulations. If starting in cold weather becomes a problem, consider using a racing gas with more light ends formulated into it. Light end chemicals evaporate at lower temperatures, aiding the starting process, but do no good for heavy load performance. Once the engine is running, there is plenty of heat in the cylinder to vaporize the heavy end chemicals.

Once all these high end, medium, and low end fractions are mixed by the manufacturers in their desired proportions, an anti-detonation rating is established for the fuel. There are three ways to figure octane ratings. If the "research" method is used, the rating will usually be higher. The "motor" method usually produces a lower rating and pertains more to high rpm and high load applications. The third method (the R+M / 2

you see on gas pumps) averages the other two for a more accurate rating. When comparing racing gasolines, be sure to note which methods were used in the rating process. Remember that you will only need a high enough octane rating to keep detonation from occurring. If 100 octane gets the job done, then 116 octane is not going to work any better. And also remember that higher octane does not mean more power.

Jetting changes may be necessary when you switch from formulations with more light end chemicals, to formulas with more heavy ends. Heavy ended racing formulas usually require leaner jetting because the fuel is denser. Also, weather influences the density of the fuel, which can force jetting changes, especially at the track under racing conditions. The fuel will usually be denser in the morning hours and less dense as the day goes on.

Tetraethyl lead is one of the ingredients mixed into racing gasoline as an anti-detonation agent. Because of health risks, Federal standards regulate the amount of lead that can be added to gasoline. Only small amounts can be used legally, and most racing gas manufacturers obey the rules. However, some backyard mixers are using dangerously high doses of tetraethyl lead in their

RB Racing made this water-alcohol injection storage tank to double as the license plate bracket. When boost pressure exceeds 5 psi, a one-way valve opens, allowing pressurization of the tank, which forces the water and alcohol mixture through another one-way valve and on to the compressor housing inlet on the turbocharger.

brews. Always handle these fuels cautiously. Use rubber gloves and avoid breathing the fumes as much as possible. Some racing teams insist that mechanics use full breathing masks when they work with racing gas. Why? Because tetraethyl lead can cause irreversible brain damage and birth defects.

Racing gasoline should be used as a last resort. It's hard to get, it's expensive, it's hard to store properly, and it prevents the use of an oxygen sensor type air/fuel ratio meter. If you can get by with 92 octane, by all means do so.

For strictly racing try methanol and crank the boost. Hahn Racecraft and Mr. Turbo both offer S&S carburetors specially modified for use with methanol. Methanol burns slower and is resistant to detonation up to amazingly high boost levels and/or compression ratios. Many Funny Bikes burn methanol, as opposed to gasoline, for this reason, but it is pretty much out of the question for street use. It is corrosive, hard to get on trips, and you will consume twice as much of it as you would gasoline. It takes approximately twice the amount of methanol to produce the same power as gasoline, and will require approximately 50 percent larger jetting (by area, not hole diameter) than for gasoline.

Water-Alcohol Injection

Aside from lowering the compression ratio and running leaded racing gasoline, the next best detonation dampener would be the addition of a water and alcohol injection system, especially when manifold boost levels exceed 12 to 15 psi. At that level of boost, every type of anti-detonation trick should be employed and water-alcohol injection is an effective method.

In the early 1930s, Sir Harry Ricardo, author of the classic textbook *The High Speed Internal Combustion Engine,* experimented with water and alcohol injection on a supercharged test engine. His early tests are still valid and modern day tests have reached the same basic conclusions.

Using a test engine set at 2,500 rpm and 7 to 1 compression ratio, the engine was run on low grade 86 octane gasoline. Slowly, supercharger pressure was applied up to the first signs of detonation, which in this case was a Mean Effective Pressure of 168 lbs per square inch. At this point the fuel mixture was enriched slightly in increments, and the supercharger boost was increased until detonation was again occurring. This process continued until a richer mixture no longer suppressed detonation. After a 60 percent increase in rich-

This is one of the two 5 psi one-way valves RB Racing uses to regulate its water-alcohol injection system.

Mr. Turbo invented the license plate type of storage tank, seen here on a British GSXR1100 turbo bike.

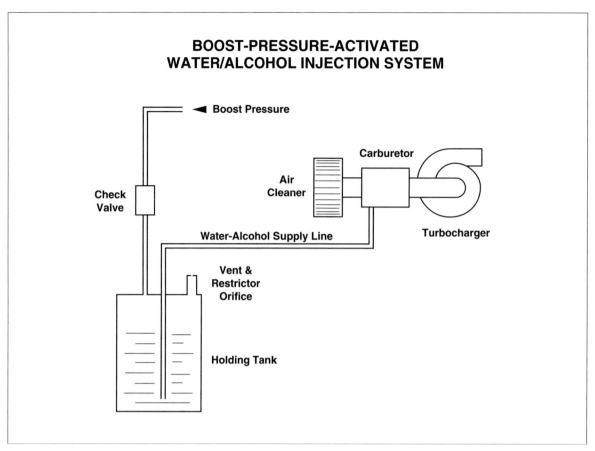

**BOOST-PRESSURE-ACTIVATED
WATER/ALCOHOL INJECTION SYSTEM**

Figure 8-2: Water-alcohol injection can be another effective method of controlling detonation. This simple draw-through boost-pressure-activated system features no moving parts. There are many variations on this design, as explained in the text. Figure 8-3 shows RB Racing's system.

ness, more fuel did not reduce detonation, and in fact, tended to increase detonation.

At this point Ricardo introduced a fine spray of water into the intake and found that the intercooling effect and steam acted as a anti-detonate, making it possible to raise the supercharger boost level to a MEP of 290 psi (which was as high as his dynamometer went). It was also found that the fuel mixture could be leaned out somewhat with the addition of water alone.

Later, Ricardo experimented with a mixture of water and alcohol, thinking that alcohol as a fuel would add volatility along with an intake cooling effect, thereby resisting detonation even further. He found that a 50-50 mixture of alcohol and water was the practical limit. Any more than 50 percent alcohol did not improve performance and could possibly promote detonation. Later testing by Bonneville racers Ted Trevor and Dick Griffin confirmed that there was no advantage to going beyond a 50-50 mix.

When should a water-alcohol mixture be injected into the intake system and at what boost level? It depends on what other precautions have been taken to control detonation and what boost level is desired. As a general rule, injection should start at boost levels two to three psi before detonation occurs, probably somewhere between 5 and 12 psi manifold pressure in most applications. Differences between the combustion chamber designs of motorcycle manufacturers account for much of this variation, but differences in ambient temperature can also account for variations for the same installation (for example, hot days might require that the H_2O/alcohol kick in sooner than on a cold day).

There are three basic water-alcohol systems in use today (with variations) for draw-through turbo systems. The most popular method happens to be the simplest. A storage tank for the water-alcohol mixture is pressurized by boost pressure and the mixture is fed under this pressure to the engine intake. This simple system has no moving parts to fail at the proverbial "inappropriate moment."

The original Crown Manufacturing design places the water-alcohol storage tank under the variable boost

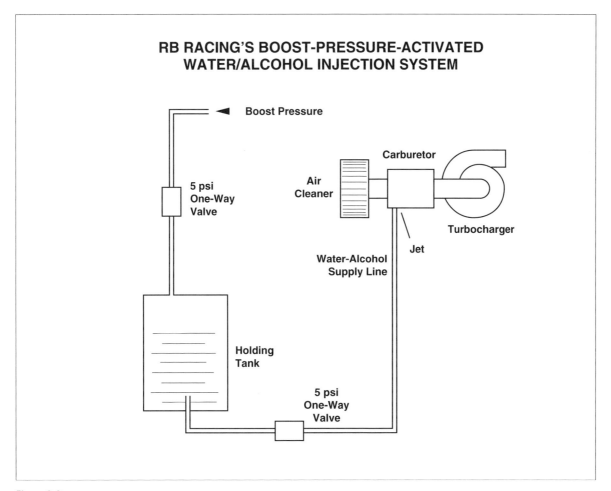

RB RACING'S BOOST-PRESSURE-ACTIVATED WATER/ALCOHOL INJECTION SYSTEM

Figure 8-3

pressure from the turbocharger. The tank is fitted with an orifice valve that bleeds off low values of tank pressure. When boost pressure increases, the orifice valve is no longer able to bleed off the higher tank pressure, allowing the tank pressure to force the water-alcohol mixture up a tube that feeds the carburetor. The tank pressure is regulated by the size of the orifice: a smaller orifice will pressurize the tank at lower levels of boost pressure and thereby inject the water-alcohol mixture sooner, and vice versa.

Dick Griffin's design is based on the Crown system, but is even simpler. A line from the intake manifold contains a restrictor jet supplying pressurized air to the holding tank. A line from the tank runs to the base of the carburetor, supplying the water-alcohol mixture to the compressor. Figures 8-2 and 8-3 show exactly how the lines hook up.

RB Racing's system runs a pressure line from the intake plenum chamber to a 5 psi one-way valve. When boost pressure goes over 5 psi, the valve opens, allowing pressurization of the water-alcohol storage tank top. A line from the bottom of the tank supplies the mixture to another 5 psi one way valve and from there to the inlet of the turbocharger in a blow-through system, or the base of the carburetor in a draw-through system.

Water-alcohol injection can also be used on blow-through turbo systems; however, a high-pressure boost-activated pump will have to be incorporated to overcome the manifold boost pressure. For example, at 15 psi boost the water-alcohol injection pump would have to put out at least 18 to 20 psi in order to inject the mixture into the manifold.

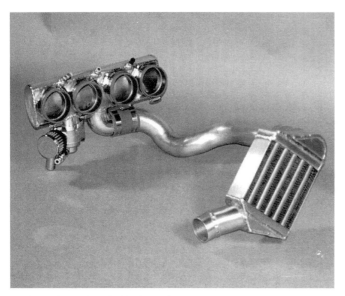

Mark Vanderwald made this beautiful intercooler system for his blow-through carbureted GSXR750. At 7 psi boost the bike puts out 145 rear wheel horsepower on a dyno, with just fan air blowing through the intercooler. If the intercooler was seeing a full blast of air, as it would when moving down the road, it could develop another five horsepower.

This closeup shot of Mark Vanderwald's intercooler reveals some of the surgery needed when certain items like fairings get in the way. Due to space limitations, people have created interesting shapes out of their intercoolers. A computer was used to determine the optimum size of this intercooler, using 7 lbs boost and total CFM as a reference. As you can see, intercoolers don't have to be big. It depends mostly on boost and the average ambient temperature of your riding area.

Intercooling

One major byproduct of compressing air is heat, which, as previously discussed, raises combustion temperature and can promote detonation. Normally, fuel needs some heat to vaporize it as it travels through the intake tract. However, too much intake charge heat can cause combustion temperatures to rise, thereby affecting the point at which detonation will occur. Lowering the temperature of the incoming charge lessens the chance of detonation, but how can you lower the temperature of fast-moving compressed air?

An intercooler cools the air flowing through it, just as a radiator cools liquid. The intercoolers most commonly used in motorcycle applications are known as air-to-air intercoolers. Outside air passing over the radiator fins cools the compressed air flowing through the inside of the radiator. Other types of coolers are more common to cars, boats, and airplanes, where the cooling medium could be ice water, sea water, engine jacket coolant, freon, or even dry ice.

The amount the temperature drops through the heat exchanger will be in direct relation to the size of the radiator, the temperature of the cooling medium (in our case, air is the medium), the flow rate of the medium, and the temperature of the charge entering the intercooler radiator. There will also be a pressure drop as the compressed air from the turbocharger passes through cooling tubes in the heat exchanger; the amount of pressure drop must be weighed against the amount of temperature drop. It wouldn't be practical to lower the incoming charge temperature to 100° if you are going to lose half the incoming pressure boost to losses in the intercooler. A properly sized intercooler should be big enough to allow the incoming charge to pass through as unrestricted as possible, yet efficiently cool the compressed charge flowing through it.

Intercoolers large enough to allow good flow can be bulky. On an automobile, an intercooler radiator can fit many places without affecting styling, but on a motorcycle it's more of a problem. The latest turbo designs mount the turbo down low on the front of the motorcycle's frame. On Suzuki GSXRs, for example, the space above the turbocharger is occupied by a massive oil cooler. Figures 8-4, 8-5, and 8-6 (overleaf) show RB Racing's solution of twin intercoolers installed on each side of the frame in the front, where they can catch high velocity air passing the bike. Their Triumph Daytona turbo system has one large intercooler mounted in the headlight location where it receives a direct air supply. The headlight is replaced with two high intensity lights mounted where the turn signals once were. On the

RB Racing mounts a massive intercooler under the gas tank of its turbo ZX-11 systems. Note the equally large intake plenum chamber supplying the four dual injected EFI throttle bodies.

A hand-fabricated aluminum hood covers the entire front of the intercooler and is supplied with cool air through the stock ram air ducting. This is a "C" model with only one duct from the single opening in the fairing. "D" models have two ducts supplying air to the intercooler.

ZX-11 system, a huge intercooler mounts under the gas tank where the ram air box was located, using the ram air intakes (ducted to a special shroud over the face of the intercooler) to supply air to the intercooler. From there, the cooled air moves on to the fuel injection throttle body(s) and in some home-built systems, the carburetors.

Intercooling on blow-through systems is relatively easy, except for space limitations. However, intercooling a draw-through system is next to impossible. The problem is that intercooling must be placed in the pressurized portion of the intake tract. On a draw-through system the pressurized portion bears the air-fuel mixture. An intercooler would tend to separate the air and fuel. On a blow-through system, the pressurized air can be cooled *before* it is mixed with fuel, eliminating the problem of fuel separation. Draw-through systems have to rely on lower compression pistons, race gas, and water-alcohol injection as weapons against detonation and its destructive results.

As a rule, a one degree Fahrenheit decrease in intake manifold temperature should result in a one degree drop in exhaust temperature. Lower inlet temperature makes it easier on the exhaust valves and cuts down on the heat rejection requirements of the engine. In addition to cutting down the heat load on the engine, intercooling increases the density of the air, allowing more air mass per minute to flow through the engine. This allows more fuel to burn, resulting in more horsepower.

If the air charge temperature is 200° F, the temperature of the cooling medium is 100° F, and the intake charge temperature is lowered to 150° F, then 50 percent intercooler efficiency has been achieved. If a more efficient intercooler can drop the intake charge to, say, 130° F, then a 70 percent intercooler efficiency has been realized. Intercooling really begins to pay off at that efficiency.

I spotted some pretty strange intercooling systems while researching this subject, but one particularly caught my eye at El Mirage. Someone had mounted an automotive radiator on the front of a turbocharged Harley and used it as an intercooler. It looked as though it may have come from a Ford Falcon. Aside from its large size, this intercooler suffers from two other problems. The brass used for the radiator fins is not the best material. Aluminum dissipates heat much more efficiently than brass, especially when conducting heat from fast-moving pressurized air as opposed to slow-moving low-pressure engine coolant. In addition, because the automotive radiator was designed for slow-moving engine coolant, the pressure drop to air flow is much higher than it needs to be.

Some experimentation will probably be necessary before you settle on the right combination of intercooler components; however, these pictures of all the various heat exchangers will get you in the ballpark. Intercooler radiators, end manifolds (caps), and spigots in every conceivable size, shape, and configuration are available from Spearco Products of Panorama City, Calif. (818-901-7851).

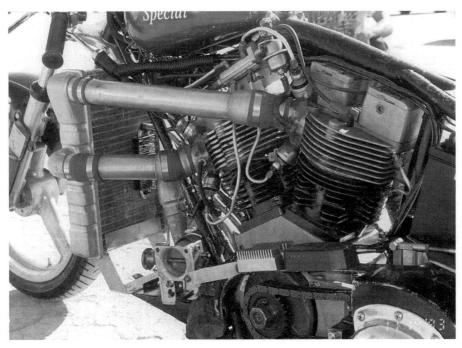

DO NOT try to use an automobile radiator as an air to air intercooler! They are too big, the pressure drop is too high, and the brass with which the fins are made does not conduct heat as well as aluminum fins.

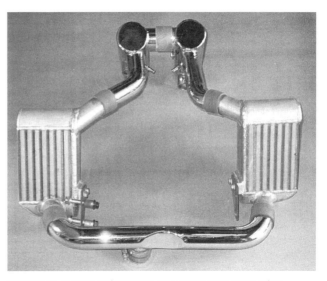

Figure 8-6: George Galipeau's V-Max sports twin intercoolers hand-fabricated by RB Racing. Note the twin plenum chambers that blow-through the stock CV carburetors.

Figure 8-4 *(above)* **and Figure 8-5** *(below):* This Suzuki GSXR1100 belonging to Henry Louie has twin intercoolers, one on each side of the engine, primarily due to the lack of usable space. This bike has logged more miles at over 200 mph than do some street bikes during their whole life. It holds the record for its class at El Mirage.

Ignition

At full throttle, any heavily boosted engine will require a high intensity spark. All the boost in the world will do no good at all if you can't ignite the air-fuel mixture. Making a spark jump the plug gap in open air, under normal atmospheric pressure, is fairly easy—even the weakest ignition system can do it. However, firing that spark under normal combustion pressure becomes a bit more difficult. Doubling or tripling the pressure via turbocharging or supercharging doubles or triples the demands on the ignition coil(s) and spark plugs.

Modern motorcycle ignition systems can handle boost levels of up to 18 lbs. However, at higher boost levels, stock ignition systems may not fire the plugs reliably. Most older motorcycles used conventional points to trigger the coils. Because an ignition coil takes time between firings to store energy for the next firing, operation at higher rpm results in a weaker spark, since there is less time between firings to store electrical energy—not what you want when turbocharging. Today's motorcycles are usually equipped with some form of electronic ignition. The triggering device is generally magnetic, with a transistor to start and stop the current flow. With no points to burn, the current isn't limited to low voltage. By using higher voltage, the coil requires less time to charge between firings, resulting in higher output voltage and a hotter spark. If you plan to use more than 15 lbs boost, you will have to make improvements to the ignition system or, as some racers say, you'll just blow the spark right out!

Spark Plugs

Spark plug technology has really improved in recent years. The high-performance aftermarket has finally realized a good thing and is marketing some innovative designs. It just stands to reason—the larger and more intense the spark, the more fuel gets burned, which adds up to greater combustion pressure and more horsepower. Or as the EPA would put it, *more efficient combustion.*

The main improvement on today's high-tech spark plug is in the ground-to-electrode design. On a standard spark plug, the ground is a single curved bar that covers the electrode. The spark is confined to the space between the electrode and the ground. Split Fire spark plugs split the tip of the ground into a "V" shape, spreading the flame over a wide area. Also, the ground does not totally cover the electrode, which exposes more spark to the combustion mixture. Magna Fire spark plugs take this design a step further: the ground is actually a circle above the electrode which lays a perfect circle arc, exposing a huge flame area. NGK makes motorcycle spark plugs with two grounds, one on each side of the electrode. All of these modern spark plugs are a vast improvement over standard plugs in a high boost level turbocharged motorcycle engine.

Ignition Wires

While upgrading the ignition system, don't forget the wires which link the coil(s) to the spark plugs.

Do not make the mistake of purchasing TVR wire, which is used in automobiles to reduce radio and television interference. In order to suppress interference, TVR wire has internal resistance which decreases the spark energy being supplied to the spark plug. Make sure you use only magnetic-suppression wire (MSW) if radio and television interference is a problem. If radio and TV interference is not a problem, use solid core wire, which offers no resistance and is the ultimate linkage between the coil and the plug. Of course, your neighbors will hate you when Oprah turns to snow on their TV screen, but they probably hate you and your power boosted bike anyway.

Coils

Most motorcycle OEM coils today are more potent than the ones used in the 1970s with points as triggers. If you own a older bike with a points type of ignition system and you are planning on turbocharging, you may get by with hotter coils, but chances are you'll need a complete BHP or similar distributor ignition system. If you own a motorcycle with an electronic, magnetically-triggered ignition system, things should be fine up to 15 to 18 lbs of boost, but only if the ignition is capable of firing a 10 mm or larger spark in open atmosphere.

Distributors, Magnetos, and Adjustable Ignition Advancers

A lot of people have the misconception that the distributor is the energy source, when really it's just an adjustable triggering device. The advantages of adapting a distributor to your turbo bike are as follows:

1. Dual points let more voltage reach the coil and allow for more coil saturation time between firings.

2. With a distributor, you only need one coil. That coil should be one of the really hot automotive high-performance types, which will punch out more energy than the typical motorcycle coil.

The ignition systems on most modern motorcycles (1986 and up) can usually handle boost levels up to 10 psi. Beyond that, it may be necessary to upgrade the coils. You may also want to consider adjustable ignition, either manual or boost-sensitive. *Above left:* Distributors and magnetos can be adapted to most motorcycle engines and will provide enough spark for more than 40 psi of boost. This type of ignition is usually seen on race machinery, either street or strip, and as shown here, it fits in right next to the carburetor on draw-through systems. *Above right:* Here's a neat magneto installation on a Kawasaki drag machine. *Below:* On a street machine, this magneto looks as good as it performs.

3. The distributor lets you adjust timing easily. In many cases, that last bit of detonation can be eliminated by simply retarding the timing a few degrees.

4. If you're the inventive type, you can design a pressure retard mechanism that will retard your timing as boost builds (as in old Corvair Spider distributors). This leaves you with stock timing for improved (or normal) bottom end performance and retarded timing while under boost when detonation is most likely.

These distributor systems for motorcycles look nice and are *hot*—but they are bulky. They are generally belt driven off the end of the crankshaft and take up valuable space where in many instances the turbocharger is located.

Magneto

Magneto ignition systems only *look* like distributors. A magneto, which is self-energizing, allows an engine to operate without a battery. Mags are usually seen only on drag racing motorcycles where boost levels can exceed 30 psi. Here are the advantages:

1. The faster they turn, the more energy they put out. They can be used without a battery on race bikes.

2. An ultra-high-energy spark, which is desirable under high boost conditions.

3. Adjustability. As with a distributor, this makes it easier to manipulate the timing. Magnetos are generally belt-driven and have the same space requirements as a distributor.

Transistorized Electronic Ignition Systems

Late model motorcycle ignition systems can often be modified to put out adequate spark energy for a boosted engine up to 18 lbs simply by adding aftermarket high-energy coils. The only disadvantage to OEM ignition systems is that they are not adjustable (due to EPA regulations) for advance or retard. Several companies are now manufacturing adjustable ignition black boxes for most Japanese four-cylinder motorcycles; Crane makes a similar unit for Harley-Davidsons. These ignition boxes make it possible to advance or retard the ignition by 10 degrees, which is more than enough for a turbocharged or supercharged engine. Rohm Performance Products of Yuba City, Calif. (916-674-9123), makes advance/retard adjustable ignition plates for Suzuki and Kawasaki motorcycles that work quite well and are simple to install.

With any of these ignition systems, if detonation is a problem, the timing can be retarded a little at a time until the problem diminishes or goes away completely. This is good to a point; however, if the timing is retarded too much, the engine will run hot and lose bottom end performance. Usually about 2 to 4 degrees is enough to take care of mild cases of detonation.

Rohm Performance Products makes these easy-to-install adjustable ignition timers for most late model sport bikes. They make it possible to retard your timing several degrees if necessary to bring mild detonation under control. You can't retard the timing too much without a loss of power, but a couple of degrees is barely noticeable.

Waste Gates

Boost levels too high for a given compression ratio will most certainly cause detonation. Waste gates indirectly control detonation by limiting the amount of pressure the turbocharger can ultimately put out. It does this by bleeding excess exhaust pressure at a predetermined manifold boost level, thereby limiting the boost pressure. Most turbochargers used on motorcycles today are capable of putting out far more boost than is needed. If the boost level is not controlled, combustion pressure will rise to the point of severe detonation. Turbochargers are usually chosen somewhat under-sized for the engines they are going on, so they will have good low end response and short lag. This means they can inadvertently be overspeeded to produce more boost pressure than might be desired.

It is possible to match a turbo exactly to an engine to put out just the desired pressure at full throttle without a waste gate. However, bottom end performance and response will suffer. To build positive boost more quickly (for better low end power), a smaller A/R ratio turbocharger should be used with a waste gate incorporated to regulate wide open throttle manifold boost pressure.

Most aftermarket waste gates are manually adjustable, some by changing internal diaphragm springs, others by turning an adjusting screw that raises and lowers tension on a spring, and still others by adjusting the length of a shaft to the spring. Most aftermarket units use poppet type valves, the standard in the industry today. See Figure 8-7 for typical construction.

OEM waste gates are usually adjustable by changing the length of a shaft that connects the waste gate diaphragm to a lever that operates the opening and closing of a poppet valve in the exhaust housing. These units can be adjusted to keep boost pressures above 10 psi, but be careful not to stretch the diaphragm. OEM waste gates can also be modified to work with a dial-a-boost controller, as can all aftermarket units. Dial-a-boost controllers regulate the amount of intake manifold boost pressure the diaphragm in the waste gate sees. Lower pressure to the waste gate means it will open later, and higher pressure means it will open

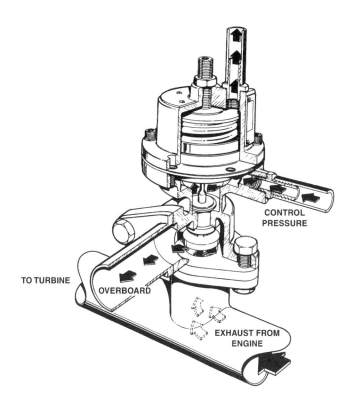

Figure 8-7: This cutaway view of a Spearco waste gate shows how boost pressure actuates the diaphragm at the top, which in turn opens and shuts the relief valve, allowing pressurized exhaust to escape into the atmosphere.

sooner. If you want to achieve higher boost levels, I recommend a good aftermarket waste gate; it will have a greater range of adjustability and can be placed just about anywhere on the exhaust system leading to the exhaust housing of the turbocharger. OEM waste gates are always attached to the turbocharger where they can actuate the built-in relief valve in the exhaust housing.

Mr. Turbo, Hahn Racecraft, RB Racing, Spearco, Turbonetics, Turbo City, and many other companies are all good sources for reliable aftermarket waste gates. Remember, waste gates are the ultimate adjuster of boost and how much detonation-free horsepower you want to put out.

OEM waste gates (such as the one shown here on a Garrett turbocharger) can be used in conjunction with a dial-a-boost controller, but are usually preset to 5 to 7 psi boost. For high boost operation it is recommended that a high-quality aftermarket waste gate be used. They are manually adjustable and can also be used with a dial-a-boost controller. Most of the turbo kit manufacturers offer waste gates, as do suppliers such as Spearco, Turbonetics, and Turbo City.

Aftermarket waste gates like this RB Racing unit can be mounted just about anywhere on the pressure side of the exhaust system leading to the turbocharger. In this example, it is mounted directly to the exhaust turbine housing.

Turbonetics makes the Deltagate Mark II waste gate. It was originally designed for automotive use; however, if you have the space available, it will work equally well on motorcycles. This is a good choice for large displacement engines that would overpower smaller waste gates. A waste gate that is too small may not bleed off enough exhaust pressure, causing the turbocharger to continue building boost. Larger waste gate valves and ports will guarantee that you bleed off sufficient exhaust to avoid overspeeding the turbocharger.

A dial-a-boost controller, shown here just to the left of the ignition switch, is used to regulate the amount of boost pressure passed from the intake plenum chamber to the waste gate. Less pressure means the waste gate will open later and more pressure means it will open up sooner. This is great on hot days when you'll want to run lower boost levels, and for when you've been challenged and need to crank up the boost.

Superchargers are often seen on drag bikes such as this Top Fueler belonging to Ron Webb. It is common to hear of boost pressures as high as 35 to 40 psi, which is no problem for screw-type superchargers in short bursts through the quarter-mile. On the street, a more practical limit of 5 to 10 psi would be prudent. Today's Top Fuel engines are based on Suzuki GS1100s or Kawasaki KZ1000s, mostly in name only. There isn't much left of the original Kawasaki KZ1000 engine on this bike, which features a billet aluminum head, hand made by Clyde Day, Webb cams, APE cam sprocket, Arias pistons, Trett crankshaft, Super Rods, Trett bottom end attached to an MCU big block (1325cc), external oil pump, Sprintex (screw-type) supercharger, MCU mechanical fuel injection, B&J transmission, ART clutch, and Mallory (dual) magneto ignition. This bike has run 6.41 seconds at 217 mph. Its long wheelbase and wide rear tire make it nearly impossible to steer in anything but a straight line. *Photo by Harold Barnett*

Choosing the Right Motorcycle for Power Boosting

Supercharging

Some motorcycle engines adapt to turbocharging and supercharging better than others; some shouldn't be power boosted at all. This chapter will help you determine which is which. Most people are interested in streetable turbo systems, with possibly a little drag racing or street racing thrown in from time to time. As described in the chapters on supercharging and turbo-charging, most of the principles of power boosting are the same, regardless of which method you use to force more air-fuel mixture into the engine. Pressure is pressure, no matter how it's generated.

Only a handful of supercharger kits are available for motorcycles: two for Harleys, three for Yamaha V-Maxes, one for the Suzuki GSXR750, and one for the Suzuki GSXR1100 and GS1100. If you want to supercharge any other bike, you're on your own. That's not

Yamaha V-Maxes make interesting blower bikes. They have a strong bottom end and a V configuration that offers an ideal location to mount the supercharger. Shown here is A.S.A.P.'s street and strip system that uses the Fageol self-lubricating Roots-type supercharger.

George Galipeau warms the sneaker a bit before blastoff on his very streetable 250 horsepower V-Max. The RB Racing system used here mounts the turbo down low and in front of the frame and blows through properly jetted stock carburetors. RB's newer systems only come with programmable electronic fuel injection, which will be the next step for George's bike.

(517-484-4080), and Magna Charger of Orland, Calif. (916-865-7010), all make supercharger kits for the Yamaha V-Max.

For street use, superchargers can also be adapted easily to inline three- and four-cylinder motorcycle engines. The blower is usually mounted behind the cylinder block in the normal carburetor location and pumps through a thin plenum chamber manifold connected to the ports on the head. The drive mechanism connects to the crankshaft, which is forward of the rider's leg, and affords ample room. Rohm Performance Products of Yuba City, Calif. (916-674-9123), makes a clean and simple Roots-type supercharger system for the Suzuki GSXR750 that uses such a drive mechanism. Horsepower Unlimited of Sophia, W.V. (304-683-5500), makes a billet aluminum supercharger system for the Suzuki GSXR1100/GS1100 using the Whipple screw-type supercharger. The finished product is one of the best engineered supercharger systems available today and is the only system to rigidly connect the supercharger to the engine block. This design also provides a belt guard, which gives it a clean look.

Mounting a supercharger on a Harley-Davidson requires a little more ingenuity. The supercharger normally mounts on the side of the engine and points forward. This means the drive at the nose of the supercharger is oriented 90 degrees from the crankshaft and will require a 90-degree gear drive to connect the supercharger and the engine. Brilhante Company (800-HOT-BIKE) uses this method and blends styling with plenty of leg room. Magna Charger makes the most aesthetically pleasing—as well as the simplest—supercharger system for Harley-Davidson big twins. The drive is unique, in that it is taken from the crankshaft on the right side of the engine where the ignition plate is located. The ignition plate is moved into the cast gear drive housing and is still easily accessible. The Roots-type supercharger is angled upward and away from the rider's leg.

V-Max bottom ends are reasonably strong and can handle quite a lot more horsepower than stock. However, at anything over 15 lbs boost, you may want to consider heavy duty rods and lower compression pis-

to say it's impossible, but you'd better have access to a machine shop, and a TIG welder, and have a general knowledge of supercharger drive mechanisms. Size and placement are the two hurdles one must cross when designing a supercharger system. The drive mechanism must not interfere with the rider's leg, and it must be aesthetically pleasing. This is one reason why the Yamaha V-Max is such a good choice for supercharging. Just like blown V-8 dragster engines, the cradle of the "V" between the cylinders is an ideal location to mount the supercharger. This gives a straight shot down to the crankshaft for drive and still clears the rider's leg. Mad Max Enterprises of Waterbury, Conn. (203-574-7859), A.S.A.P. Racing Products of Lansing, Mich.

Sitting still is the best way to check out RB's V-Max turbo system. Twin intercoolers reside on each side of the front frame down tubes just above the turbocharger. Coupled with 8 to 1 Arias pistons it has seen 18 psi boost on more than one occasion. The only problem is traction. This bike will blow away the rear tire at anything over 12 psi in any gear, at any speed. Best mind your manners around one of these things.

tons. Suzuki bottom ends are capable of handling twice the stock horsepower, and possibly even more, without modification. Like any power plant, though, if ultra-high boost levels are to be attained then all the normal bottom end strengthening measures should be taken, including installation of lower compression pistons. Harley bottom ends are moderately strong. Boost levels over 15 psi may require heavy duty rods and crank assembly, plus special head gaskets and base gaskets, along with lower compression pistons, just to be safe.

Kawasaki has always had a reputation for strong lower ends, all the way back to the original Z-1. Early Kawasakis (like GS Suzukis) had roller bearing bottom ends and split, two-piece crankshafts that were pressed together. Because turbocharged motors can create enough torque to twist the crankshaft out of alignment, the crankshaft components must be welded to prevent this from happening. Any of the KZ Kawasaki inline four-cylinder engines would make a strong blower motor. Just ask any Kawasaki Top Fuel bike owner.

Kawasaki ZX-11 engines are strong and can be boosted to reasonably high levels without internal modifications. A problem getting proper lubrication to the number three rod journal can be rectified by sending the oil pan to Mr. Turbo for modification. I recommend this, even if the engine is not boosted.

Whenever you are power boosting street legal motorcycles, whether by supercharging or turbocharging, stock cams work best. An exception is pre-Evo Harley-Davidson Sportsters—stock cams have too much overlap and duration. One solution is to install Harley 45 flathead cams, which can easily be modified to fit shovelhead Sportsters. Another option is to call Leineweber Enterprises of Yucca Valley, Calif. (619-364-4432), which specializes in blower and turbo cams for Harley-Davidson motorcycles. Some factory race replica and full-on race bikes may have inappropriate cam

Twin plenum chambers supply air to the stock (re-jetted) V-Max carburetors on this early RB Racing system.

Turbocharging

Almost any modern 500cc or larger motorcycle can be turbocharged for all-out, high-boost operation. You would naturally use a stronger crank and rods, low compression pistons, lockup clutch, possibly a big block with a pro-turbo head, and any other number of strengthening and performance-oriented items. For lower-boost street machines, it's nice to be able to bolt on a turbo system and go riding, which is what most people would like to do. If you own a bike for which a pre-engineered kit is already available, you're in clover; the rest of you may be forced into designing your own system. This should be no problem if you are mechanically inclined and armed with the right information. This section will cover turbo two-strokes, turbocharger placement, bikes for which turbo kits are available, ideal bikes for turbocharging, porting, and cam timing.

Turbocharging Two-Stroke Engines

One of the questions I hear most often is, "Can you turbocharge two-strokes?" The answer is yes—but that technology is still in its infancy at this time. Some people are successfully using turbochargers on two-stroke racing snowmobiles, and now and then you'll hear of somebody in Europe turbocharging a 125cc two-stroke to some amazing amount of horsepower. Most of the automobile companies are experimenting with various types of two-stroke "smogger" engines, some of which are turbocharged.

It is difficult to lubricate a turbocharger on a two-stroke motorcycle properly. Two-stroke motorcycles are lubricated by mixing oil with the fuel. As the oil-fuel mixture passes through the crankcase on its way to the intake ports, it deposits enough lubricant on the roller bearings and moving parts to assure a reasonably long life. Plain bearing turbochargers require a supply of high-pressure oil to keep the bearing(s) properly lubricated. Since two-stroke motorcycle engines don't have the high-pressure lubrication system common to four-stroke engines, the problem then is how to lubricate the turbocharger. It's not an insurmountable obstacle, but it would require locating a mechanically driven oil pump with an oil reservoir somewhere on the machine.

On rotary valve two-strokes, it is easy to alter the intake and exhaust timing of the engine. Just like a four-stroke engine, milder port timing (same idea as less duration and overlap in a four-stroke) helps to trap more of the pressurized air and fuel in the cylinder for

timing for pressure boosting; however, normal factory street grinds are usually the best. Gasoline or alcohol drag bike engines can usually take a little more overlap and exhaust cam duration, but most racers leave the intake cam stock or near stock. Supercharged Top Fuel engines usually run a lot of lift, duration, and overlap. Of course, they are putting out over 35 lbs of supercharged and nitro-fueled boost and 1,000 horsepower, so this would be expected. Turbocharged engines, on the other hand, generate greater exhaust pressure and function best with mild cams. See the Cam Timing sidebar later in this chapter for additional information.

RB Racing built this K100 BMW racing turbo system for Matt Capri several years ago. In 1997 Capri broke the class record at El Mirage by running over 206 mph with a strong side wind. With lakes top-end gearing it has run mid 9's at over 150 mph in the quarter-mile on a street tire and no wheelie bar. Imagine what it would do with lower gearing! Notice the half fairing in this picture. The bike was running in the high 190 mph range with a full fairing *(see photo below),* but when Matt switched to the smaller fairing which reduced frontal drag, the bike went much faster. Just proves the old adage—less is more.

RB Racing made this slick street turbo system *(above and opposite page)* for the BMW R1100RS Boxer. Believe it or not, with stock gearing and in street trim, this bike will run the quarter-mile in 10.30 seconds at 132 mph—about the same as a brand new Kawasaki ZX-11. It is intercooled and uses an RSR electronic control unit in place of the stock BMW Motronic box so fueling can be programmed. The turbo fits nicely up under the left side cylinder, offsetting the shaft drive on the right side of the bike. This motorcycle is a blast to drive, especially when you want to whip a GSXR1100 or something.

greater combustion pressure. Intake and exhaust timing can also be altered on engines with a piston port induction system, but it is a little more difficult. Two-strokes with radical (top-end-only) port timing will probably have to be tamed down a bit to be turbocharged successfully. Two-strokes which are set up for higher torque at lower speeds have milder port timing and *may* be fine as is. Some two-strokes used in snowmobiles and watercraft have mild port timing for more bottom end torque and have been successfully turbocharged with no port timing changes at all. Adjustable exhaust port gates like those on Honda's new clean-burn two-stroke engine also show great promise for turbocharging.

In Chapter 3, I mentioned the Aerodyne turbocharger. This particular turbocharger is self-lubricated and does not require a high-pressure supply of oil from the engine. This one feature alone makes the Aerodyne

turbocharger ideal for use on two-stroke engines and is the turbocharger of choice among snowmobile racers.

Another great feature of the Aerodyne turbocharger is the VATN exhaust turbine system. This design makes the turbocharger appear "small" and responsive to the engine at low speeds, and "large" on the top end for greater top end efficiency. Both characteristics are important when turbocharging two-stroke engines.

Turbocharging Four-Stroke Engines

Most four-stroke engines over 500cc can be turbocharged without many problems. Installation is a matter of fitting, more than any other factor. So let's consider a few examples. From a placement point of view, V-four motorcycles are the most difficult to turbocharge. The Yamaha V-Max has a strong motor, big displacement, etc., etc. However, it's *all* engine and there's no fairing to hide anything under, so where do

Above and opposite: Mr. Turbo's new kit for the Honda 900RR features the Aerodyne self-lubricating turbocharger. How much power can a street turbo system like this put out? Check the dyno chart *(at right)* and then figure this is one of the lightest bikes on the market. In this case, 225 horsepower adds up to mid-nine-second quarter-mile ETs at over 150 mph. Or look at it this way—205 mph, top end!

we locate the turbocharger? Down low and in front of the frame—between the frame and the front wheel. On a V-Max, this locates the turbocharger too far away from the intake ports to draw-through a carburetor, so you will have to blow-through the stock carburetors, or an aftermarket electronic fuel injection system. Kawasaki originated this style of system in the early 1980s with the 750 Turbo. Other kit builders in recent years have added intercooling, but the idea of mounting the turbocharger in this location is the same. It makes sense: the closer the turbocharger is to the exhaust ports, the more responsive it will be.

This arrangement also puts the turbocharger below the level of the crankcase, which means you will have

to fabricate a siphon oil drain system. An alternative would be to use an electric siphon pump, which is a simple, low-cost method of oil return if you have the amperage to work with. Westech Development of Wimberly, Texas (512-847-8918), distributes an industrial strength electric pump that has proven its reliability over the past three years. It is made by SHURflo and has even been used on NASCAR race cars to circulate rear-end oil through an oil cooler. A more expensive solution would be to use an Aerodyne self-lubricating turbocharger, which is still somewhat of an unknown quantity in the world of four-stroke turbo bikes at this time. A few kit builders (First Choice, Mr. Turbo, and Hahn Racecraft) are now making Aerodyne-equipped systems, so time will tell how reliable they are over the long haul. Read the sidebar on "Things you need to know about turbocharger lubrication" in Chapter 3.

A blow-through design will usually allow the use of an intercooler, which dramatically reduces the temperature of the compressed air before it enters the combustion chamber, thereby increasing horsepower. Read the sidebar on "What you should know about compressing air and generating heat" in Chapter 3 and the section on intercooling in Chapter 8.

Let's assume (for less of a hit on your pocketbook) we choose to use blow-through carburetion, since only minor modifications are necessary to pressurize the carburetors. This means a bypass type of fuel system will also have to be devised, including a high-pressure electric fuel pump and a boost-sensitive fuel pressure regulator. As an alternative, you might also consider electronic programmable fuel injection. It is definitely the wave of the future; however, it is quite a lot more expensive (average cost $2,500 for a four-cylinder motorcycle engine) than designing your own blow-through carburetion system. Read Chapter 4 on fueling and Chapter 5 on electronic programmable fuel injection for more details.

Basically, a turbocharger, its lubrication system, an intercooler, and a fueling system are the meat of such an installation. If you're a good craftsman, you can turbocharge a Yamaha V-Max with minimal help from outside sources for about $2,000 to $3,000. To have such a system custom built would cost in the neighborhood of $4,000 to $5,000. Other V-4 motorcycles besides the V-Max would use the same kind of system.

With V-twins, you have the option of building a simple draw-through design. The engines are narrow enough to locate the turbo on the side, placing it much closer to the intake port(s) and exhaust ports. Mr. Turbo makes a simple draw-through system for Harleys that

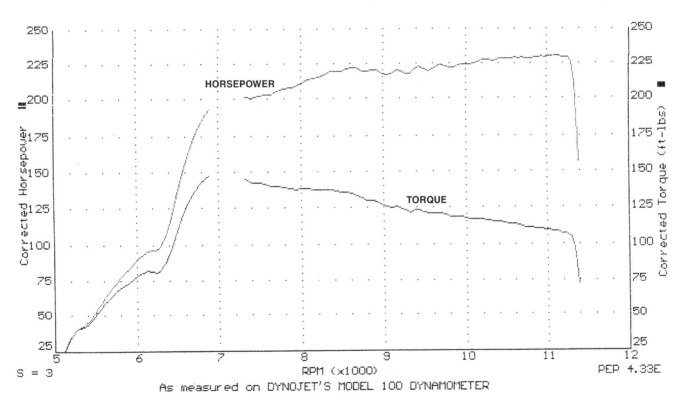

As measured on DYNOJET'S MODEL 100 DYNAMOMETER

S = 3

PEP 4.33E

ORIENT.008   86.1 °F   30.46-0.62 in.Hg.   0 ft.   CF=0.99   RPM/MPH=75
    1100CC ENGINE,CARRELLO RODS,9:1 PISTONS,30LB INJ.,55LB REG,C-16 FUEL,
    AS RAN AT 205 M.P.H. AT UFO SHOOTOUT.BOOST - 15LBS   B POT - 7:30
    USE 5TH GEAR.   BOOST-15LBS

Mr Turbo. 4014 Hopper Rd, Houston, Texas 77093 (Tel) 713-442-7113

Westech makes a nice, stealthy, low-boost turbo system for the ZX-11 that blows through a modified stock air box *(right)* and through the re-jetted stock carburetion system. Note the addition of the extra air chamber and intake snout on the side of the air box. They also make a similar system for the ZX-9R and have plans for other bikes in the future. This system, at approximately 5 lbs boost, will crank out 190+ horsepower, high-9-second ETs at 150 mph, and nearly 200 mph on the top end. They offer systems from 4 psi to 10 psi.

mounts on the right side of the engine. It's a fairly low-boost system that will take a stock Evo to over 100 horsepower.

Another likely candidate for a simple draw-through system would be the Suzuki 1400 Intruder. If you keep the boost down to the 10 to 12 psi range, there's no reason a turbo system couldn't be bolted onto either of these stock engines. But, remember that "simple" may not be the best. Blow-through carburetion and fuel injection allow the use of intercooling and an unrestricted intake tract. You will always be able to blow more air through multiple carburetors or fuel injection throttle bodies than you can draw through (as an example) a single 38 mm carburetor.

RB Racing's blow-through, electronically fuel injected system can turn your street Harley into a 135 to 225 horsepower asphalt-eating monster. They mount the turbocharger low on the left side of the front cylinder, which points it forward in an aesthetically pleasing design that blends right into a Harley. Intercooling is optional on all their systems.

PCS of Daytona Beach, Fla. (904-253-2586), is manufacturing blow-through carburetion turbo kits for the Ducati M-900s and 900 SSs that feature all stainless steel exhaust. The turbocharger mounts up high and in front of the engine. At this time, they are not offering intercooling, but these are relatively low boost systems running on stock compression engines.

It is important to remember that V-twins, due to their staggered firing order and exhaust pulsations, in a blow-through format will require a large plenum (approximately twice to three times the engine displacement) just prior to entering the intake manifold (throttle body), or pressurized carburetor. The plenum acts as a pressurized storage tank between firings and makes a full gulp of air available every time a piston goes down on an intake stroke. The plenum smoothes the flow of air and fuel into the engine.

Hahn Racecraft at one time made a competition system that propelled their gas-only big twin race bike to nearly 170 mph in the quarter-mile. As you can see, there is plenty of performance potential left in that Harley.

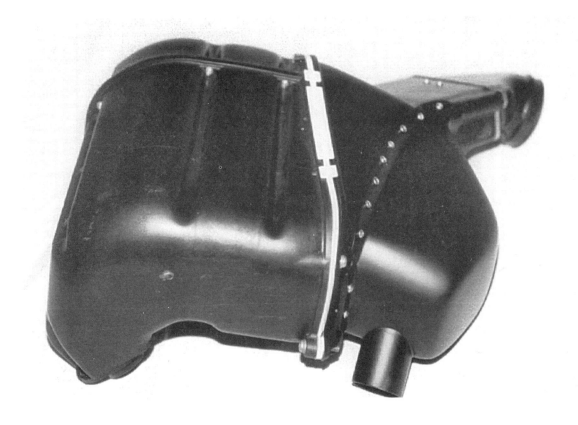

If you want to liven up any "V" configuration motorcycle and a kit isn't readily available for your particular machine, you can always design your own system or have one custom-fabricated.

Inline four-cylinder motorcycle engines are the easiest to turbocharge. Any of the major brands would be treated in basically the same manner. There are two ways to go: simple draw-through, or the more exotic blow-through. In a draw-through system, the turbocharger is located where the carburetors once were and blows directly into a log type manifold. These systems are the most popular because they are simple (one carburetor) and economical (a kit can usually be purchased for $3,000). Draw-through systems *will* exhibit a little more lag, due to the longer path of the exhaust system to the turbocharger and the more indirect path the air and fuel travel to get to the combustion chamber. These differences may be minimal, but nonetheless, draw-through systems are not quite as responsive as blow-through designs, though today's more responsive turbochargers alleviate the problem somewhat. Another disadvantage to draw-through designs is that intercooling cannot be incorporated; aside from racing gas and a lower compression ratio, water-alcohol injection is your only effective tool against detonation.

Blow-through systems are a little more complex and expensive, but a lot more efficient. The turbocharger usually mounts down low and in front of the frame, between the frame and the front wheel. This puts it in an easily accessible location closer to the exhaust and also makes it possible to intercool. The turbo would normally blow through either a single or dual intercooler arrangement with the cooler air ducted to the mouths of the pressurized carburetors or fuel injection throttle body(s).

Four companies manufacture turbocharger kits for inline four-cylinder motorcycles. Mr. Turbo makes both carbureted draw-through and injected blow-through kits for Suzuki, Kawasaki, Honda, Yamaha, and Harley-Davidson motorcycles. Hahn Racecraft specializes in Suzuki and Kawasaki brands and will custom-build turbo systems for just about anything. RB Racing makes kits for Harleys, Suzukis, Kawasaki ZX-11s, Triumph triples and fours, and BMW R and K bikes, but they will custom-build systems for any brand of motorcycle. RB makes strictly blow-through electronic fuel injection kits for all of their motorcycle turbo systems. Westech makes low-boost systems for Kawasaki ZX-11s and ZX-9Rs that blow through the stock carburetion system.

American Turbo-Pak started all this turbo mania stuff in the 1970s by producing systems for KZ Kawasakis, many of which are still in operation today. This early example had the log style exhaust manifold, which was later changed to a "Spyder" 4 into 1 collector style. Early KZ1000s, and even the police version still being made, are excellent material for boosting. Parts are readily available. They have a strong bottom end (once the two-piece crank is welded) and still power many all-out drag bikes.

BMW horizontal twins, especially the newer R1100RS models, respond to turbocharging quite nicely. RB Racing's kit for the Boxer is capable of boosting its way through the quarter-mile in 10.38 seconds at nearly 130 mph! The R1100RS turbocharger is placed under the left side cylinder. This offsets the drive shaft side and makes for more even weight distribution. The stock EFI is modified for blow-through operation by use of RB Racing's electronic fuel injection controllers the RSR ECU and receives air through a single intercooler. It's fun to go looking for big game on this bike.

No matter what the motorcycle brand or model, turbocharger placement must be your prime consideration. Most vertical twins, triples, fours, and sixes have adequate room for the turbocharger behind the cylinders. If you choose to go draw-through, the Rajay 300 series turbo would be about the largest (dimensionally speaking) you would use in any normal motorcycle application. On inline four-cylinder motorcycles, even the Rajay fits nicely where the carburetors and air cleaner are normally placed.

The IHI, Mitsubishi, and Garrett turbochargers are small in diameter compared to the Rajay and are easier to mount on a motorcycle. The latest trend in mounting the turbo on a typical four-cylinder or "V" configuration motorcycle is, as described, to put it in front of the frame and down low, similar to the factory Kawasaki 750 Turbo. This puts it in a location for easier access, closer to the exhaust for improved efficiency, low for a better center of gravity, and out from under the seat or gas tank where heat buildup can sometimes be a problem.

Draw-through systems in which the turbocharger is mounted higher than the crankcase present no oil drainage problems, whereas blow-through systems usually mount the turbo lower than the crankcase and therefore will require a siphon type system to return oil to the crankcase.

Some perimeter frames make it difficult to place the turbocharger in the carburetor/air cleaner bay and may

Don Vesco built this beautiful twin turbo system for Kevin Draper's Top Fuel Harley. Twin Garrett turbos feed the 160 cubic inch engine. Of course there isn't too much Harley left in the engine as it is billet everything. An example of fine workmanship throughout, this bike has produced some low-seven-second quarter-mile times (alcohol only) on early shakedown runs. Once the bugs are worked out they are hoping for times to improve into the six-second bracket.

force you to locate the turbocharger at the front of the bike, in which case you will probably choose to go with a blow-through system.

The growing trend of blowing through pressurized carburetors or electronic fuel injection is interesting from several standpoints. The turbocharger can be mounted in a more accessible location, while throttle response is greatly increased, further reducing turbo lag. By going to a blow-through design, the builder can choose from a greater selection of turbochargers. Any small turbo can be used in a blow-through application as long as it is sized correctly (proper CFM range) on the compressor side and has the proper A/R ratio.

Above and opposite: **RB Racing's new Harley system is, in a word, beautiful. It is also the most high-tech turbo system you can buy for Milwaukee's finest, featuring electronic programmable fuel injection and stainless steel exhaust headers. Intercooling is optional. This bike recently completed a 4,000-mile journey with no system failures whatsoever—and even at low boost levels, it easily outpulled all other bikes on the tour, including Yamaha's latest beast, the Royal Star. At only five pounds boost this bike put out a whopping 120 horsepower to the rear wheel.**

Above and opposite: **RB Racing's ZX-11 system features a huge Turbonetics 800 CFM turbocharger and an equally large intercooler that mounts under the gas tank. It is fed fresh, cool air through the ram air duct in the front of the fairing. It also features RSR electronic programmable fuel injection (two injectors per cylinder) and is estimated to be good for approximately 380 horsepower in street trim.**

Above and below: If you are mechanically inclined and you don't have the cash for a turbo kit, or nobody makes a kit for your particular bike, have no fear. You can make your own system, as Gary Evans did for this water cooled GSXR1100, for quite a lot less than a kit—and you can learn something at the same time. He chose to blow through a set of Keihin 39 mm flat slide carburetors, which are well sealed for the job and have worked flawlessly. The bike has been dyno'd at slightly over 200 horsepower to the rear wheel with the RHB-52 IHI turbocharger. A larger RHB-6 is used for bigger numbers.

Above and below: Mark Vanderwald made his turbo system as a college project. He chose the Suzuki GSXR750 (1990) because of its known bottom end strength and parts availability. His plan was to run the stock compression on no more than 7 psi boost and blow through the re-jetted stock CV carburetors. His mechanical engineering professor liked it enough to give him an "A" for his efforts and the school rewarded him with a degree. How does it perform? Like a stocker until you hit boost, at which point it is putting out 145 rear wheel horsepower (7 lbs boost) and performs like a Grand Prix bike that gained a little weight.

Above and below: **RB Racing built this prototype Triumph Daytona turbo system for Matt Capri and is now offering it to the general public. Capri has ridden this bike to 198 mph at El Mirage dry lake and someday when some more traction can be found, it should go much faster. On asphalt (with a boost leak) it has gone 202 mph, making it the first street Triumph to ever hit the magic 200 mark.**

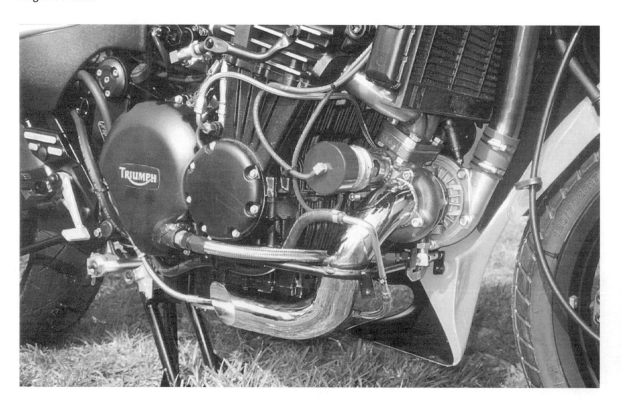

Full race, supercharged, nitro-burning motorcycle engines can be brutal on bottom ends. One way to solve the rod problem is to make your own—like this billet piece. Looks like it would work in a small block Chevy.

Brilhante makes this clean Roots-type supercharger system for big twin Harleys. A 90-degree nose drive is needed to get everything pointed in the right direction. Note the S&S Shorty carburetor.

Which Motorcycles Make the Best Turbo Bikes?

There are several things to consider when planning to turbocharge your motorcycle.

1. How strong is the bottom end? Some bikes have an excellent reputation for super-strong bottom ends that can take abnormal amounts of stress. However, an engine with weaker-than-normal internal parts doesn't necessarily prevent you from turbocharging. Stock rods can always be replaced with stronger aftermarket items. Two-piece cranks can be welded. Forged pistons can replace OEM cast pistons. Wrist pins, rings, valve springs, and numerous other parts known to be weak can be replaced with stronger aftermarket items.

2. Is a kit made for your bike, and if so, is it a blow-through or draw-through design? The few available kits are generally made for the brand and model motorcycles with the best reputation for strength and durability. If a kit isn't made for your particular motorcycle, there may be a good reason. The main difference between blow-through and draw-through systems is *price*. If your budget is tight, go with the lower-cost draw-through system and possibly suffer the erratic idle and, in some cases, poor transitioning qualities.

Mr. Turbo makes a universal turbo kit for inline four-cylinder motorcycles. They supply you with the turbo and hardware pieces for a complete system, but you will have to do some of the fabrication work yourself, or job it out. For instance, all the exhaust header U-bends and straight sections will need to be configured and welded, but after that it is a fairly easy job with no special machine work required.

American Turbo-Pak also made systems for the Honda CBX. Though it is recommended that the stock rods be replaced with Carillo pieces, these make excellent turbo bikes. They must have sold a lot of these kits because I hardly go out for a ride without spotting one someplace. Mr. Turbo still offers a kit for the mighty CBX if you want to bring your horsepower specs up to date.

Harleys can be successfully turbocharged with both draw-through and blow-through systems available from several sources. This is Mr. Turbo's draw-through carburetion system. The turbocharger mounts on the side of the engine, about where the stock carburetion system was located. It draws air and fuel through either a single Mikuni flat slide or an S&S Shorty carburetor, and can boost power to the century point with no problem.

Above and below: **First Choice Turbo Center** is marketing turbo kits for Harley big twins and Sportsters that feature the Aerodyne self-lubricating, variable vane turbocharger. Aerodyne turbochargers can be mounted either vertically or horizontally and in the case of these systems, they are mounted vertically and on the left side of the front cylinder. There is no need for a waste gate because the variable vanes do the regulating. The big twin system is intercooled while the Sportster must make do with warmer intake air due to a lack of space for the intercooler radiator. Both systems blow through modified Mikuni 40 mm flat slide carburetors. Big Twins can be boosted to 100 to 140 horsepower in street trim; we have no figures on the Sportster.

. . . Which Motorcycles Make the Best Turbo Bikes? . . .

Bikes you can get kits for:

Kawasaki
- 900–1000 Z-1 *(1, 2)
- GPz *(1, 2)
- J-Model *(1, 2)
- Ninja 900 *(1)
- KZ1300 *(1)
- ZX-11 *(1, 3)
- ZX-9R *(3, 9)

Suzuki
- GS1100 *(1, 2)
- GS1150 *(1, 2)
- GSXR750 *(1, 4)
- GSXR1100 *(1, 2, 3)
- 88–90 Katana 1100 *(1)

Honda
- CBX *(1)
- CBR900RR *(1, 3, 4, 5, 9)
- XX Blackbird (4)

Yamaha
- YZF-R1 *(4)
- V-Max *(3, 8)

BMW
- K100 (8 valve & 16 valve) *(3)
- R1100RS Boxer *(3)

Harley-Davidson
- Big Twin Evos (all models) *(1, 3)
- Big Twins and Sportsters *(3, 7)

Ducati
- M-900 (Monster) *(6)
- 900CR *(6)
- 900SP *(6)

*KEY

(1) Mr. Turbo (281-442-7113)

(2) Hahn Racecraft (708-851-5444)

(3) RB Racing (310-515-5720)

(4) American Turbo Systems (941-403-0198)

(5) Team Mr. Honda (915-545-2453)

(6) PCS (904-253-2586)

(7) First Choice (716-226-2929)

(8) Mad Max (203-574-7858)

(9) Westech (512-874-8918)

Mr. Turbo's ZX-11 injected turbo kit has boosted this bike to more than 230 mph and will reel in the quarter-mile in the low nines at over 160 mph. It also won the Daytona Bike Week dyno shootout and still holds the record at 459 horsepower (with a little nitrous assist). It is our understanding that Mr. Turbo will soon be offering fully programmable electronic fuel injection, which should create a user-friendly system.

. . . Which Motorcycles Make the Best Turbo Bikes? . . .

Motorcycles that would make ideal turbo bikes, but for which no kits are available:

Kawasaki
- ZX-7 & ZX-7R
- ZX-6
- ZR1100
- ZRX1100

Suzuki
- GSX1300R
- RF900
- Bandit 1200
- TL1000 and TL1000R

Honda
- CB1000
- Goldwing

Yamaha
- FZR1000
- FZR750
- FZR600
- Virago
- GTS1000

Ducati
- 916

Harley-Davidson
- Buell S-2 Thunderbolt - Competition Motorcycle (208-344-2580) will custom fabricate systems for Buell/Harleys.

Moto Guzzi
- LeMans 1000 (eight valve)

Above and opposite: Hahn Racecraft's latest entry in the turbo wars is this Aerodyne-boosted system for the water cooled Suzuki GSXR1100. It blows-through programmable electronic fuel injection and intercooling is an option. This bike is capable of low-nine-, high-eight-second quarter-mile sprints at more than 160 mph without a wheelie bar and on a street tire.

. . . Which Motorcycles Make the Best Turbo Bikes?

While these motorcycles would be ideal candidates for power boosting, there's always someone who will want to turbocharge a Honda VT500 or a RD400 Yamaha. If you are in that group, try to stick with what's available if you want immediate results. We will inevitably see a 120 horsepower VT500 Honda—that is for certain. I should mention that numerous shops across the country specialize in custom turbo installations. For instance, RB Racing in Gardena, Calif., will turbocharge just about anything, as long as it's a four-stroke and you can handle the expense of a custom-built state-of-the-art system, including electronic programmable fuel injection. Specialty machine and fabrication shops, such as

Kirby's Motorcycle & Machine of Grover City, Calif. (805-489-8693), will custom-build whatever you desire. Carl Pelletier's Competition Motors of Boise, Idaho (208-344-7580), specializes in turbocharging Harley-Davidson big twins and Sportsters, including Buell models. Extreme Sport Bikes (909-825-0101) is a highly experienced company, specializing in custom race and street turbo systems for motorcycles and sand drag cars.

And there's always your own two hands. ■

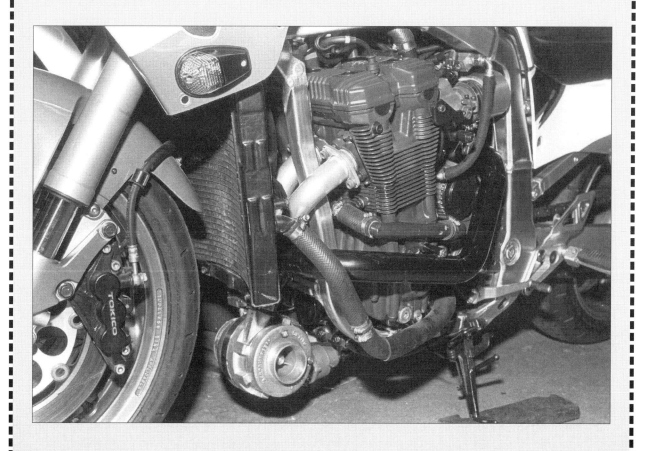

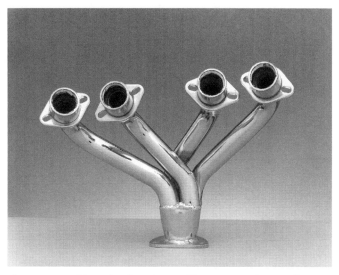

These rotational firing headers, designed by RB Racing for one of their early draw-through turbo systems, help smooth the exhaust flow into the feeder pipe that leads to the turbo mounted behind the cylinder block.

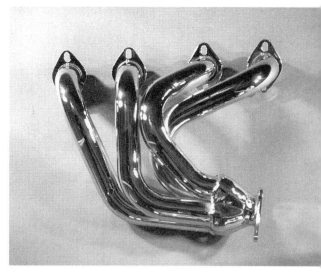

These equal length four-into-one draw-through headers immediately turn left, shortening the path the feeder pipe must take to the turbocharger behind the cylinder block.

One would think these headers are just another draw-through system design. Actually, they are designed for a blow-through Triumph Daytona 1200 and are extremely short. The turbocharger mounts directly to the flange.

Shovelhead Sportsters had exhaust spigots that were less than ideal, even to hang a stock exhaust system on. Even worse, they just won't seal, no matter what type of clamping arrangement you use. Exhaust flange adapters can be made easily from heavy wall steel tubing and two-bolt exhaust flanges that can be purchased from any muffler shop. The adapters weld to the head and provide a perfect seal for turbocharged motors.

One of the first turbo kits for a motorcycle was produced by American Turbo-Pak for the KZ Kawasaki. It had a simple log manifold that was compact and featured a short route back to the Rajay turbocharger.

Mr. Turbo still makes kits for KZ1000s that feature equal length, four-into-one headers. Shown here is a ZR1100 system.

Here's a blast from the past. Many years ago, RB Racing made draw-through turbo systems for the Honda CBX and twin turbo systems for the Suzuki GS1100. Bob Behn at RB is a master pipe monger, as shown in these rare photographs. Things have come a long ways since those days.

GS Suzukis make great turbo bikes. The engines have extremely strong roller bearing bottom ends and the bike looks mean as can be in drag racing mode. Note the banana pipe off the turbo. Most turbo motors are quiet in comparison to normally aspirated engines because the exhaust must first pass through the turbocharger turbine housing before exiting into the atmosphere.

Cam Timing

Usually stock cams make the best turbo cams, with the exception of some older shovelhead Harley Sportsters. Those machines have fairly radical cam timing, which is less than ideal for turbocharging.

The criteria for a good turbo cam are pretty basic. The less overlap and duration, the better. If both valves are open for too long a period at the same time (overlap), you lose a lot of boost potential right out the exhaust pipe. Today's engines, with their free-flowing heads, need less overlap and duration to achieve a competitive power figure. With the exception of special racing models like Honda RC30s and such, most modern motorcycle engines have cam timing suitable for turbocharging or supercharging.

An ideal turbo cam has approximately 15 cam degrees of overlap, 7.5 degrees each side of TDC. The duration of opening should be 220 to 240 crankshaft degrees. The duration is based on readings taken at 0.002 inches off the heal of the cam. Be aware that many cam grinders give duration and overlap readings at 0.050 inches off the heel of the cam. Do not use these readings, as you will end up with more overlap and duration than is acceptable. Remember, when the lifter is 0.050 off the heel at zero lash, the valves are 0.075 off their seat (assuming a typical rocker arm leverage of 1.5 to 1). All cam modifications should be checked after partial assembly of the engine, using a degree wheel on the crankshaft and a dial indicator on the cam or cam follower.

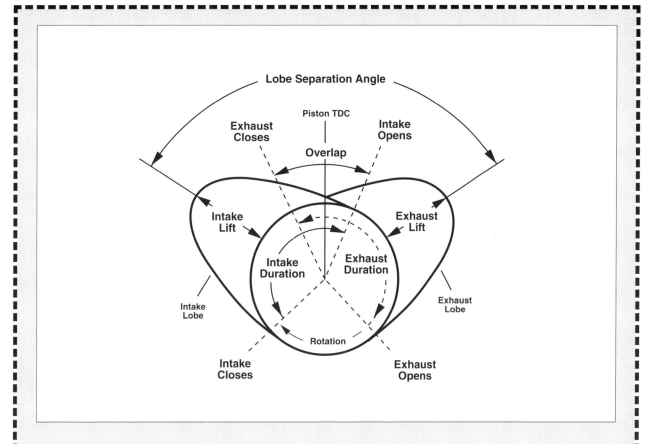

. . . Cam Timing

Lobe-separation angle is another way of expressing overlap. It is usually expressed as the number of *crankshaft* degrees between the intake and exhaust lobe center lines. If the exhaust lobe centerline is 114 crankshaft degrees before top dead center (BTDC), and the intake lobe centerline is 106 crankshaft degrees after top dead center (ATDC), adding the two numbers together and dividing by two (to get cam degrees), will produce the lobe-separation angle measured at the camshaft. In this case, $106 + 114 = 220$ and $\frac{220}{2} = 110$ degrees. Lobe-separation angle is just another way to express valve overlap and is the best way to define the relationship between exhaust valve closing and intake valve opening. As the lobe-separation angle becomes tighter (from 110 degrees to 106 degrees, for example), this moves the intake and exhaust lobe centerlines closer together, increasing the amount of valve overlap. Going the other way, moving the lobe centerlines farther apart decreases the amount of valve overlap. Turbo motors will benefit from a moderate increase in lift. Increasing

lift will allow more air and fuel to enter the cylinder without necessarily increasing overlap and duration.

Racing is another story. A little more lift certainly helps, but some people actually run a few more degrees duration to get the cooling effect of the intake charge passing through. It helps the exhaust valves live longer in high-stress, high-heat situations.

Turbo cams are available for Harleys, but because the cams in most other OEM motorcycles are fine just the way they are, nobody's making any new strides in turbo cam technology. If you want to turbocharge your Harley, contact Leineweber Enterprises. They have been making supercharger and turbo cams for Harley-Davidsons for years.

If you have already put a set of Yoshimura or other high performance cams into your engine, you may as well swap them back for the stock sticks. A stock valve train is a lot easier on parts and will give you reasonable low end performance while the turbo is kicking in.

■

Porting and Head Work

Porting (especially for competition) is recommended, as its effects are the same whether turbocharging or not. The larger and more obstruction-free your ports and valves are, the more air and fuel you will be able to move through the engine. But for the street, stock intake geometry and parts are usually just fine. After all, anything over 250 horsepower goes up in tire smoke, even at highway speeds. You can only transmit so much power through a street tire before it loses grip.

Anything over 15 lbs boost may require the use of a solid copper head gasket. Ultra-high boost levels may also require copper "O" ring seals. Aftermarket stainless valve springs, sodium filled exhaust valves, bronze guides, and increased oil flow through the head are also worthwhile modifications.

Higher valve spring pressure is necessary only with a higher lift cam. Most modern sport bikes are capable of all the rpm your turbocharger system needs. There's no point in stressing an engine far beyond its stock rpm potential just because you can. If your bike came equipped with an rpm limiter, do yourself a favor and leave it operational. The idea is to create more power up to your normal rpm limit—there is no need to spin the engine any faster. ∎

What book on power boosting motorcycles would be complete without "Mad Mel" Mandel's turbo GS Suzuki-powered 1969 Honda? You might say this bike is the complete transformation project. It was originally powered by a potent turbocharged Honda CB750 engine. When the old Honda wheezed its last breath, Mel had Vance & Hines install a Suzuki GS pro turbo motor (which is now sporting a 1400cc big block). Overkill? You bet—and that's the way Mel likes it. Horsepower is estimated to be in the 350 to 380 range. This bike is so clean you can literally eat off it. Not bad for a 21-year-old motorcycle.

Above and below: **Personal Cycle Service is now producing IHI turbo systems for the Ducati Monster, 900CR and SP models. Set to run at 3.5 to 5 lbs boost, it should be good for a 30 percent increase in power on a stock motor.**

Honda CX500T

CHAPTER 10

Turbo Bikes of the 1980s: Compressed Collectibles

Ever wonder what happened to those factory turbo bikes of the early 1980s? Most of them were crashed or thrashed, but a few of them survived to become collectible classics. Recent publicity has stimulated renewed interest in these models, but surprisingly, the activity is not from longtime owners removing dusty covers from forgotten two-wheelers. It's from new thirty-something owners who missed turbo mania the first time around.

Perhaps buyer reluctance in the early 1980s was due to the magazine reviews—the editors weren't kind to turbos. They called them overweight, underpowered, two-wheeled flash bikes bristling with unproven technology that added nothing to performance and a lot to the $5,000 price tags. Or perhaps the turbo bikes represent adolescent unobtanium—the objects of high school fantasy. Whatever the reason, many new owners are joining the turbo ranks. Longtime owners kept them for their exclusivity or their proficiency as sport-tourers, or considered them a market segment Japanese manufacturers neglected for ten years after the turbos were introduced.

Honda CX500T

The first turbo unveiling was in April of 1982: the Honda CX500T. It was a 575-pound top-heavy style bike with water cooling, a turbocharger, electronic fuel injection with two computer controllers (for ignition and fueling), an anti-dive fork, dual-piston calipers, composite rims, aluminum swingarm, single-shock suspension, and LCD displays. It was a technological *tour de force*. With its fully integrated body work and gold anodized wheels, it was a styling exercise as well.

It featured an upright riding position and fairing that covered all but the extremities. The high-rpm-dependent, 18-psi-boost motor lacked bottom end power, making it a handful in town or on a twisty road. But once up to speed, it was a fine open road cruiser, able to digest large portions of tarmac without the backache normally associated with sport touring bikes.

Yamaha XJ650L

Suzuki XN85

Yamaha XJ650L

A month later, Yamaha unveiled its version of the future with a visit to the past. Based on a 650 Seca, the Yamaha XJ650L used blow-through carburetors on a stock engine with strengthened internals, the world's smallest turbocharger (39 mm compressor wheel), and a tall, Star Wars-like fairing. It was a tall, thin motorcycle that hid its 567-pound weight well. Its off-boost power was comparable to contemporary 750s and once the waste gate was disconnected—doubling the boost to 15 lbs—its on-boost rush was as strong as a liter-size bike. The engine upgrades yielded a bulletproof mill unaffected by the high boost pressure. More than a few of these models are now approaching 100,000 miles without major engine work.

This bike has a cammy motor in a frame with too much flex, fork tubes that are too skinny (36mm), and too little braking power—but with one of the best fairings ever designed. It's cool in the summer and warm in the winter. It allows riders to go without rain gear except in the most drenching downpours. The Yamaha's *forté* is comfortably covering 500+ miles of two lanes in a day.

Suzuki XN85

The Suzuki XN85 came six months after the Honda. Surprisingly, its most appealing feature wasn't the turbo. It was the razor sharp steering of the 16-inch front wheel. Declared the best handling motorcycle ever built, it compares favorably with contemporary 600s.

It had anti-dive forks, fuel injection, a bikini fairing, and an aggressive riding position. It operated at medium boost—10 psi—but you couldn't tell. It had no off- to on-boost difference and had the same power everywhere, which made for smooth but unexciting performance. This characteristic made it a favorite of the twisties crowd, as there was no fear of uncontrollable wheel spinout on corners, a trait of the other turbos. There also wasn't any of the strong high-speed acceleration that normally makes turbo bikes so addicting.

Honda CX650T

Fifteen months after the CX500T, Honda followed with the much-improved CX650T. It had a lot more bottom end and a turbo that built pressure at lower rpm (2500) than anyone else's. And it finished with an urging that enabled it to demolish even the mighty GS1100, making it the roll-on king.

Honda CX650T

Kawasaki ZX750E

As good as this bike was, it shared a fatal flaw with its stablemate. The oil-cooled stator couldn't withstand the heat produced by the turbo motor and failed with regularity every 20,000 miles. Its internal mounting required engine removal, which required fairing removal, which required disconnection of all wires to swap stators. It's an eight-hour nightmare or a $400 donation to your local Honda dealer—not including a $350 stator.

Honda followed the CX650T with an '83 model that had an 11 psi waste gate, a one gallon larger (5 gallon) gas tank and a slight change in graphics.

Kawasaki Axe

The next factory turbo was from Kawasaki, introduced in September of 1983 and produced in '84 and '85. It was the last and the best. It used a Gpo engine, a KZ650 cylinder head, and a decent amount of boost (10 psi) to attain the goal everyone else had been trying for—a medium-weight (556 lbs) motorcycle with liter-class power.

The ZX750E was the first 10-second production motorcycle that could do more than just go straight. It was a total package with its strengthened frame and swingarm, high-stress engine components, and full-coverage fairing. The only thing it lacked was looks. To the untrained eye it was nothing more than a GPz750, with its only distinguishing feature the wraparound aluminum fairing brace that doubled as a turbo protector.

By mounting the turbo unit only inches from the exhaust ports, turbo lag was minimized. With its large-for-a-turbo displacement and quick spool-up, it was strong from idle to its 150+ mph top speed. Its only shortcoming was a temperamental throttle position switch and weak fuel pump that sometimes made it a rough runner below 4,000 rpm.

Kawasaki Z1RTC

Kawasaki aficionados will note the K-company was the first to mass-produce a turbocharged motorcycle: the '78–'79 Z1RTC. This is true, but those bikes were KZ1000s modified stateside, not factory produced. They were the product of Turbo-Cycle, Inc., a joint venture between American Kawasaki and American Turbo-Pak, whose employees fitted ATP kits and sent

Before the GPz750 Turbo, Kawasaki worked a deal with American Turbo-Pak to produce kitted turbo bikes that would be sold through Kawasaki dealerships with a full factory warranty. This 1979 Z1RTC model is one of the repainted 1978 models. The 1978s were light metallic blue—leftovers were repainted black and sold as '79s.

the finished product to dealers with a full factory warranty.

The 1978 Z1RTC was painted ice blue metallic to distinguish it from other models. Despite a ten-second quarter-mile, it didn't sell well. Its on-off switch performance and one-dimensional capability appealed only to the drag strip crowd. In 1979 the leftover '78s were sent to the paint shop, stripped, and painted black. These repainted Z1RTCs were sold as 1979 models.

A decade and a half after the first factory turbos, what can be said about them? Each had its own personality and shortcomings, but all were ahead of their time. The fully integrated fairings and body work (except for

the Suzuki), and fuel injection systems (except for the Yamaha) are features found on few models today.

To their proud owners today, these bikes offer relief from the unbelievable pricing of today's models while providing membership into an exclusive club. None of them had the low weight and high performance of the ideal motorcycle. What they had was a uniqueness—unequalled then or now.

For more information on the factory turbo bikes contact Robert Miller at the Turbo Motorcycle International Owners Association at PO Box 385, Westtown, PA 19395 or call 610-431-4257.

Table 10-1
Production Turbo Bikes — BHP at Rear Wheel

RPM	Honda CX500T	Yamaha XJ650L	Suzuki XN85	Honda CX650T	Kawasaki ZX750E
2500				12	
3000		18		18	14
3500		21	22	23	22
4000		23	27	29	28
4500	10	23	34	38	34
5000	16	27	42	50	44
5500	24	32	49	65	60
6000	28	42	55	74	70
6500	35	53	60	77	80
7000	43	65	63	77	85
7500	56	71	67	80	90
8000	63	71	71	80	95
8500	66	70	71	81	96
9000	68	64	70	75	93
9500	69		67		
10,000	67				
¼ mi. ET	12.38 sec.	12.49 sec.	11.99 sec.	11.75 sec.	11.13 sec.
¼ mi. speed	106 mph	105 mph	110 mph	112 mph	120 mph

The Suzuki XN85 was another 650 attempt at liter size horsepower. What it lacked in horsepower, it made up for with exceptional handling characteristics. The engine was fueled by electronic fuel injection and, like the Honda, was ahead of its time.

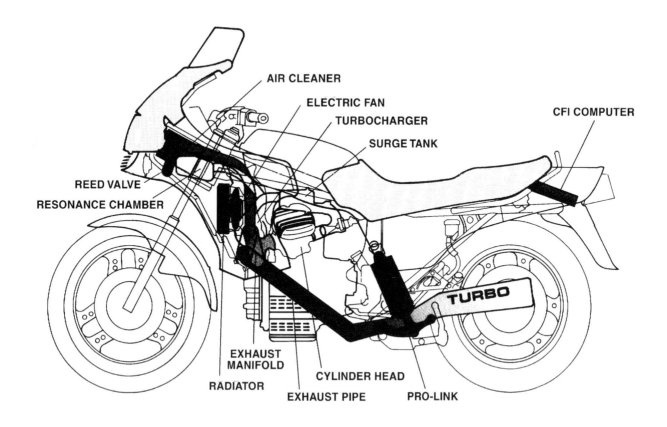

AIR CLEANER

ELECTRIC FAN

TURBOCHARGER

SURGE TANK

CFI COMPUTER

REED VALVE

RESONANCE CHAMBER

EXHAUST MANIFOLD

RADIATOR

CYLINDER HEAD

EXHAUST PIPE

PRO-LINK

TURBO

This diagram shows exactly where the major components were located on the Honda CX500. It was well laid-out for easy maintenance and accessibility—with the exception of the troublesome stator assembly.

YAMAHA TURBO SYSTEM

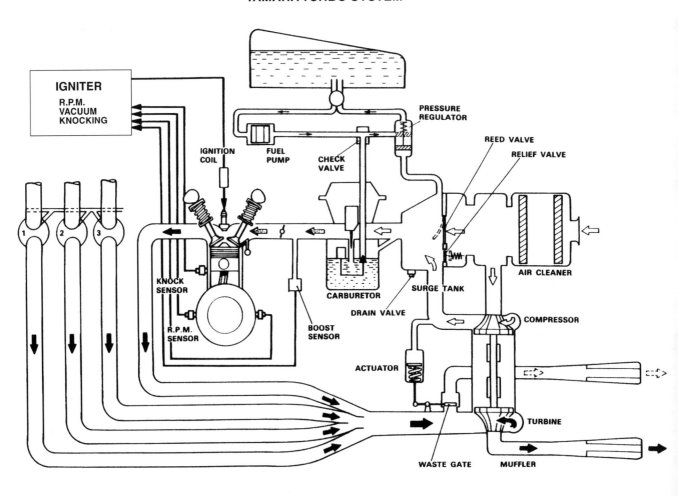

Yamaha made the only factory blow-through carburetion turbo bike, the XJ650L. The bike also featured one of the smallest turbochargers ever built, with later versions putting out 11 psi boost. These bikes were best suited for long distance touring and had the most advanced fairing of all the factory turbo bikes. Note that if boost pressure falls below atmospheric pressure, a reed valve in the intake path allows fresh air to enter the carburetor directly, bypassing the turbocharger.

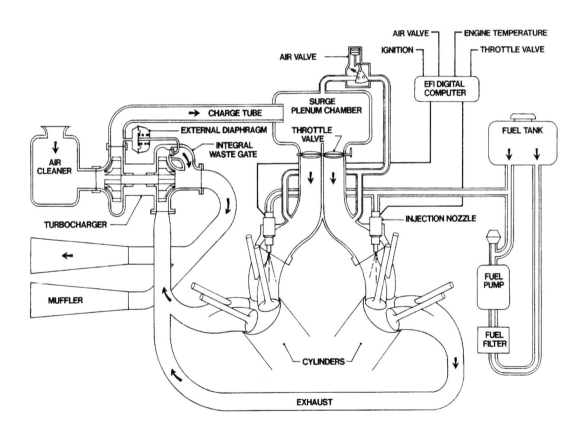

The Honda turbo system was complex and state-of-the-art in the early 1980s. At 18 lbs boost, the 650 version was as quick as a stock Suzuki GS1100.

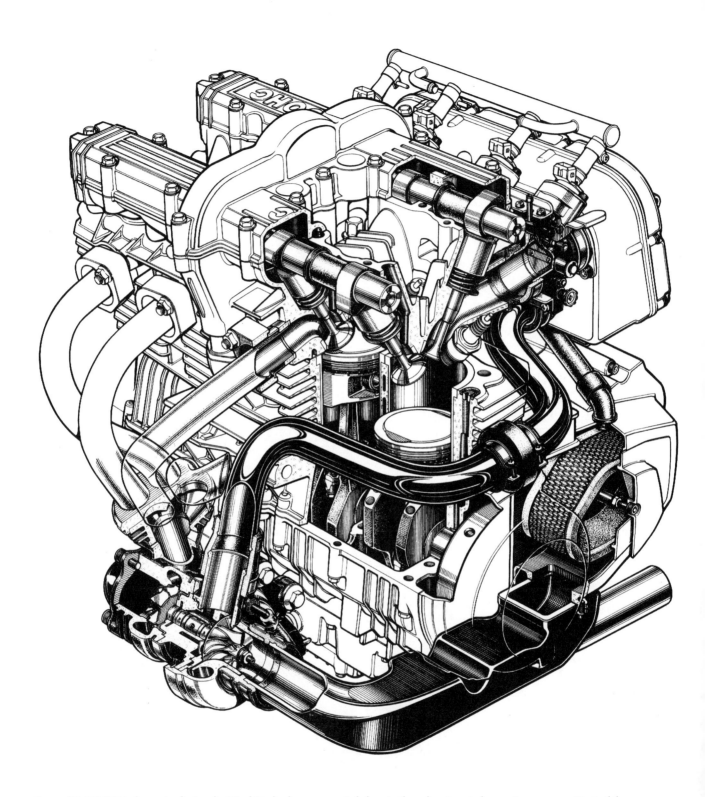

Kawasaki's GPz750 turbo motor featured a Hitachi turbocharger mounted close to the exhaust ports for greater response. Most of the four-cylinder turbo kits made today are patterned after this system. The standard GPz engine was strengthened considerably to handle the 100+ crankshaft horsepower.

Directory of Suppliers

As you explore the possibilities of turbocharging, supercharging, and nitrous oxide power boosting, you will want to get acquainted with the key suppliers of parts, equipment, and services who might be of assistance to you. Following is a list to get you started.

Aerocharger Turbo Systems
8 Apollo Drive
Batavia, NY 14020
Phone 716-345-0055
Fax 716-344-5623
Markets the only self-lubricating turbocharger. Manufactures kits for Harley big twins and Sportsters.

American Turbo Systems
3435 Enterprise Ave. #50
Naples, FL 34104
Phone & Fax 941-403-0198
www.americanturbo.com
Manufactures turbo kits for the Honda XX Blackbird, CBR900RR, Suzuki GSXR1100, & Yamaha YZF-R1.

A.P.E.
1010 W. Oak Street
Burbank, CA 91510
Phone 818-842-4952 or 800-824-1825
Fax 818-842-9032
Manufactures internal engine parts for supercharged and turbocharged motorcycle engines.

Arias
13420 S. Normandie Ave.
Gardena, CA 90249
Phone 310-532-9737
Fax 310-516-8203
Manufactures low compression forged pistons.

A.S.A.P. Racing Products
2415 Clifton
Lansing, MI
Phone 517-484-4080
Supercharger systems for Yamaha V-Max motorcycles.

Camden Superchargers
401 M East Braker Lane
Austin, TX 78753
Phone 512-339-4772
Fax 512-339-4795
Manufacturer of Roots-type superchargers.

Competition Motors
3602 ½ Chinden Blvd
Boise, ID 83714
Phone 208-344-7580
Fax 208-344-2311
Custom Harley turbo and injection systems.

Dyno Jet
200 Arden Drive
Belgrade, MT 59714
Phone 406-388-4993
Fax 406-388-4721
Carburetor jet kits.

ET Performance
3805 Mariana Way
Santa Barbara, CA 93105
Phone and Fax 805-563-2386
Custom EFI systems for Harleys.

Extreme Sport Bikes
12210 Michigan Ave., Suite 3
Grand Terrace, CA. 92313
Phone 909-825-0101
Custom turbo systems and products.

Fageol Superchargers
1255 Hayden Lane
El Cajon, CA 92021
Phone 619-447-1092
Fax 619-593-7294
Manufacturer of Roots-type superchargers.

Hahn Racecraft
110 Kirkland Circle - Suite J
Oswego, IL 60543
Phone 630-851-5444
Fax 630-851-5514
Turbo kits for Suzuki and Kawasaki motorcycles.

HKS USA
2355 Miramar Avenue
Long Beach, CA 90815
Phone 310-494-8068
Fax 310-494-1768
Manufactures intake pop-off valves.

Horsepower Unlimited
P.O. Box 605
Sophia, WV 25921
Phone and Fax 304-683-5500
Custom turbo services for Kawasakis.

J.E. Pistons
15312 Connector Lane
Huntington Beach, CA 92649
Phone 714-898-9763
Fax 714-897-5636
Manufactures forged low-compression pistons.

K & N Engineering
P.O. Box 1329
Riverside, CA 92507
Phone 909-684-9762
Fax 909-684-0716
Manufactures air cleaners and air/fuel ratio meters.

Kirby's Motorcycles & Machining
944 Griffin Street
Grover City, CA 93433
Phone and Fax 805-489-8693
Custom turbo installations and machine work.

Leineweber Enterprises
P.O. Box 335
Yucca Valley, CA 92286
Phone 619-364-4432
Fax 619-364-3402
Manufactures turbo cams for Harleys.

Mad Max Enterprises
35 Harpers Ferry Road
Waterbury, CT 06705
Phone 203-574-7859
Fax 203-574-5237
Supercharger kits for Yamaha V-Max motorcycles.

Magna Charger
6262 Newville Road
Orland, CA 95963
Phone 916-865-7010
Fax 916-865-7875
Supercharger kits for Harley-Davidson big twins and Yamaha V-Max motorcycles.

Mikuni American
8910 Mikuni Avenue
Northridge, CA 91324
Phone 818-885-1242
Fax 818-993-7388
Supplier of low pressure fuel pumps, Cagle fuel pressure regulators, and carburetors.

Mr. Turbo
4014 Hopper Road
Houston, TX 77093
Phone 281-442-7113
Fax 281-442-4472
Turbo kits for various motorcycles.

MTC Engineering
428 Shearer Blvd
Cocoa, FL 32922
Phone 407-636-9480
Fax 407 631-8804
Manufacturer of low compression pistons and provider of drag racing specialty services.

Nitrous Oxide Systems, Inc.
5930 Lakeshore Drive
Cypress, CA 90630
714-821-0580
Fax 714-821-8319
Manufactures nitrous oxide injection systems.

The Nitrous Works
1450 McDonald Road
Dahlonega, GA 30533
Phone 706-864-7009
Fax 706-864-2206
Manufactures nitrous oxide injection systems.

PCS
594 Ballough Road
Daytona Beach, FL 32114
Phone 904-253-2586
Fax 904-253-3578
Manufactures turbo kits for Ducati motorcycles.

Pingel Enterprises
2076 11th Avenue - Unit C
Adams, WI 53910
Phone 608-339-7999
Fax 608-339-9164
Manufactures high-flow fuel valves.

Powerdyne
104-C East Avenue K4
Lancaster, CA 93535
Phone 805-723-2800
Fax 805-723-2802
Manufactures centrifugal superchargers.

ProCharger
14014 W. 107th Street
Lenexa, KS 66215
Phone 913-338-2886
Fax 913-338-2879
Manufactures centrifugal superchargers.

RB Racing (also called RSR)
1625 W. 134th Street
Gardena, CA 90249
Phone 310-515-5720
Fax 310-515-5782
www.rbracing-rsr.com
Manufactures motorcycle turbo kits and EFI systems, and provides custom performance services.

Rohm Performance Products
3120 Industrial Drive
Yuba City, CA 95993
Phone 916-674-9123
Fax 916-674-9145
Manufactures supercharger kits and adjustable ignition advancers.

Spearco Performance Products
14664 Titus Street
Panorama City, CA 91402
Phone 818-901-7851
Fax 818-785-4362
Manufactures several turbo installation products.

Summit Racing Equipment
1200 SE Blvd
Tallmadge, OH 44278
Phone 330-630-3030
Fax 330-630-5333
Supplier of Mallory pressure sensitive fuel pressure regulators.

T.M.C. Group
2 Rands Lane, Armthorpe
Doncaster, South Yorkshire DN3 3DR
ENGLAND
Phone (44) 130-283-4343
Fax (44) 130-283-3969
Manufactures nitrous oxide injection systems.

Team Mr. Honda
3401 N. Mesa Street
El Paso, TX 79902
Phone 915-545-2453
Fax 915-545-2457
Manufactures turbo kit for Honda CBR 900RR.

Turbo City
1137 W. Katella Avenue
Orange, CA 92867
Phone 714-639-4933
Fax 714-997-1196
Supplier of miscellaneous turbo installation products.

Turbonetics
5400 Atlantis Court
Moorpark, CA 93021
Phone 805-529-8995
Fax 805-529-9499
Supplier of various brands of turbochargers and providers of custom turbo modifications.

TWM Induction
325 Rutherford Street - Unit D
Goleta, CA 93117
Phone 805-967-9478
Fax 805-683-6640
Supplier of air/fuel ratio meters.

Vortech
5351 Bonsai Avenue
Moorpark, CA 93021
Phone 805-529-9330
Fax 805-529-7831
Manufactures centrifugal superchargers.

Westech Development
P.O. Box 875
Wimberley, TX 78676
Phone 512-847-8918
Manufactures turbo kits for Kawasaki ZX-11, and
ZX-9R motorcycles.

Whipple Industries
3292½ N Weber Avenue
Fresno, CA 93722
Phone 209-442-1261
Fax 209-442-4153
Supplies Opcon Autorotor screw-type superchargers.

WhiTek
P.O. Box 337
Arroyo Grande, CA 93421
Phone 805-481-7710
Fax 805-481-0901
Manufactures EFI systems for Harleys.

Wiseco
7201 Industrial Park Blvd.
Mentor, OH 44060
Phone 800-321-1364
Fax 216-951-6606
Manufactures forged low compression pistons.

Publications

Powertech and Turbo Bike Magazine
P.O. Box 800725
Valencia, CA 91380
Phone 661-255-3426
Fax 661-255-1593
Features extreme performance motorcycles and high-
tech, how-to articles.

Streetfighters Magazine
Trident House
Heath Road
Hale, Altrincham
Cheshire WA14 2UJ ENGLAND
Phone (44) 161-928-3480
Fax (44) 161-941-6897
Features extreme performance motorcycles.

Other Publications

Auto Math Handbook
by John Lawlor
HP Books
Tucson, Ariz.
ISBN 1-55788-020-4

Automotive Supercharging and Turbocharging
A Technical Guide
by John D. Humphries
Haynes Publishing
ISBN 0-85429-880-0

Chilton's Guide to Turbocharged Cars and Trucks
by Mike Stone
Chilton Book Company
Radnor, Penn.
ISBN 0-8019-7397-X

Racer's Encyclopedia of Metals, Fibers & Materials
by Forbes Aird
Motorbooks International
Osceola, Wisc.
ISBN 0-87938916-8

Turbochargers
by Hugh McInnes
HP Books
Tucson, Ariz.
ISBN 0-912656-49-2

Turbomania
by Bob Tomlinson
CB Tech Dept.
Farmersville, Calif.
ISBN

Organizations

Turbo Motorcycle International Owners Association
PO Box 385
Westtown, PA 19395
Phone 610-431-4257
Fax 610-431-1404

Glossary

aesthetics How something looks; eye appeal.

aftermarket parts Parts made by companies other than the original manufacturer of the equipment for which the parts are intended.

ambient Surrounding; as in ambient temperature.

air density Density is the ratio of the mass of an object to its volume, in this case, air. Generally speaking, higher altitude and/or hotter air will result in lower air density.

air/fuel ratio So many parts of air to so many parts of fuel, by weight. 14.7 to 1 would mean there are 14.7 parts of air to 1 part of fuel by weight.

air priority valve Attaches to blow-through intake plenum chambers to allow the engine to breathe normal air until positive boost is realized.

air velocity How fast air is moving. Usually mentioned in relation to the flow through carburetor venturis or fuel injection throttle bodies.

A/R ratio A calculation to determine the size of a turbocharger exhaust turbine scroll. Defined as the ratio of the area of the incoming gas opening in the scroll, divided by the radius from the center of the shaft to the center of the opening. Indicates ability to flow a certain amount of exhaust. Small A/R ratios allow less exhaust to flow through, but at a higher speed.

aromatics A combination of molecules from chemicals that make up gasoline. Explained fully in Chapter 8.

aspiration Breathing, as in air.

ball bearings Bearings made of rolling balls; lubricated by low pressure oil.

BARO A fuel injection term that means barometric pressure sensor.

Bernoulli Principle The physical principles describing the pressure differences arising from air flow around an object.

benzene An aromatic chemical used as an octane enhancer in racing gasoline.

BMEP Brake Mean Effective Pressure. See definition in Chapter 6.

BTU British thermal units. A measure of the energy content of fuels. Used in calculating combustion temperature.

blow-through Means blowing just air through carburetors or fuel injection throttle bodies.

centrifugal compressor A term used to describe a driven-impeller supercharger.

CFM Cubic feet per minute. Used to describe what volume of a fluid will pass through a channel in one minute, such as air passing through superchargers, turbochargers, carburetors, etc.

closed-loop An electronic fuel injection term used to describe a speed-density design as opposed to a flapper valve and hot wire flow meter system. Explained fully in Chapter 5.

compressor housing A turbocharger component that is responsible for taking in air, compressing it and sending it on to the engine. On the opposite side of the turbocharger from the turbine housing.

compressor map Used to calculate turbocharger efficiency. Explained in Chapter 3.

CV Constant velocity; a type of carburetor.

detonation A term used to describe uncontrolled combustion of fuel prior to the intended (proper) ignition timing.

draw-through Drawing air and fuel through a carburetor, as in turbocharging or supercharging.

dyno or dynamometer A device used to determine the amount of horsepower an engine is producing.

ECU Electronic control unit; used in electronic fuel injection systems.

EFI Electronic fuel injection.

efficiency The ratio of the effective energy (or power) output of a machine to the energy (or power) expended in producing it. In turbocharging and supercharging, it is the ratio of the energy added to the intake air stream (in the form of increased pressure), to the energy expended to drive the supercharger or turbocharger. The efficiency of a turbocharger or supercharger can never be 100 percent, since there are losses due to friction, incomplete air sealing, gear losses, and so forth.

EGO Exhaust gas oxygen, as measured by lambda probe sensors, or oxygen sensors used in electronic fuel injection systems.

endgas Unburned hydrocarbons; as those contained in engine exhaust.

EPA Environmental Protection Agency. An uncontrolled, self-regulating government agency. An organization akin to "Big Brother."

floating bearing A bearing that is suspended by oil film under high pressure and is used in some turbochargers as a shaft bearing.

forced induction Forceable adding more air and fuel to an internal combustion engine, such as supercharging or turbocharging.

fuel injector A device that is triggered by an ECU to open at predetermined times to allow fuel to flow into the intake port.

fuel rail A manifold which supplies fuel to a row of fuel injectors.

gear drive Refers to a type of supercharger drive mechanism. A gear-driven supercharger, as opposed to a belt-driven supercharger.

gravity-feed Supplying fuel to a carburetor by a downhill path and gravity.

horsepower What you are trying to increase by reading this book.

heavy fractions A term used to describe slower evaporating chemicals used in making racing gasoline.

impeller A laded wheel that spins inside the compressor housing of a turbocharger or centrifugal supercharger and compresses air.

isopentane A chemical contained in olefins and paraffins used in making racing gasoline.

isooctane A chemical contained in olefins and paraffins used in making racing gasoline.

intercooling A term used to describe the cooling of compressed air before it enters the combustion chamber.

junk food You'll eat a lot of it while building your power boosted motorcycle.

kinetic energy The energy needed to increase the velocity of an object or fluid. Conversely, the motion energy of a moving object or fluid, which will be given up as its velocity is reduced.

knock Another term used to describe detonation, or uncontrolled combustion.

KPa Kilo Pascal, a metric unit of pressure. A pressure of 1 KPa is equal to 0.145 psi. A pressure of 1 psi is equal to 6.895 KPa.

lag A term used to describe the delay time for a turbocharger impeller to spin up to speed.

LED Light emitting diode, as used in air/fuel ratio meter lights and other electronic devices.

light fractions Fast evaporating chemicals used in making racing gasoline.

MELTDOWN What your engine will suffer as a result of excessive detonation.

MAP Manifold absolute pressure; a term used with electronic fuel injection sensors.

mass flow A measure of air flow through an electronic fuel injection system.

medium fractions Chemicals that evaporate at temperatures between light fractions and heavy fractions used in making racing gasoline.

methanol A type of alcohol fuel that is sometimes used in racing to eliminate the possibility of detonation.

motor method One of the methods used to determine the octane rating of gasoline.

multi-stage A term used to describe certain nitrous oxide systems, waste gates, and clutches.

nitromethane A high energy fuel used in some classes of drag racing. It has the ability to produce its own oxygen as it burns.

N_2O The chemical term for nitrous oxide.

nitrous oxide A liquefied gas that contains oxygen and is used as a fuel supplement to increase horsepower.

normal aspiration In reference to engines breathing normal air with no power boosting.

OEM Original equipment manufacturer. Refers to the original maker of a piece of equipment, such as a motorcycle. The original maker of a product.

oxygen sensor A device used to measure the oxygen content of engine exhaust; used to signal either an air/fuel ratio meter or electronic control unit in an electronic fuel injection system.

octane rating A measurement of gasoline's ability to resist detonation.

olefins Chemicals (alkenes) used in making racing gasoline.

paraffins Chemicals (alkanes)—including octane, isooctane, butane, pentane—used in the formulation of gasoline.

peak pressure point The point in the stroke of a piston moving within an internal combustion engine at which the greatest level of combustion pressure is realized.

plain bearing Non-roller, non-ball bearing; requires high pressure oil for lubrication.

plenum chamber A large capacity intake manifold that usually supplies pressurized air, or air and fuel to the engine.

pop-off valve Used to relieve pressure spikes in a intake system. Usually attaches to a plenum chamber.

power boosting A term used to describe turbocharging, supercharging, or nitrous oxide injection.

pre-ignition Ignition of air and fuel before the intended (proper) ignition timing occurs. It is usually caused by hot spots on the piston or combustion chamber.

pressure drop A loss of pressure in a flowing gas or liquid due to restrictions in its path.

pressure ratio Used in determining proper turbocharger or supercharger size and efficiency. The results of a formula used in deciding what compressor housing to use in a particular turbo installation.

pressure regulator See *regulator, deadhead-type pressure* or *regulator, bypass-type pressure*

PROM Programmable Read-Only Memory. An electronic memory device used in storing and recalling the correct amount of fuel for any set of operating conditions in electronic fuel injection systems.

PROM map A multi-dimensional chart that shows what information is on a particular PROM chip or memory chip.

quick-cash access Something you will need when building a power boosted motorcycle.

ram air induction The ability to gain a mild supercharging effect by directing air from the front of a motorcycle through ducting that attaches to the air box or air chamber, to the carburetors.

redline The maximum allowable speed of an engine—something you will hit regularly after power boosting your motorcycle.

regulator, deadhead-type pressure A deadhead-type pressure regulator operates to maintain a controlled pressure within a fluid stream by restricting flow between the source and its destination. As applied to fuel pressure regulators, this type of pressure control tends to heat the fuel flowing to the carburetors or fuel injectors, since the pressure drop across the regulator expends some energy. With this type of regulator, the fuel flowing from the fuel pump exactly equals flow to the carburetors or fuel injectors; the pressure at the pump is reduced to that required at the destination through the inline restriction of the regulator.

regulator, bypass-type pressure A bypass-type (also called "return-type") pressure regulator operates to maintain a controlled pressure within a continuously flowing fluid stream by sending excess fluid back to its source (for example, the fuel tank). As applied to fuel pressure regulators, this type of pressure control tends to keep a fresh supply of cool fuel flowing to the carburetors or fuel injectors, with excess fuel being routed back through a petcock and standpipe at the bottom of the fuel tank. With this type of regulator, fuel flows from the fuel pump in excess of demand; the excess is simply returned to its source.

research method One of the methods used to determine the octane rating of gasoline.

roller bearings Bearings made of rolling cylinders; lubricated by low pressure oil.

rotary compressor A supercharger that contains rotors, as in a Roots design.

scavenge pump A pump used to return draining oil from a turbocharger to the crankcase of the engine.

screw compressor A supercharger that uses large intertwining screws instead of rotors to draw in and compress air.

short shifting Shifting gears early in order to control wheel stands or wheel spin.

slide carburetor A carburetor that uses a flat or round slide for throttle control. A non-CV type carburetor.

sliding vane compressor A supercharger that has one offset rotor that contains blades (vanes) that trap and compress air.

speed-density EFI An electronic fuel injection system that is preprogrammed to a set of rpm, load and throttle angle (N-Alpha) values which totally control fuel delivery.

spool-up time Also called turbo lag time. The time it takes a turbocharger to get up to speed.

stagnation zone   The location on a moving vehicle where maximum pressure is obtained for a ram air system. Usually dead center of a motorcycle's fairing.

stoichiometry   The determination of proper proportions of components for chemical reactions, as in the ideal air/fuel ratio for combustion.

supercharger   A mechanically driven air pump.

tetraethyl lead   A lead based chemical that is used in racing gasoline as an anti-detonate.

toluene   An aromatic chemical that is used in formulating racing gasoline.

TPS   Throttle position sensor; used in electronic fuel injection systems.

turbine housing   The exhaust housing for a turbocharger.

turbine wheel   A bladed wheel contained in a turbine housing which turns when exhaust is forced past it. In turn, it drives a shaft and, at its other end, a compressor impeller.

turbocharger   An   exhaust-gas-driven   supercharger.

VAC   Vacuum-atmospheric pressure sensor. Used in electronic fuel injection systems.

VATN   Variable vane turbo nozzle, a term used to describe a movable vane assembly in a turbocharger. Movable vanes adjust the amount of exhaust which can pass through an exhaust turbine housing.

velocity stack   A slightly funnel-shaped cone that attaches to the inlet of a carburetor, fuel injection throttle body, inlet opening to a compressor housing, or supercharger, and is used to smooth the flow of air.

venturi   The smallest part of the throttle bore in a carburetor.

volumetric efficiency   A rating that describes how efficiently an engine can consume air and expend exhaust gases in relation to pressure drop, port, and combustion chamber design.

waste gate   A device used to control exhaust flow through a turbocharger. It is used to control boost level.

water-alcohol injection   A device used to inject a mixture of water and alcohol under pressure into the fuel-air path to control detonation.

xylene   An aromatic chemical used in blending racing gasoline.

Index

About the Author

Joe Haile is a native Californian lucky enough to have grown up in a racing family during a period when hot rodding was coming back after "the big one," World War Two. His father (Joe Haile, Sr.), a UCLA graduate mechanical engineer, was an avid drag and Bonneville racer—which naturally meant young Joe would follow in his footsteps. The family 1953 Studebaker was constantly being modified and raced on weekends, and when go-karts became the rage, Joe Jr. successfully competed, driving Carretta karts.

When Studebaker came out with the supercharged Golden Hawk, his father purchased one of the engines and promptly installed it in the '53. Later, Joe Jr. installed the same engine in his grandmother's 1951 Studebaker Starlight Coupe. It was his first experience with pressurized engines, and his fascination grew from there. The blown '51 Stude ran 102 mph in 13.90 seconds—fast for a street car in 1964, and definitely not bad for only 289 cubic inches. It was an ugly car, with a bullet nose grill and a wraparound rear window that kids used to make fun of. That was, of course, until they got their doors blown off.

Then came college, an AA Degree in commercial art, and his first job working for the Bendix Corporation's Electrodynamics Division proposal art department as a rookie. During that time and for the next three years, he attended the Art Center School of Design to hone his artistic skills. After that came a '66 high-performance Ford Mustang (no blower), a 427 Corvette (didn't need a blower), and then his first turbocharged vehicle, a 1966 Corvair Spider. More commercial art jobs eventually led to publication art direction and, at the same time, the start of Joe Haile Engineering. His new company specialized in producing high-perform-

ance speed equipment for Harley-Davidson motorcycles, which included Mikuni carburetion systems, the first two-into-one headers for Sportsters, special exhaust flange adapters and, finally, turbo kits based on his own Rajay-turbocharged Harley Sportster. Then along came a new organization called the EPA, real fun people who specialized in putting businesses like his out of business—which they did. Back to art direction.

Joe was, over a period of 18 years, art director of *Popular Off Roading, Big Bike Magazine, Air Progress, Air Classics, Sea Classics,* various railroading magazines, *Big Valley Magazine,* and later a designer/production artist on *Motocross Action, Dirt Bike* and *3 & 4 Wheel Action.* All this culminated in his first self-published book, *Turbo Bike,* in 1991, then *Turbo Bike Volume Two,* both instructional manuals on how to turbocharge motorcycles.

Based on the success of the first two books, he decided to try publishing his own magazine, *Turbo Bike & Motorcycle Performance.* He's still at it. The magazine, originally biannual but now annual and renamed *Powertech and Turbo Bike Magazine,* is steadily growing as power boosting becomes more popular. Considered an expert in the field of abnormal aspiration, Haile is constantly consulted on a variety of projects by professionals and amateurs alike, and has written numerous technical articles for other publications including *Motorcycle Consumer News, Rider,* and *Streetfighters.* His own magazine has quite a following (it is addictive). Anyone wishing to subscribe or purchase back issues can call 661-255-3426, 24 hours a day.

Other Books of Interest

▼ Maintenance and Technical

Motorcycle Basics Manual *by Pete Shoemark*
Whichever motorcycle you own or work on, this excellent manual will help you understand the inner workings of each of its functional systems. The author covers basic two-stroke and four-stroke engine cycles; fuel systems; exhaust systems; ignition systems; transmissions; lubrication and cooling systems; wheels, tires and brakes; front suspension and steering; frame designs and types; rear suspension; electrical systems; and much more. This is much more than a how-to-fix-it book. It takes you into the design of motorcycle components so you know how things work, not simply how to replace them.
Paper, 8-1/4 x 10-3/4 in., 164 pp., 394 illus.

BASIC $23.95

Motorcycle Carburettor Manual *by Pete Shoemark*
This classic book presents the basic principles of carburetor operation and takes you through the practical aspects of overhaul, tuning, and correcting improper adjustments. Covers a wide range of carburetor types, including slide, constant velocity, and fixed-jet carbs. Refers to carburetors made by Amal, Bendix, Dellorto, Gurtner, Keihin, Lectron, Mikuni, SU, and others. An extremely practical guide every serious motorcyclist should have.
Paper, 8-1/4 x 10-3/4 in., 117 pp., 237 illus.

SHOE $23.95

Motorcycle Electrical Manual *by A. Tranter*
This book offers a comprehensive presentation of motorcycle electrical systems. Included are sections on: essentials of electricity, principles of ignition circuits, coil and battery ignition, magneto ignition circuits, electronic ignition systems, spark plugs, DC generators, alternators, lighting and signalling circuits, starter motors, batteries and wiring systems, and much more. A very helpful and practical guide that will help you unravel the mysteries of electrical systems.
Paper, 8-1/4 x 10-3/4 in., 125 pp., many illus.

MELEC $23.95

Motorcycle Electrics Without Pain *by Mike Arman*
Many books approach the subject of motorcycle electrics by discussing theory first, theory second and theory third. The author of this book contends that is unnecessary and, more often than not, doesn't fix a broken machine. In this book, you'll learn about only a few basic circuits which, with some minor modifications and minor variations, make up all motorcycle electrical systems. In short, anyone can fix electrical systems if they have a good basic understanding of these circuits.
Arman's book provides specific, step-by-step procedures on fixing most motorcycles, allowing you to quickly and accurately troubleshoot and repair almost any electrical problem in almost any motorcycle. Arman's quick-witted and humorous prose, sprinkled generously through this book, makes it entertaining and easy to read.
Paper, 8-1/2 x 11 in., 64 pp., 105 illus.

ELEX $11.95

Machinery's Handbook (25th Edition)
by Oberg, Jones, Horton, Ryffel, Green, & McCauley
The *Machinery's Handbook* is the most authoritative metalworking resource available. Engineers, machinists, and do-it-yourselfers have been consulting this comprehensive reference guide for over 75 years. This 25th edition features many new and expanded components, including sections on new materials, motion control systems, tool life estimates, logarithm and trigonometry tables and electrical discharge machining.
Other sections of the book discuss mathematics, strength of materials, balancing, plain and anti-friction bearings, springs, shafting, cutting tools, screw thread systems, cam design, gear ratios, die casting, and numerous other important topics.
Hardbound, 5 x 7-1/4 in., 2,550 pp., many illus.

MACH $80.00

Scientific Design of Exhaust and Intake Systems *by Philip Smith and John Morrison*
For years, engineers, engine designers, high-performance tuners, and racers have depended on the information in this book to develop the maximum potential from their engines. This authoritative book will lead you through complex theories to an understanding of how to design exhaust and intake systems for your own particular application.
Dr. John C. Morrison is one of the foremost authorities on the analysis of the induction and exhaust dynamics of high-speed engines. Together with Philip Smith, he gives a thorough explanation of the physics that govern the behavior of gases as they pass through an engine, and the theories and practical research methods used in designing more efficient induction manifolds and exhaust systems, for both competition and street use.
Softbound, 5-1/2 x 8-1/2 in., 274 pp., 185 illus.

DESXI $22.95

Motorcycle Tuning: Four-Stroke *by John Robinson*
Engine development is slow and expensive, but the results can be very rewarding. Although it is impossible to make all-round engine improvements, other than those gained by careful assembly to stock tolerances, improvements on one area of four-strokes can be traded for losses in another. Increases in high speed power can be balanced against losses in low-speed power, engine flexibility and reliability.
In this book, the technical editor of *Performance Bikes* explains how various stages of engine tuning are reached, and describes typical development work with enough theory to devise a practical development program for your own modifications.
Paper, 6 x 9-1/4 in., 152 pp., 70 illus.

MTUN4 $35.95

▼ Workshop Setup & Practices

How to Set Up Your Motorcycle Workshop
by C. G. Masi

This informative, comprehensive book will help you set up your motorcycle workshop to make the most of available space, and equip it with the tools necessary to get the job done. Whether you plan only to keep your bike clean and in good repair or you want to become more seriously involved with restoration, customization or even a professional repair shop, this book will show you how it's done. If you have more ambitious goals, you'll find guidelines for setting up painting, welding and even metal fabrication operations.

Masi explains the basic principles of motorcycle workshops, and helps you determine what your needs are. He offers ideas on planning and designing your motorcycle shop and practical advice on what equipment you'll need, as well as which tools are needed for electrical work, motor work, and chassis work. Masi offers helpful suggestions about which tools to keep with your bike, which tools you'll need in emergency situations, and valuable hints and tips on which tools to purchase, which tools you can fabricate, and best of all, how to use them. Many amusing anecdotes and examples recount real-life experiences.

Sftbd., 8-1/4 x 10-1/2 in., 160 pp., 205 illus.

MASI $24.95

Motorcycle Workshop Practice Manual
by Pete Shoemark

This manual is a practical guide on workshop techniques written for the do-it-yourself motorcycle enthusiast. Readers will benefit from the wealth of information given by the author, who has written many of the other Haynes workshop manuals.

Using an easy-to-follow format, amply illustrated with over 300 line drawings and photos, the text is divided into six chapters covering the workshop, tools, workshop techniques, engine and transmission work, frame and suspension work, and electrical and ignition work. Examples of the topics covered include cylinder head overhaul, electrical testing, bearing removal, and more. Useful data is given in the appendix and a glossary of technical terms is in included.

Paper, 8-1/4 x 10-3/4 in., 143 pp., 300 illus.

MWORK $23.95

▼ Restoration

Motorcycle Wheel Rebuild Video

This informative video covers all of the fundamentals for wheel rebuilding. Lacing a wheel, truing a rim, tire mount and dismount, and static balancing are some of the major topics covered. The demonstrations are clear and easy to follow and are filled with tips to help you do the job properly and easily. The production quality is a bit rough, as is often the case with highly specialized videos. Despite this drawback, whether you're involved in a rebuilding project or just want to learn the details of mounting a tire, this video will help you get the job done right.

Video, VHS in., 63 min. pp., color illus.

MWRV $29.95

The Motorcycle Restorer's Workshop Companion   *by Geoff Purnell*

Here's a handy guide to the techniques you'll use restoring motorcycles. Included is information about: tools and their use, metalworking, working with timber, casting and pattern-making, lathe work, work with sidecars, achieving professional finishes, and much more. In order to do a professional job of restoring motorcycles, you need to learn and apply many skills. This book will get you off to a running start.

Hardbound, 7-1/4 x 9-1/2 in., 168 pp., 150 illus.

MRWC $32.95

Restoration of Vintage & Thoroughbred Motorcycles   *by Jeff Clew*

The popularity of old motorcycles has exploded over the past ten years. More people are beginning to recognize the craftsmanship and distinctiveness of these rare beauties and, in contrast to today's complicated machines, the simplicity of their design. However, many admirers have been reluctant to purchase a favorite vintage machine because they've never tackled a restoration project before. Fear no longer! This book was written for you.

Clew covers every stage of restoration from selection and purchase of the machine through each separate aspect of technical work, not only allowing the owner to produce a fully ridable machine but also, if desired, a fully accurate 100-point concours winner. The first edition of this book came out in 1976. This second edition brings the restorer up-to-date with the developments in restoration techniques and, through numerous illustrations, how these can be applied to the greatest benefit, particularly when dealing with more modern machines. Clew uses illustrations and pictures extensively for easy comprehension. Whether you own a 1914 Triumph, a 1931 Rudge, or even a 1962 Ducati, this book will save you time, money, and agony as you go about restoring it to its original state.

Hardbound, 7-1/4 x 9-7/8 in., 221 pp., 282 illus.

RESVT $36.95

▼ Painting

Jon Kosmoski's Kustom Painting Secrets

Learn from the master. Jon Kosmoski takes you step by step through preparation and painting of several automotive and motorcycle projects. You'll learn the skills as well as the tricks needed to achieve professional results. He covers shop setup, spray guns, paint stripping, preparation of the work, painting sequences, types of primer, applying paint, paint gun adjustments, pinstriping and flame painting, candy finishes, applying graphics, marbleized finishes, how to paint engines, and much more. Emphasis is given to paint materials manufactured by Kosmoski's company, House of Kolor. His paints are used widely by builders and customizers. For more on Kosmoski's techniques, see our videos "Kustom Painting Secrets–The Video," and "Cycle Flame Painting."

Paper, 8-1/2 x 11 in., 128 pp., 208 illus.

KOS $22.50

▼ Clymer and Haynes Manuals

Clymer and Haynes motorcycle manuals are comprehensive aids to maintenance and repair for a wide variety of motorcycles. Clymer manuals cover more of the recent models while the Haynes series tends to cover more of the classics. Each manual makes heavy use of photos and technical illustrations to help you visualize the work you will be doing. Manuals contain a section on troubleshooting, maintenance, lubrication, and tune-up. These motorcycle repair manuals are among the very best tools you can have as you begin working on your "pride and joy." Each book was written from practical experience. The editors actually purchase the motorcycle, tear it down and rebuild it while taking notes and photographs about the process.

These books often contain helpful hints not found in the factory manuals. Make a manual the first special tool you buy!

Whitehorse Press stocks every motorcycle repair manual available from these two publishers, a collection covering thousands of different makes and models.

NOTES:

NOTES:

NOTES:

▼ **NOTES:**

NOTES:

▼ NOTES:

NOTES:

▼ **NOTES:**